Warlike Sketches

1939-1945

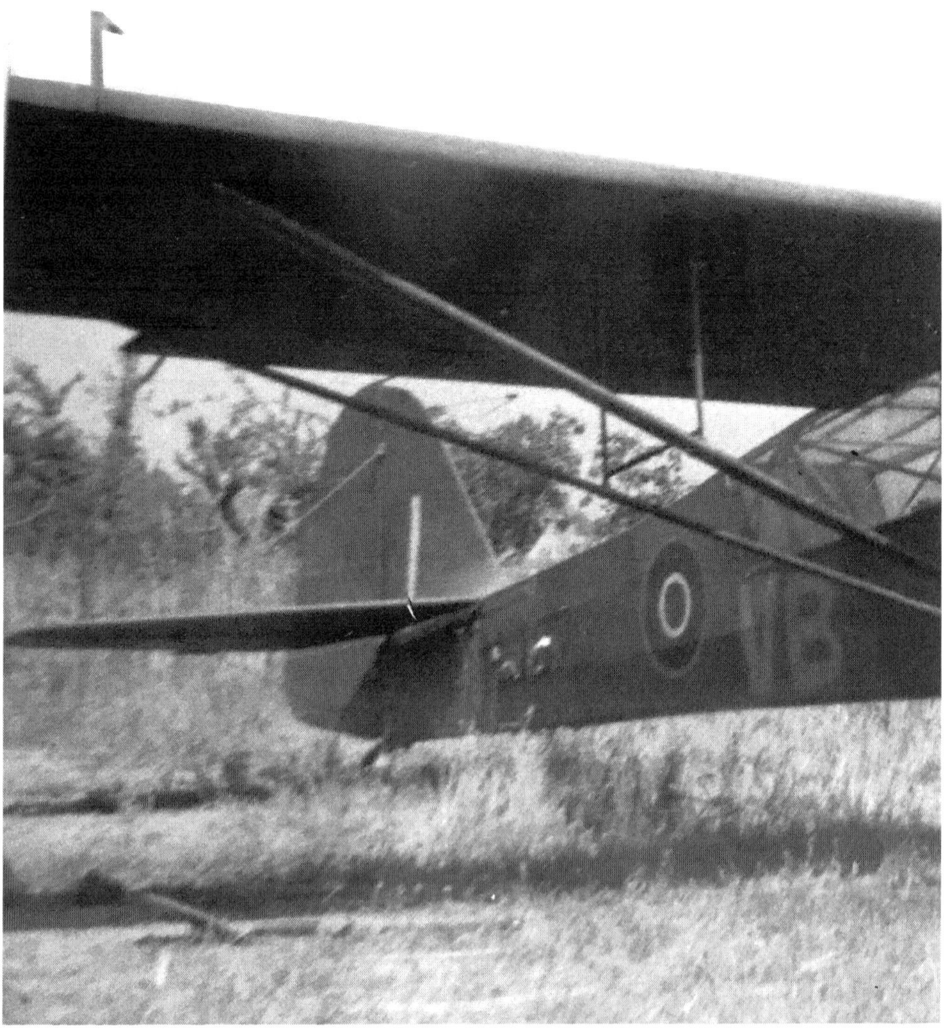

Warlike Sketches
1939-1945

by Arrol Macfarlane

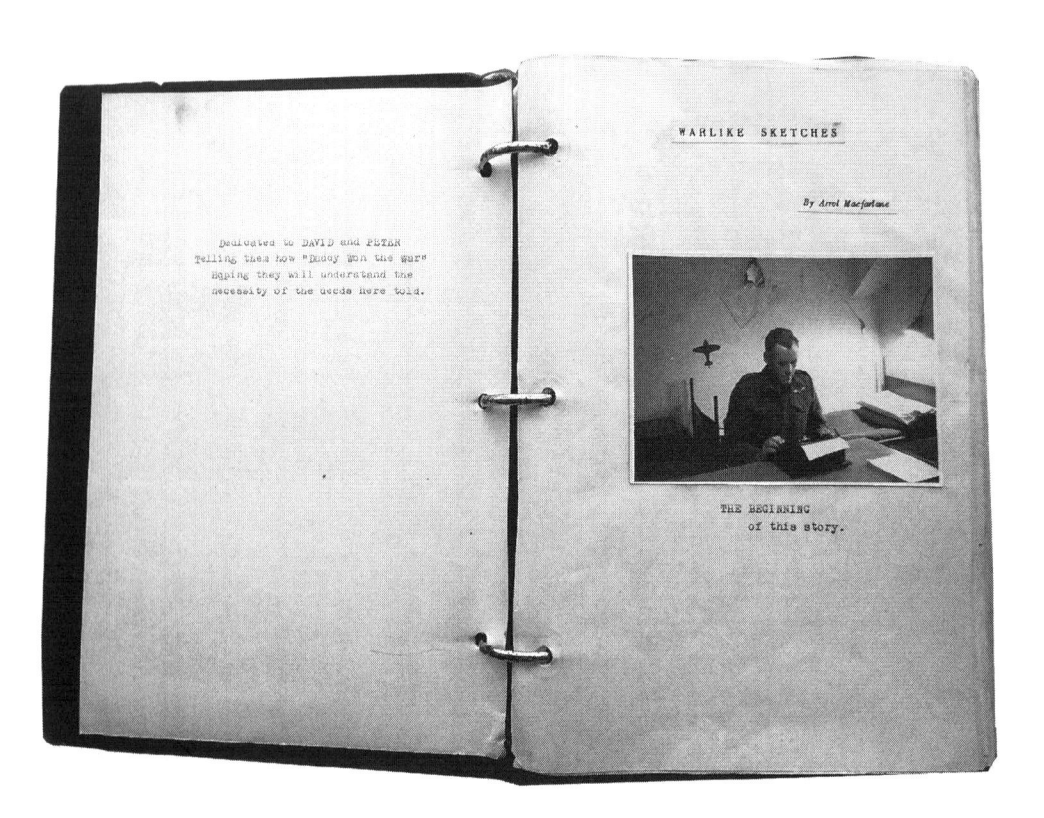

Original typeritten text copyright © 1955 by Arrol Macfarlane (1911-1998)
Printed Edition Copyright © 2016 David Arrol Macfarlane and Peter Macfarlane
All rights reserved.

ISBN-13: 978-1537112718
ISBN-10: 1537112716

Contents

7	The Why and the Wherefore
8	Joining up and initial training in England and Wales
27	Fourteen months in Scotland
42	Air Observation Post training
61	To North Africa to join 657 Air OP Squadron
79	Flight from Algeria to Italy
106	Into action at Cassino
127	From Cassino to the Arezzo Front
158	The Arezzo Battle and the capture of Florence
174	The Gothic Line Battle
205	The Ravenna Front
260	Move to Northwest Europe
282	With the Occupation Forces in Germany
309	The Way Home
316	Glossary
317	War Travels
319	About the 2016 Edition
322	List of Maps and Photographs
324	Index

Dedicated to DAVID and PETER
Telling them how "Daddy Won the War"
Hoping they will understand the
necessity of the deeds here told.

The Why and the Wherefore

Having written two accounts of hiking trips in the Nahuel Huapi area, which evidently amused the family and odd friends who read them, it seemed a good idea to start another effort in this line and thereby ward off boredom.

At the time I was in Germany with the Occupying Forces, having been abandoned by my flying pals who had returned to England, and I had recently "acquired" a portable typewriter.

Possessing a diary, kept throughout the War, a Log Book for flying details and maps of all my battle areas, it was just a question of key bashing, or so it seemed.

However, soon I was in difficulties. The tale seemed endless even though I endeavoured to stick to essentials, and wrote laconically with a minimum of detail – but that did not make for interesting reading. There was a stack of interesting material. I doubt if anybody had a more varied War career than I. Starting as a Medium and Heavy Gunner I soon found myself with a 18-pounder for anti-invasion purposes. Then dressed up in First World War uniform riding horses with a crack North West Frontier Mountain Regiment. Next step was with Light A A [*Antiaircraft*] and before I knew it was V. P. (Vital Point) Commander of Kinlochleven, on the west coast of Scotland. Was later impressed into a Mixed Heavy AA Regiment, with the ATS [*Auxilliary Territorial Service*] and Radar wizardry and, in desperation, volunteered for Air Observation Post work, wriggling in by a fluke. Was briefly attached to an Armoured Regiment and drove tanks, then to an Infantry Regiment and foot slogged. Then out to North Africa, Sicily, Italy, sitting over all battles starting from Cassino, to end up with Monty's 21st Army Group battling in Holland.

During my Air OP time I fired practically every type of gun in those theatres of war, even working with the only Italian Artillery on our side. So there was really much to relate.

Anyway, I hope the result, which took some fifteen years to finish (it was lying around untouched for years) is readable and not too long nor too short. The kind reader should refrain from criticizing style, if any, and spelling. It must be borne in mind that the whole job was done on a German typewriter.

VOYAGE TO THE UK, JOINING UP AND INITIAL TRAINING

The Beginning of this Story

It all started, I suppose, when Chamberlain gave his famous broadcast on September 2nd 1939, announcing to the World that we were at War with Hitlerite Germany.

This news caught me in Argentina, away up in Esquina, Corrientes. I heard the dreaded news via a squeaky radio in the back room of the Shell Agent's *almacén*. I was a Shell Zone Inspector at the time. Having volunteered some time back I visualized sundry telegrams flowing from the Embassy and, even though it had rained heavily and roads were considered impassable, set off nevertheless for my base camp in Paraná, Entre Ríos. It took me the better part of 16 hours to cover the 380 km but my trusty Ford got me home safely and then promptly stripped her gears in front of my digs. Truly a faithful steed.

All my initial fears, however, went for naught. Many long months of patient waiting were to elapse before anything happened. By that time I had been transferred back to Buenos Aires and there I managed to get things moving.

It was on the 27th of July 1940 that a party of us sailed on the *Almeda Star* after a series of hectic parties. We found we were to travel in super luxury as, with only six passengers on board and all bachelors, we were each given a stateroom. Sailing with me were Duncan Cutts, Mike Henman, St. J. Makin, Wee Willie Wilson and Dennis Hall.

We had rather a scare when nearing Rio. A vessel was sighted which was thought at first to be a raider. On nearer approach she proved to be friendly. After that we were impressed into keeping watch throughout the hours of daylight for possible submarines, or other hostile vessels and, nearing the UK, also for enemy planes. We had for armament only an ancient 3 inch gun mounted in the stern and an erratic Lewis Gun to ward off all nasty comers.

On board the *MV Almeda Star* - Cutts, Makin, Wilson and self

Our destination was Tilbury. As we sailed along we heard about the Stuka raids on shipping, magnetic mines being strewn around, submarines appearing in ever increasing numbers, stalking the approaches to the UK. Lastly, should we survive all these perils, long range guns were firing from Calais and dominating the Channel through which we were expected to pass.

We refuelled at St. Vincent, Shell of course, where we could be sure spies had seen us and passed the word along to some hungry submarine pack. We were a juicy morsel, carrying precious meat. However, the days went by and nothing happened. A heavy storm struck and lasted four days. This was a blessing in disguise as submarines could not operate successfully in that weather. I was on the topmost bridge doing my spot of lookout when I saw a marvellous sight. The majestic Rodney, with escorting destroyers, slid past at high speed smashing her sharp bows through the waves in grand style.

Later a Sunderland flying boat located us and passed a message on the Aldis lamp. We were ordered to proceed via the north of Ireland to Liverpool, and a good thing too under the circumstances.

The *Almeda Star* was extremely lucky that trip and we made our destination port on the 22nd August 1940 without further mishap. Her luck was not to last and two trips later that lovely ship was lost with all hands somewhere in the North Atlantic.

With no intention of losing time Makin, Hall, and myself groped our way to Lime Street Station getting our first experience of the blackout and caught an evening train for London.

At the crack of dawn we were in London, too early to contact people. We settled down in a *café* for a plentiful English breakfast. At a reasonable hour had a tussle with the various buttons of a telephone booth and managed to ring up my Aunt Dolly living out in Grove Park, which gave her a great surprise as she had no idea I was in England. On arrival at her house I was made very welcome and this became my headquarters for the rest of the War.

As can be imagined there was plenty to talk about and all the latest family news was exchanged over sundry cups of tea.

Two days later, after checking in with the Volunteer Committee at River Plate House, went along to Scotland Yard for an interview with Captain Plum to see what I could do to help win the War. I was too old for flying duty with the RAF, I was an ancient 29 at the time, and ground duty did not appeal to me. Capt. Plum did his best to persuade me to join a Guards Regiment, but wasn't successful. My choice was the Artillery where some amount of science is required. As I was a big chap the Medium and Heavy variety was suggested and accepted and it was arranged that I should join the 21st Medium & Heavy Training Regiment at Larkhill, Salisbury, at my convenience. Just fancy that. Decided to take a modest weeks holiday before joining up officially on the 2nd September, exactly a year from the day War was declared.

Joining Up, Initial Training 11

Fargo Camp, Larkhill, with two Barbadians and a local.

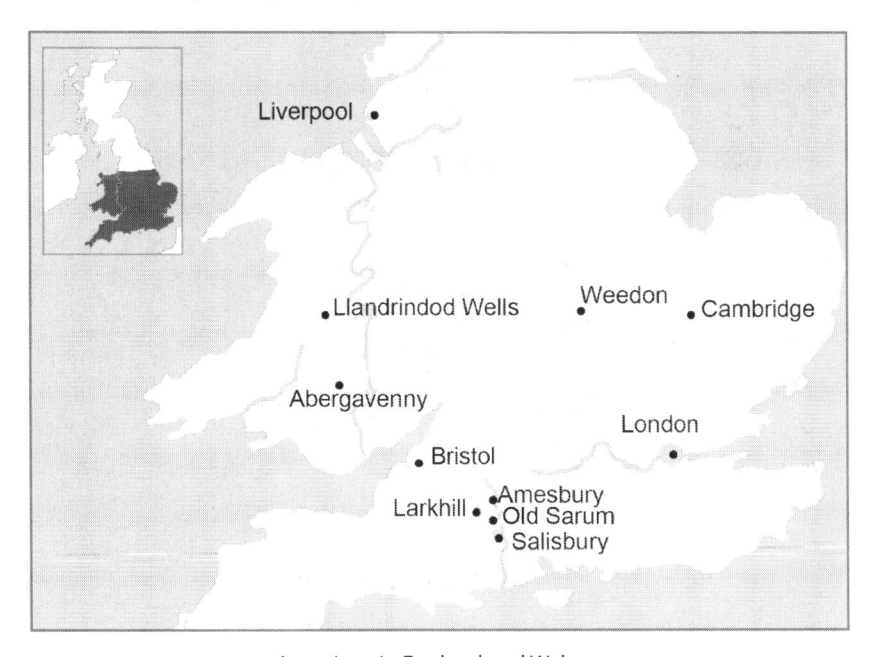

Locations in England and Wales

Joining Up

And so it came about that I found myself travelling to Salisbury in the company of two Barbadians by name Ward [2 *Sept. 1940*]. They were brothers and also volunteers and we were to join our Regiment between intakes of conscripts and this proved to be extremely advantageous and undoubtedly changed the course of my private War.

We changed trains at Salisbury for Amesbury and there a truck awaited us. My first night in camp was most unorthodox. I was taken around by a decent Sergeant and introduced to three other Argentinians, Handley, Charlesworth, and Davidson, who were all in the elite 9 Squad where Specialists were formed. Having been shown to my own outfit, 7 Squad, promptly left to keep a date with the *criollos* and we sat around drinking beer, sitting on the grass as the evening was mild, chatting about Buenos Aires and the likes till nearly midnight, and way past lights out. They weren't very regimental. As I was still in civvies [*civilian clothes*] got away with it without any trouble.

Had an interview with Major Ferguson, the Camp Commander, the following morning and was told that my only hope of becoming an Artillery Specialist, my aim in life at that moment, was to pass my trigonometry exams with high marks as all artillery work is based on this science. This was rather awkward for me as I had never done any trig. at school. But nevertheless I set to learn as much as possible before the next intake arrived a week later. The major was extremely helpful. He lent me books on the subject and even coached me personally. He also had me shifted to 8 Squad, which meant that I would automatically be a candidate for No. 9 and all I had to do to attain my desire was to pass the exam. On the strength of my having been in the Argentine Army, where I reached the exalted rank of *recluta incompleto* I was made an Acting Unpaid (Unwanted) Lance Bombardier and, as such, had the high honour of marching my bunch of types to and from parades.

The new intake arrived. Amongst them were many under-graduates who were all clamouring to enter "9 Squad" and room was limited to 25. The dreaded exam came up and about 50 sat for it.

Thanks to my recent cramming, and the fact that Army trig. differs exceedingly from the normal kind, I managed to pass with flying colours getting 64 and 70 on the written and oral exam respectively; thus wriggling through where many of the Varsity chaps failed.

Commenced training in earnest on gun drills, director work, range finding, range tables, and all the works that make up the art of gunnery.

Introduction to Air Raids

Right from the start, and with monotonous regularity, the Luftwaffe would attack London at sundown. While I was staying at Grove Park, my cousin Cathie and I would walk to the edge of the common in the evenings and watch for the pin-points of light, pretty against the darkening sky, that denoted ack-ack fire in the distance. The sirens would start up away in the distance and, as the raiders approached, so would the nearby ones burst forth into their wicked moaning crescendo. Then we would walk back to *Mount Blow* where my Aunt Dolly would have the kettle on for the inevitable cup of tea with which every Londoner welcomed these raids.

They had an Anderson shelter in their garden, an uncomfortable damp affair, and never used. Instead we would sit around in the front room, with the blackout curtains properly drawn, listening to the odd bomb falling, mostly at a respectable distance, and to the occasional tinkle of descending fragments of ack-ack shells. The twins, then but a few months old, were parked in their pram under the stairs. They were there when a bomb hit the corner of the adjoining semi-detached house and demolished it leaving Mount Blow in a sorry mess. At the time the family were in the sitting room but nobody was hurt although the ceiling fell down on them and all the windows blew in.

By then I had joined my Regiment in Larkhill. When I heard the news I asked for and obtained a 48 hour pass. Fargo Camp had been thoroughly plastered with incendiary bombs a few nights previously and we had spent a hectic night putting out the fires, though luckily most of them fell in open spaces, but it was a good thing Jerry

[*Germans*] did not follow up with HE [*High Explosives*] as they often did. However the very night I went to London he returned with HE and made a real shambles of that camp. A direct hit on a spider (5 huts joined to a common bath hut) killed many of the boys and a lot of the other spiders were damaged by near misses. In my hut, darts left in the dart-board were forced right through by the blast, and the overhead cupboards were emptied of their contents which fell upon the sleeping chaps. And so I missed two nasty bombing incidents.

Initial Training

Training went on apace as replacements had to be found quickly to build up the British Army again after the disastrous European campaign which had ended with the retreat from Dunkirk [26 May–4 Jun 1940]. At that time manpower was ahead of the equipment. The Invasion Season was on. Much has been said about the lack of weapons and people are apt to think that reports were exaggerated. I can state that my personal weapon for quite a while was a rudimentary Mark I pike made out of an old bayonet stuck into the end of a bit of piping. Later on we were issued a few rifles with 20 rounds of ammunition.

The 6 inch Howitzers used for training were 1914 vintage with steel wheels. They lacked clinometers and other gadgets to make them normally usable but they could be, and would be, fired over open sights if necessary.

For the purpose of this invasion I was on the gun crew of an ancient 18 pounder gun together with some old timer NCO's and we were reasonably prepared should the balloon go up.

Things were jittery and twice we stood to thinking the invasion had really started, Hitler undoubtedly lost a golden opportunity. He could have literally walked right through the British Army had he come over with but a few tanks.

We were happiest going on schemes which took us roaming over Salisbury Plains. It is not the prettiest part of England but I doubt if anyone appreciated the scenery more than I, it was so different from that to which I had been accustomed. As a Specialist I was kept very busy solving problems and was not bored.

Gunnery is quite an art and is really interesting. However, I never got the opportunity of seeing a gun fired. A funny way to train a soldier with a War on, but expect that they could not spare the ammo. Also there were no Medium or Heavy guns available, and we only saw one modern gun when it was specially brought from a line regiment for this purpose and we looked on whilst "professional" gunners put on a show.

All this running around and fresh air gave me a terrific appetite and here it was that I found myself at a disadvantage compared with the local lads. For the first month or so, and until my tummy shrunk to austerity size, I was positively hungry and the only thing that saved me from collapsing (or so I thought) was the good old NAAFI [*Navy, Army and Air Force Institutes*] where one could buy dinner of sorts for about 1/6 [*1 shilling and 6 pence*]. The dinner served up free by the Army wasn't worth queuing up for, often consisting of bread and dripping – 'orrible stuff. We were given a good solid breakfast, stacks of odd cups of tea during the day, a good lunch, tea at about 17·00 hours with, maybe, bread and cheese plus jam and then naught but the above mentioned dripping to see us through until the next day.

The NAAFI was a cheerful place with somebody perpetually banging away at the piano – and banging is the word. Here I met another hungry fellow called Massey, a lowly budding driver. Despite his Kings College education he had not made the grade into 9 Squad. We were wont to eat together and went for pleasant rambles exploring the countryside, imbibing many a gallon of beer at the local pubs. The best was an ancient one in Amesbury, reputed to be over 400 years old. The ceiling of the main bar was so low that I could only stand upright in one spot which I commandeered whenever necessary.

The year was advancing and it was getting colder and colder. Salisbury plains are definitely one of the coldest spots in the British Isles and doing guard duty at night was something unpleasant, especially after the snows came and it was icy underneath. The clothing issue was good and warm, but even so one returned from a two hour stretch out in a blizzard frozen stiff and trembling.

Cathie Bonner and the twins in Portpatrick

Leave – Waterloo Bridge and Scotland

I managed to wangle a spot of leave while I was still at Larkhill and I will always remember arriving in London very late on a cold, sparkling clear moonlight night and walking across the bridge from Waterloo Station in the middle of a noisy air-raid with Jerry planes obviously pretty well overhead. The Houses of Parliament looked beautiful bathed in moonlight and serenely majestic, daring Jerry to drop a bomb. Searchlights disappeared into the clear sky and scores of glittering diamonds pinpointed the heavens as ack-ack shells sought out the enemy. The noise was deafening. The pulsating roar of planes overhead, the sharp crack as anti-aircraft guns fired from all around and, more ominous, the tinkling of jagged bits of steel falling, and falling swiftly, on the metalled roadway and roofs. Needless to say I was wearing my tin hat. There weren't many people strolling across Waterloo Bridge at that time and I did not linger.

That leave I went up to Scotland for the first time to visit the family who had evacuated to Portpatrick after their house had been

In Mountain Battery rig.

badly damaged. Thoroughly enjoyed my stay and there it was I met Fred Bonner, Cathie's husband, he was then a Lieutenant in the Ordnance Corps.

When I returned to Larkhill I found that Jerry had, once again, bombed them with shattering results, leaving many spiders demolished and twenty more of the lads dead.

With this blow, there weren't enough huts for all the survivors and we were sent off posthaste and prematurely to a transit camp in Derby, where we arrived by train on the 21st January 1941, after spending four and a half months of training on the plains.

In which I Join the Modern Army

After a few days of doing nothing much at Derby, what remained of 9 Squad was hauled out on parade to decide upon our destination. Name places were given but not units, and most of the lads chose places near their home towns. It did not much matter to me where I went and I took what remained. This turned out to be a place called Weedon. I had never heard of it but it seemed to be in pleasant country.

Next day we were on our way. Arrived at Weedon [*21 Jan 1941*], lugged our kit out of the station and there we received a shock. An ancient mule-drawn carriage awaited us. For better or for worse we were in a crack Mountain Battery that had done deeds of glory in the North West Frontier battling with naughty tribesmen.

Our modern battle-dresses were taken away to be replaced by 1918 war uniforms consisting of SD [*Service Dress*] jacket, breeches and puttees and an SD peaked cap. And we wore spurs. Making the best of things as is my wont, I managed to have a jolly good time during my five months with this ancient outfit.

The famous school of equitation, where we were stationed, had been built in the days of Queen Anne and had been occupied by Cavalry Regiments until they were motorised quite recently. To begin with we slept in converted stables, thick walled affairs – cold and clammy. After a while, when I went up in the world and became a Lance Bombardier, I made my abode in an attic, nice and draughty but at least we could see the sun, when it decided to shine. We slept on the floor on palliasses filled with straw, with a pillow to match. After a while my slumbers were sometimes disturbed by the noise of beasties nibbling away at the straw. Nothing lousy, mind you, just noisy. At first I thought it could be mice by the racket they made, but after duly jumping with army boots on the offending pillow no visual or odorous evidence appeared to support this theory, so it must have been something smaller. Of course I could have changed the straw but that meant lugging the thing all the way down umpteen stairs and out to the stables; not justified really as the wee beasties remained friendly.

Slept beside our Bugler and a Jewish chiropodist. The former was up there for strategic reasons as he had but to stick his head out of the nearby window to do his stuff, at that unearthly hour of the morning when armies start stirring, then he would nip back to bed again whilst we dressed and shivered and went out on parade.

What I enjoyed most was the riding. This was done properly in the ancient school, reputedly one of the best in Europe. Our teacher, Captain Hanse was also one of the best. He was a short tubby chap, so tubby that he had to use a step-ladder to mount. Nevertheless, he was the cat's whiskers as regards riding and training horses. He had taught the King to ride as also Lord Wavell and charged umpteen guineas for the privilege, so I was certainly getting my money's worth.

Capt. Hanse had a hard time of it because most of his pupils were Cockneys who did not know one end of a horse from the other when he took them over. The troops in a Mountain Battery do not ride as it is their job to lead the mules, and it was the signallers and us Specialists who were being taught. It was hard going and Capt. Hanse was not a mild mannered man. The horses were better trained than the men and would obey his orders long before the riders could react, and that undoubtedly helped. Whenever things went wrong, and that was often, he had us draw up our horses in line abreast and make us scramble over the first and under the next, and so on. The horses never moved. Later on he went one better and would give the order "Mount two up" whilst we were trotting around in a circle. This meant dismounting, sprinting to catch up with the horse two ahead then mounting on the move. We got quite adept at this.

Best of all was the jumping and riding on schemes. As I was about the only chap who could stay on a horse it was my job to chase and collect runaways. This was quite a privilege as nobody was allowed to move faster than a trot without the express permission of an officer.

Naturally I took full advantage of this and galloped many a pleasant mile over this marvellous English countryside before catching up with the elusive horse. Remember chasing a runaway horse right through the thick traffic on the Great North Road, and what chaos we caused as the runaway zig-zagged through, caring naught for the right of way.

I was given Horatio, a 17 hand chestnut for my own. Amongst other things had to care for the beast, water, feed and groom him twice a day.

By then it was midwinter and it snowed frequently. I remember enjoying many an early morning ride on a quiet sunny day through a beautiful forest where every tree was etched in snow, each twig and branch outlined in white. Every morning before breakfast we would walk our horses quietly through these pretty glades, usually on surcingle and blanket, and leading another.

As a Specialist I was nominated Range Finder for the Battery and in charge of these Barr & Stroud instruments. They were long tube affairs, about 5 feet in length. This put me onto quite a good racket. Obviously I had to practise a great deal to gain experience and every morning I would draw one out of the stores and carry it around all day. By this means I could evade being put on any duty as, when it became strategically necessary, I had to go off and practise, "the Major had said so." To do so I had to choose a spot with a long view. This would take me a good distance from camp and assured me a pleasant contemplation of some wizard scenery in this land of Squires and Spires.

Thought up another good one and volunteered to help the Home Guard work out ranges from all their invasion strongpoints. This meant being picked up by some Home Guard Officer, usually a squire, and doing the job between cups of tea and pints of beer, dependent on the time of day. It was not a bad war effort, in fact.

Capt. Hanse wanted to know why I had not put in for a Commission. Told him I was getting my pay made up by Shell and the more pay I got the less I'd receive as Income Tax interfered. However, he threatened to put me up for one regardless.

Weedon was a small sleepy village and, believe it or not, it did not boast a pub. This must be a record. However, it did have a YWCA Hostel which afforded a pleasant shelter, a quiet spot to read or write letters and where one could get the odd cup of tea and more if desired. To make use of the place was obliged to become a member and so it came about that I possess a membership card of the Young Women's Christian Association. Worse was to happen before I ended my Army career.

Northampton was 7 miles away with a fairly frequent bus service. On days off we would hie there to do a flick, eat decently and sometimes go for a swim in an indoor heated pool. Sometimes we managed to miss the last bus and walked the 7 miles back to Weedon – we were tough in those days.

Our total establishment of mules arrived. Big brutes they were and wild. The Major nominated me official interpreter as they were Argentine mules. Did the gunners have fun and games getting them accustomed to carrying weights! Training went on inside the school which was well covered in a thick layer of peat. At first dummy weights were employed in lieu of the equipment, to prevent damage to delicate instruments. Later, when they were supposed to be reasonably trained, I saw many a brute roll over and over in the peat, making a mess of some lovingly polished piece of gun.

Although it seemed impossible, these mules were eventually trained thanks to the know-how of the North West Frontier old sweats. Then it was fascinating to see a gun literally flow together and come into action. The famous Screw Gun, a 3·7 inch Howitzer, was carried on seven mules. When "Action" was ordered these were placed in a circle and the gunners got to work like well oiled pieces of machinery. The man in charge of the axle would place it in the air at the right height and level and let go, knowing that the two wheels would appear on each end before it had time to fall. Also the pivot was moving fast towards its lawful place atop the axle and arrived a split second after that piece was put in place. The breech block which also carries a short part of the barrel would follow, and the rest of the barrel would be screwed on. Some 94 seconds after the command "Action", a round would be up the spout.

Then we began training in earnest. The way we travelled was on our flat feet leading the animals. Everybody walked, including Officers and Specialists, and our usual speed was four miles an hour. We would go pretty far, sometimes as much as 20 to 25 miles in seven or eight hours during which time, at best, we would eat haversack rations. These schemes included going into action with us Specialists climbing up the nearest hill followed by the signallers lugging their No. 21 wireless set and probably laying wire. And after all this, on return to barracks, we would have to attend to our horses, water, scrub and pad them and make them nice and comfortable and only then could we go along and sit down to a meal. The Officers were worse off as they had to see us fed as also carry out a foot inspection before they could follow suit.

I lost Horatio, for some reason or other, and adopted Gwen, another 17 hand brute. Both were excellent mounts, ex hunters, and good at jumping, except that Gwen could not see ditches and unless carefully lifted would fall short and somersault. This could be awkward for me in view of British Army's way of riding with boots stuffed well into the stirrups. Consequently my large sized boots would get stuck and there was danger of being dragged, however I was mighty lucky as we somersaulted many times and I always managed to get my feet clear.

Here it was that I met Robert E. Way, a weird type and a good friend of mine to this day. He owns a large Estate near Newmarket and should, by rights, have been producing much needed food. But he was crazy about horses and insisted on going to War with them. He had been in the Cavalry until he suffered a serious fall and ended up in hospital. When he got out and returned to Weedon he discovered to his horror that his Cavalry Regiment had been mechanized. He then tried to get into this Mountain Regiment but without success due to his broken bones, and they would only take him if he joined as a regular, and this he did.

And here he was doing duty as Battery runner, which meant he could ride a horse. His style was terrible. He would slouch in the saddle his narrow shoulders forming the top of a large curve, and his toes would point in. But he could surely ride and volunteered to look after the most savage horse. And these brutes could be pretty mean without trying very hard. Mary was one of them. She had the next box to Gwen and I would hear Way whispering endearments into her ear and every now and then there would be a loud crack as one of her hooves would miss him and strike the wooden side. In between she would try biting and the odd yelp of pain meant she had scored.

He had bad luck. After sticking it out in the Battery for over three years, one of which was spent roughing it up in the wild mountains of Scotland, where they went on schemes through snow and sleet with but one blanket to sleep with at night, he got rheumatism, not surprising, and was thrown out.

This Unit too was unlucky. After training all along for mountain warfare, and this lasted practically throughout the war, they eventually went into action – guess where – in Holland, supporting the Rhine crossing. And to add insult to injury, they were ordered to leave their horses and mules behind in England and were flown across. After firing their guns for a couple of days were flown back, and that was the sum total of their warlike activities during World War II.

We Move to Wales

I managed to wangle two leaves whilst I was stationed at Weedon and spent one roaming around visiting friends in London and SE England. On the second one I went up to visit the family then living in Portpatrick.

When I returned from Scotland the Major called me in and told me I had been officially put up for a Commission and had to report to the Northern Command Board at Leicester for the usual interview. Luckily in those days there were no Officer's Selection Boards and Pre O.C.T.U. [*Officer Cadet Training Unit*] Courses with their psychological and hardship tests. This was just a pleasant chat and a lot of questions. School attended shook them as they certainly had never heard of old B.D.S. [*Belgrano Day School*]. However, there was one snag. There were no vacancies in Field Artillery, my choice. Rather than get stuck in Heavy Stuff, which would mean a Coastal Battery, I requested to be put up for Light Anti Aircraft, at that time doing noble work in the Western Desert where they very frequently took on an anti-tank role. Likewise they were pretty busy dealing

As Cadet in Llandrindod, Wales

with all sorts of raiders down in South East England.

Shortly afterwards orders came through that we were to commence training in Mountain Warfare and were to proceed to Wales for this purpose. The 15th July 1941 found us, plus horses, travelling west. We had spent 5 months in Weedon and it was high time we had a change of scenery. We arrived before dawn at Abergavenny, detrained our steeds, and walked the six miles to Newydel Camp in the shadow of the Sugar Loaf mountain.

The first few days were pleasant enough and we enjoyed riding to the top of the Sugar Loaf every morning before breakfast. This called for some tricky riding as we went bareback and it was quite a job to avoid sliding over the horses neck on the way down, especially when leading another horse. But then the rains came and the camp turned into a quagmire. We thereafter sloshed around all day with mud up to our ankles.

And yet rides and walks on the odd sunny day up in the hills were extremely pleasant and I cannot complain too much about that period. I was lucky in only having to put up with a fortnight of this dampness and then I said cheerio to my horsey pals and caught the ration lorry for Llandrindod Wells, via Breckon.

OCTU days [Officer Cadet Training Unit]

My arrival [*30 July 1941*] dressed "à la 1914" caused some merriment but I soon found a friendly QM [*quartermaster*] who put me up to date with a battle-dress issue.

The squad I was destined to was comfortably quartered at the Brynawel Hotel and our classrooms were the local Cinemas. There was plenty of swotting to be done and the atmosphere was most scholastic.

Found that I was one of four types who could ride a motorcycle, having possessed a speedy Norton in my youth. I promptly volunteered to act as Don R [*Despach Rider*] on schemes. This meant that we could chase ahead, always through beautiful country, and were relatively independent. Once the message was delivered we could quickly repair to a friendly pub whilst the other lads were busy manhandling the heavy Bofors through fields.

Our only weapon, as Light Ack Ack gunners, was the 44 mm quick firing Bofors with accompanying predictor and we soon became proficient in handling them. When we finally went on full scale schemes, with all our transport, Don R'ing wasn't so funny. We then acted as traffic cops which meant shepherding them past a cross roads then catching up and going through the convoy travelling through the narrow sunken lanes so typical of Wales. This was dangerous sport. We would make dashes from vehicle to vehicle whenever a slight widening of the lane permitted but often we were caught between a tractor and the gun and there wasn't much room there. Any skid on the loose surface of the lane would have been unpleasantly fatal. Quite a few Don R's were lost this way.

After five months of cramming and sweating at exams, what remained of our original Squad attended a full ceremonial parade after which we were allowed to put up our solitary "pip" [*second lieutenant*]and thus I became an Officer and a gentleman (by act of Parliament).

During my stay in Wales I thoroughly explored the Wye Valley and many a pleasant tramp through those delightful hills, also roaming as far as the Cotswolds.

The Ways of the Army

Before leaving OCTU we had been allowed to request postings and I had put in for South East England where Light AA was having lots of fun and games with sneak raiders.

When I reached Aberdeen to join my Regiment together with another chap I had requested a prompt posting overseas. Another man, also new, had asked to be allowed a few months in the U.K. as he had just got married. Within a fortnight that poor chap was on a troop ship bound oversees and us two volunteers remained, to eventually become the sole remaining survivors from that particular intake.

After six months of exploring Scotland with this Light AA Regiment I asked the MO [*Medical Officer*] to give me a medical and I took the Certificate to my Commanding Officer and demanded an immediate overseas posting.

He'd look into it, he told me.

A week or so later I was called up for an interview with the Brigadier General of Scottish Command. He was looking, he told me, for suitable candidates for Mixed Heavy AA. I was most annoyed and told him straight that I had not come all the way from Argentina to while away my time in Scotland and less to be mixed up with a girlish mob. He was a decent chap and refrained from clapping me in irons or sending me before a Court Martial, which he could have done for insubordination, but all he could do was to put me at the bottom of his list where I would be quite safe.

A month later I received a signal to report to 158 Mixed Heavy AA Battery. I only managed to get out of that fix by volunteering repeatedly for Air Observation Post work, which I eventually wangled.

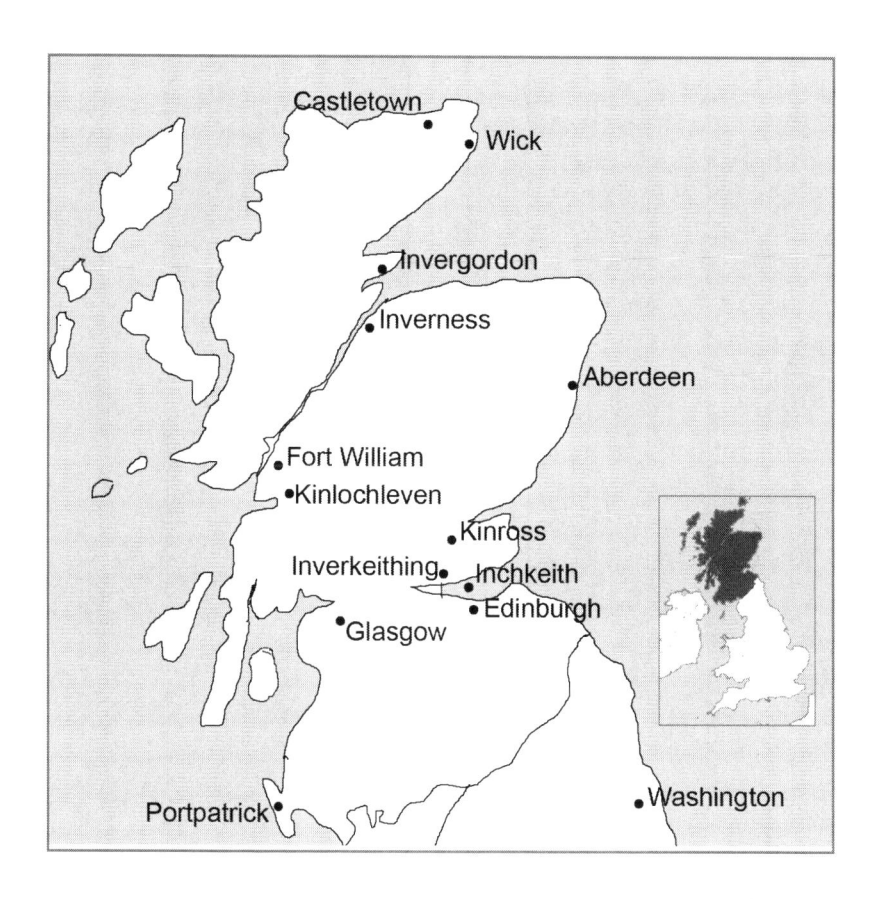

FOURTEEN MONTHS IN SCOTLAND

Getting to Know Bonny Scotland

And so I joined the 95th Light A. A. Regiment then stationed in Aberdeen. Soon after I was sent as a one man Advance Party to Inverness to take over a new commitment. Had a pleasant ride in a utility with my batman and no sooner had we got through than it snowed heavily and all roads were blocked for days. Hence spent a pleasant week living in digs in pretty Inverness, doing nothing until HQ eventually caught up with me. Then I was ordered to take a couple of trucks and join a Battery stationed in Fort William.

It was the 1st of February 1942 when I started off with two 15 cwt trucks along the Long Lochs. These particular trucks were completely open, did not even sport a windscreen but only a small windshield and were, consequently, pretty draughty. It had, as I already mentioned, snowed heavily and we were the first vehicles to attempt this trip; we crept along slowly crushing through the snow. The day was sunny and bright and I thoroughly enjoyed this, my first real journey through the Highlands, skirting the beautiful lochs with gentle hills, moulded in white, prettying the scene. Snow was so bad that we came upon several small herds of deer seeking for any fodder that might be around.

We completed the trip without difficulty and I reported to my new CO in Fort William.

My Very First Command

The next morning the Battery CO took me along to Kinlochleven, some 22 miles away, and nominated me 'C' Troop Commander and also VP (Vital Point) Commander of this wee place which, however, housed the huge and only aluminium processing plant in the whole of the British Isles and whose safety was absolutely indispensable if we were to keep on producing planes. This, with but one "pip" up and earning a mere pittance. It seemed that I was a big shot!

My Command consisted of four gun-sites each with Nissen hut and cook-house beside its Bofors gun and Kerrison Predictor, all sited strategically around the aluminium factory. Two were placed on commanding heights on either side of the vulnerable pipelines that brought water from the large loch to feed the turbines of the hydroelectric power plant. Another was sited up in the hills to the North, near the Mamore Forest Hotel and the last on the shore of Lochleven near the village. My Troop HQ was an old wooden frame school house and the Mess, which I shared with 2/Lt. Glaysher was the well known Tartan Hotel where we spent a wizard winter with all the comforts including hot-water bottles and an early morning cup of tea brought in by bonny wee Vera.

Fourteen Months in Scotland 29

Ben Nevis

Scotland, near Kinlochleven. Mountain climbing on motorbike

My normal mode of transport was by motor bike and I had a 350 cc Ariel with which I used to visit my gun sites. It was tricky going up the mountain tracks especially in slippery weather, and I used to go into Fort William once a week to fetch the men's pay. Enjoyed these trips and I managed to lower the standing record for the 22 mile run to 25 minutes, equivalent to 52 mph, not bad on those winding roads. And not often enough I roamed around the nearby highlands and did some mountain climbing, also on my motor-bike.

That particular Command was a favourite inspection spot for visiting Brass Hats because of the Tartan Hotel lunch invitation that went with it. Hence had more than average need for spit and polish – and we were more apt to find trouble.

With plenty of action in the Desert, where our types were indulging in the highly unhealthy sport of hunting German tanks, Light AA replacements were urgently needed and frequent postings were requested from us static troops. Whilst other Troops would send off their worst men and so keep up the standard of their troop, I sent off the best and soon I was having trouble keeping up to minimum efficiency with the very green replacements. However, as I had lunch with visiting Generals and did them proud, I could explain my case beforehand and, I must admit, I was always understood.

Nothing occurred to bestir the quietness of that pretty neighbourhood. As VP Commander I was expected to give out the prizes at the local Whist Drives, where also did tread many a measure even daring the Dashing White Sergeant. The only time we received an air warning RED was when we were in the middle of an attack by the Fort William Home Guard. It was about 19.00 hours and pitch black and the Home Guard were attacking lustily and throwing thunderflashes that went off with a loud bang and a mighty flash that could be seen for miles around. I was at the lochside gun-site controlling the defence when the warning came through and I set off at the double for my HQ. Of course I was promptly captured and it took me some time to persuade my captors that I wasn't trying to pull a fast one and that the warning was real. We all stood at alert but the raid petered out and nothing came over. Actually putting that strategic plant out of action could have been easy. Jerry had but to land a couple of paratroopers up on the topside loch where one man stood guard with a shotgun, and a demolition charge would have been sufficient to put the whole place out of action plus wiping out Kinlochleven; but they missed their chance or lacked information.

Whilst at Kinlochleven I was sent on a weeks Gunnery Training Course in Edinburgh where I was billeted at the Grosvenor Hotel.

In Which I Command Three Troops in 24 Hours

All good things come to an end and on the 25th March 1942, after nearly two months spent in such pleasant surroundings, we were on the move.

Batteries had recently been cut down from four to three troops and my 'C' Troop was to be deployed south. Thus it happened that I handed over my first command to a stranger and proceeded to Fort William where I was put in charge of 'D' Troop for the move North to Caithness.

The Regiment was heading for Wick, which is situated on the topmost tip of Scotland, where we were to give air defence to several aerodromes. En route, whilst still on board the train, the Colonel made me Troop Commander of 'A' Troop which I was to deploy around the Coastal Command drome up there. And so it happened that I actually commanded three Troops in the space of 24 hours. Surely a record.

I hardly had time to settle in when I was sent on another Gunnery Course, this time to Kinross which finished up a fortnight later in Edinburgh.

And then I went off on another spot of leave this time doing London and touring all over beautiful rolling Surrey with friends in their car. On the way back spent a couple of days in Glasgow getting to know it a wee bit better.

Un-lethal Front Line Troops

When I returned to Wick and reported to HQ I found that once again I was being shifted and was ordered to take over command of

'C' Troop then defending the RAF drome at Castletown. Was horrified when I got there, after mushing through deep snow, to find we were living in tents. Far too cold for my likings. I lost no time in getting on friendly terms with the Station CO and persuaded him to lend us one of his dispersal huts, solidly built of brick, and we moved in without further ado.

Studying our position, I was then OC Land Troops in the area, meaning us and some searchlight boys. Found that there was absolutely nothing between ourselves and Jerry over the way in Norway. In fact, any commando type raid could easily land on any of many sandy beaches, and there was nothing to stop them climbing the easy cliffs and destroying all the planes. That is except us.

It was early May by then and so far north the lengthening days extended first light and dusk to practically 24 hours and my men had to stand to continually. And we had to be on our toes.

A fantastic touch was added to this dramatic situation when a signal came through from Army ordering pick helves to be issued to all sentries in the UK and that rifles would NOT, repeat NOT be carried. Needless to say that order was NOT obeyed and not only did my merry men go on sentry duty with a rifle and 60 rounds of ammo but had one "up the spout" contrary to other standing orders.

Our four Bofors were sited around the aerodrome perimeter, camouflaged to some extent by the odd hedge, but devoid of any shelter. To give my lads some chance of surviving a ground attack, decided to put up a sand-bag breastwork. Sand-bags were obtained and had the lads fill them at a handy quarry. We had inherited a large three ton Fordson lorry which had been "found" by the previous outfit, no questions asked and nobody knew who it belonged to. With friends in the local Workshops and Petrol-point, I managed to get it serviced and fuelled off the record and it came in pretty useful carrying sandbags around. We had no driver so I nominated myself official *chofer* and the boys kept me busy.

I had trouble at first as the Fordson wouldn't corner properly. The front wheels had a habit of leaving the ground like a circus car. I then discovered we had made a slight miscalculation on the load factor and instead of carrying three tons of sand, it didn't look much when loaded, we were actually taking something like seven tons.

This old truck was pretty fast and we used it as a "liberty wagon" to take the lads, when off duty, into the nearest town. Nobody ever checked up on this vehicle and, when we left, we handed it over to the incoming unit.

In this way the sandbagging was carried out in record time and we were complimented on a good job of work quickly done by the local Brass Hat.

Still had doubts about our ability to cope with possible invaders so indented for some hand grenades. Nobody, including myself, had ever handled or thrown one of these nasty things, and we had a rather amusing, if bloodcurdling time teaching ourselves the drill.

I rounded up all available chaps and with my Troop Sergeant we climbed down to the sea shore. There we placed a ring of old paraffin tins as a target and from behind a small sand dune I proceeded to demonstrate how it should be done. Holding a grenade firmly in my right hand I proceeded to pull out the pin then letting the handle click open, that started the fuse ticking; counted three mighty fast and got rid of the damn thing quick. A vicious crack and the whine of bits and pieces flying overhead followed at the correct three seconds later.

That was the easiest part. What was far more scarifying was teaching the lads and watching some of them fumbling around with nervous fingers whilst I stood in front of them ready to take mighty fast action should he drop the thing with the fuse already ignited. The thought of a feeble throw and the grenade falling out of reach on the near side of the sand dune and maybe rolling gently towards us, was most disconcerting. All the lads had three throws each and there were no accidents, but some of my grey hairs date from that afternoon.

Here I managed to wangle a trip in a Maggie [*Miles M.14 Magister is a British two-seat monoplane*] and it whetted my appetite for flying. These aerodromes were defending the fleet at Scapa Flow and it was from here that torpedo bombers carried out many daring raids on the enemy.

In which I become a Headmaster

The Regiment was ordered to move to the Firth of Forth area there to take over two gun-sites, which meant that one Troop would be out of a job. The obvious candidate was 'C' Troop, of which I was then OC and it seemed something new was cropping up in my varied Army Career.

We entrained on the 21st May 1942 and arrived in Edinburgh early the next morning. There the Colonel put me in charge of the Battery HQ in addition to my own Troop. Had the Sergeant Major line them up in Princess Street and then, at the head of this mob, I proudly marched them along this famous thoroughfare. The awkward part was I hadn't a clue where we were heading for and the SM marching behind me had to whisper loudly whenever we had to turn a corner. And so we arrived at Forest Hill Drill Hall, an ancient granite edifice many hundreds of years old, which was to be our home for the next couple of months.

And so I became a Headmaster and organised classes consisting of map-reading, signalling, military law and we had plenty of PT. On every decent afternoon organised a route march up to Arthur's seat, the hill that dominates Edinburgh. I took some of the classes myself but mostly delegated the job to my NCO's.

I did not sleep in this grim and gloomy Drill Hall, but in comfy digs in front of the Edinburgh Hospital and it was a pleasant change to be in such civilized surroundings. Made the most of this opportunity to explore this most beautiful city and before eventually leaving got to know it pretty well.

Whilst there I was appointed Liaison Officer to liaise between Home Field Forces and 36 Brigade in case of invasion.

'A' Troop was stationed at Portobello, a suburb of Edinburgh, and I thought it would be a good idea if we were to build an assault course then fashionable, on a vacant spot of wild ground nearby, planning to take my own men along for a spot of toughening up. There was a railway embankment running through, a bridge, a stream and a lovely pond. Charted out a wicked course and with my merry men set to to make it. Victims had to climb the steep embankment, slide down a rope from the bridge, negotiate a rope bridge across the stream and then were expected to tip-toe precariously over upright stakes placed unevenly across the pond.

I had just finished the course, and managed to try it out once, when we were on the move again. Just as well too because a delegation of irate mothers from the neighbourhood complained to the CO that their bairns were trying out our assault course and kept falling into the pond.

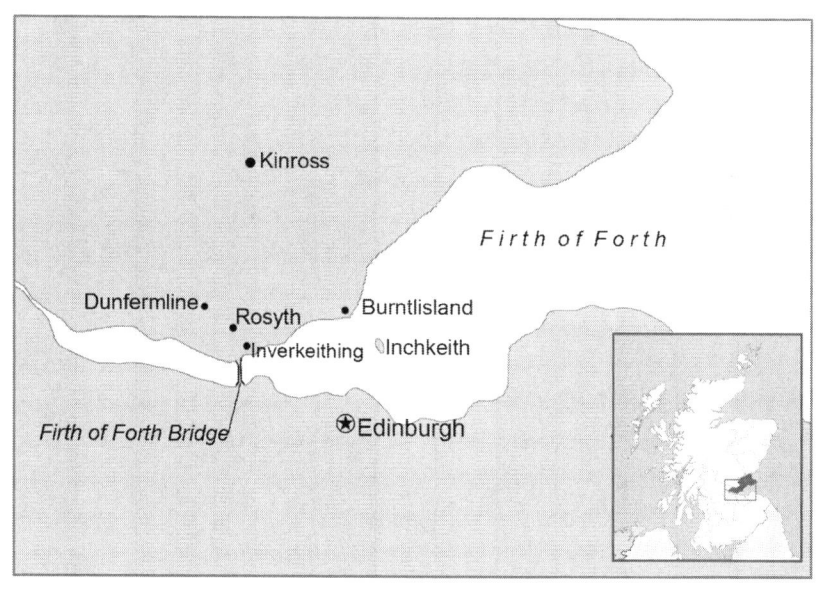

Firth of Forth and Inchkeith, the "Fortified Island."

Life on a Fortified Island

My next stop was Inchkeith, a wee island in the middle of the Firth of Forth with a beautiful view of the famous bridge built by my namesake.

Here I found we had to man ancient 3 inch 1914 vintage guns instead of the usual Bofors. The drill for these guns was completely different; we did not have predictors but made use of rangefinders, a larger edition of ones used during my Mountain Battery days and also built by Barr & Stroud. Not having a known range to check their accuracy, I borrowed a "director" from the Coastal Battery chaps who shared the island and by the process of triangulation worked out several ranges to prominent objects either side of the Firth.

To make training easier and, as most of the lads had never seen a shot fired (nor had I), invented an "observation of tracer" training gadget and built it with a spare sheet of frosted glass, some wood, brass, and a 6 volt battery and bulb. It worked fine and the instructor could easily give a fair likeness of a shell arcing towards a plane and could show a hit or a variety of near misses.

Once a week the Coastal Defence people would try out their electric contact mines spread around the Firth and for the next couple of days we would have fresh lobster and plenty of fish on our menu. The mighty explosion would knock out all living creatures in the neighbourhood and it was an easy matter to haul in stunned fish if one had the use of a boat.

Our lads were living in Jane huts, rather flimsy affairs made of wood, and we shared the mess with the Coastal Battery Officers, there to man the immense 9·2 inch Naval guns. Training had been done by means of a small one pounder gun strapped to the barrel of these monsters but it was decided to try out the big guns themselves. The island is a small one and guns and huts were pretty well intermingled, some being placed in not too secure positions, a fair distance below the gun, but in its firing arc. Huts in this position were evacuated as the blast could well deafen a man; and just as well. The first shell went off with a thunderous roar and two of the Jane huts simply collapsed.

Luckily the German Navy kept away whilst I was there nor did any nasty plane disturb our peaceful existence.

A Church of Scotland hut appeased our insides with cups of tea and rock cakes and, it being then June [1942], the weather was delightful and I enjoyed many an evening chatting with pals over a pint whilst watching a beautiful sunset outline the majestic Forth bridge. Once we saw the *Anson*, the mightiest battleship then afloat, slip by quietly one evening on her maiden run out to sea.

Unsuccessful Evasive Action

And here it was that I got ants in my pants and asked the MO to give me an overseas medical. This I handed to the Colonel with my sixth request for an overseas posting. Rommel was on the rampage in North Africa and had pushed the Eighth Army right back into Egyptian territory. Someone had to go there and help push them back.

My next step, as already related, was an interview with the Brigadier when he threatened to put me in with the ATS [*Auxiliary Territorial Service*] and I protested vigorously on the score that, as a volunteer, I should be allowed some say in the matter.

My protests were to no avail. Three weeks later, after another leave spent in London, plus a few days spent with my old 'C' Troop in Burntisland, where our Mess was a famous whisky distillery, I found myself reporting for duty to 158 Mixed Heavy AA Regiment at Dunfermline. I was assigned to 540 Battery then stationed at Donibristle.

The second half of August 1942 was spent learning my new trade and from the 2nd to 23rd September I attended a Course at the 7 AA Division School in Washington N.C. (Newcastle) where they tried to teach us in three weeks what, in peacetime, takes two years.

The tempo of that Course was terrific. We had to learn all about three types of Heavy AA guns, two complicated predictors, two rangefinders and several even more complicated Radar systems, the latter, then called GL [*Gun Laying Radar, an early model*], very hush-hush. All morning was spent in the classroom and in the afternoon we did practical exercises, usually strenuous gun-drill. We found it was no use trying to study in the evenings, our brains could not absorb any more. However, our tummy's power of absorption was not impaired and stacks of good beer was put down during nightly pub-crawls.

Managed to wriggle through the exams in fair order and then we were all given another fortnight leave to recuperate.

With the Lassies in Bonny Scotland

My new Battery, 158 Mixed Heavy AA had their gun-sites sited near Inverkeithing, on the North side of the Firth of Forth Bridge and guarding the important Naval Base of Rosyth.

At first it was highly disconcerting giving out orders and having a squeaky girlish voice answer but, all in all, the change wasn't that bad. Far worse for the old Army Sergeants, too old for overseas, relegated to these girly regiments, to have to drill them. It was highly amusing seeing them trying to line them up, a quite impossible operation in view of many obviously protruding parts. At best they could get the fronts more or less in line but you could see them shudder when they glanced behind.

It was then October and the breeze that habitually whistles up the Firth of Forth was frigid when it hit morning parades. The girls' hats would fly off and lines were wavy as they leaned forward into the wind. When I was Orderly Officer I endeavoured to hurry up these parades and soon had things down to a fine art and only about five minutes were taken for the whole thing.

With GL (Radar) we were on duty 24 hours and every third night or so, had to sleep in the underground Command Post run by ATS [*Auxiliary Territorial Service*]. As things were peaceful we had a bed down there and would have a good sleep, getting up once during the night to do the rounds of the guns to see that all was well. The girls would keep me well supplied with cups of tea. These duties were not dreaded.

At first light and dusk complicated drills had to be carried out to line up each of the four guns with the predictor, the predictor with the GL, the GL with the Plotting Table and so on. I was the only officer who could do it by heart, having just come out of school so to speak, and for 25 minutes would give a series of orders over the Tannoy [*loudspeaker*]. Now and again we would ask a tame plane to come and act as target and we would have some fun pretending. It was uncanny to squint through the small telescope attached to the side of the G.L. receiver and see the plane unerringly cut by the cross threads.

One fine clear day I went along to Turnhouse drome and hitched a ride in the Oxford acting as target. For a couple of hours enjoyed viewing Scotland from on top.

Spent a week at Kinross attending an MT [*Motor Transport*] Course and on my return was made MT Officer and my main job was to check trucks and cars driven and maintained by ATS. The motors were usually spotless with all copper parts polished and shining but such things as gearboxes and differentials were apt to be empty of oil. Still they did a good job and were keen, and I couldn't be awfully strict with them.

Best job was cook-house inspection as one was sure of being bribed by sundry cups of tea, not NAAFI variety, and homemade cakes.

ATS quarters were NOT, repeat NOT inspected by Orderly Officers and only the Junior Commander and her hench-girls could do this duty.

On November 6th 1942 took up residence with 548 Battery away up in Invergordon, thus exploring another part of bonny Scotland.

The Colonel and his rather ancient Senior Commander were pantomime fans and the main object of the unit, or so it seemed, was to put on a first rate show that Christmas. Many times I could not properly carry out the dusk lining up drill because key members of the Predictor or Plotting Table were at rehearsals. So what, thought I, the likelihood of a Jerry plane ever coming around those parts seemed remote. I volunteered once again for Mobile AA.

Just about then an Army Order came out calling for volunteers for Air Observation Post Pilots. Did not know what it was all about but it obviously meant flying and it did seem a possible escape route. Promptly sent in a signal volunteering for the job and was surprised when I received a quick reply ordering me to appear before a Selection board at Larkhill. Wondered what I had let myself in for. Other chaps had volunteered for the Commandos, Parachutists, SAS and the likes all of which seemed sort of risky, besides I was too old for such fun and games. However, a few hours before I was due to catch my train south the first signal was cancelled.

Followed up with a written application but time passed and nothing happened.

Life in the ATS was real cushy. We had at least one ENSA [*Entertainment National Service Association*] show a week, two cinema evenings and the rest was taken up by whist drives and dances. Fratting was allowed. The girls were first class as they had to be brainy types to handle the complicated instruments. The men, on the other hand, were generally speaking, old and decrepit and unfit for front line duty, hence a good time was had by the few "young" officers.

Whilst up in Invergordon managed to play a few games of rugger and one final for the Navy against the RAF losing 9 to 0.

An interesting job came my way and that was putting in a new type of Plotting Table as nobody else seemed to understand its complicated layout. This also meant calibrating it, a lengthy business and that kept me happy for a while.

We all had a pleasant Christmas and one cold and frosty evening joined a group singing Carols. Just fancy. On Christmas day we had fun and games as O.R's took over the morning parade and us Officers were ordered into the ranks. The Colonel and Senior Commander were placed under arrest for having dirty buttons and marched off to the Guard Room. Of course we had to serve the troops an ample lunch complete with turkey and plum pudding, while getting our legs pulled mightily. It was a happy unit but rather unwarlike.

Went on another Gunnery Course at Kinross and, on the 16th January on another leave with Aunt Dolly and family in London they having returned to their home after a brief exodus up North.

Farewell to the ATS

Started off by enjoying my leave and going to as many wizard shows as possible. Managed to see all the best ones and also looked up friends in neighbourhood counties. Generally exploring the pretty English countryside.

However, wasted no time in making my way to River Plate House and there asked Mr. Graham, whose job it was to look after us volunteers, and he did it very well, to try and use his influence to get me into this new Air OP racket. He rang up his friend Captain Plum at the War Office, explained my request, and was told I hadn't a hope in hell as there were all of 380 applicants and only some thirty were required. My hopes of wriggling out of the ATS were thoroughly squashed and had no option but to make the most of it, finish my leave and then go back and enjoy a life of ease. So I thought.

Two days later the "hope in hell" materialized. There is a saying that covers such events. A telegram arrived at Grove Park ordering me to report for a RAF medical on the following Monday.

And so it came about that I went along to Imperial House on Kingsway and was given a pretty thorough examination. My eyesight was A1 a necessary prerequisite for this job but I was out for size as maximum permissible for flying duties is 6' 4" and I'm 6' 5 ½." However, persuaded the Doc that he couldn't be sure of the latter figure as the scale didn't go up that far and he put me down at the maximum.

Went back, this time to 541 Battery in Donibristle, to await my release. It did not take long and on the 23rd February 1943, after seven months in this mixed outfit, said goodbye to all and sundry and set off once again for Salisbury Plains back to the real gunnery, wondering whether I had done the right thing.

All in all I suppose I could not complain as I had spent 14 months in Scotland, touring around extensively, getting to know the land of my fathers and the wizard countryside.

Phase two of my Army Career had finished.

Locations in England and Wales

AIR OBSERVATION POST TRAINING

The Real Adventure Commences

On arrival at Larkhill [*23 February 1943*] discovered I was one of twenty interviewed by the CO of the Air OP [*Observation Post*] Training School.

Training consisted of concentrated OP exercises with plenty of miniature range work. My previous experience came in handy and I managed to more than hold my own at exams, obtaining 75 and 80% for written and oral, respectively. We did plenty of real firing on the plains, the first time for me, and found it difficult to correct shots on such a featureless terrain. But the others were likewise handicapped.

On the 31st March the gunnery course finished and of the

twenty entrants only thirteen remained to continue on the EFTS [*Elementary Flying Training School*].

Another leave in London followed where I met my old pal J. E. Walding co-owner with me of the notorious craft "Holy Smoke" a name soon to become famous – but more of that anon.

Enjoyed another wizard leave and was in fine fettle when the time came to head for the Flying School.

In which I Fulfill a Lifelong Ambition

On the 7th April 1943 I reported to the 22nd EFTS – RAF at Cambridge with Headquarters at Marshall's Aerodrome on the outskirts of that beautiful city.

Once again twenty of us made up this particular Course, thirteen survivors from Larkhill and seven others who had been hanging around waiting for us to arrive.

We were all billeted in private digs. I had a comfortable room with a family towards the other end of the town and a bus would pick us up in the morning and return us in the evening.

During the morning we sat in classrooms and learnt all about navigation, meteorology, signalling including Morse, aerodynamics, etc., etc. In the afternoons we FLEW. It was early Spring and the weather could not have been better nor more stable. Three of us shared a plane and between flights, whilst waiting for the others to come in, we would lie in the sun and dream.

The very next day after arriving we were all in the air on our first trip in our training plane, the sturdy Tiger Moth, and for the first time in history, I handled a plane. It was easy.

Two days later we were initiated into the joys of spinning. Horrible it was at first. Practically everyone that day had to make use of the bucket and mop kept at our dispersal hut for obvious reasons. Glad to say I was spared that.

On the eighth day and with 8.50 hours of flying time to my credit the Instructor climbed out of the front cock-pit and gave me the traditional "Take her away. She's all yours."

Marshall's aerodrome is a huge roughly circular expanse of lush grass, lovely to land on. With plenty of space to fool around with, flying was really easy. And so it was I found myself taxiing along and eventually pushing on full throttle. The engine made a lovely roar as it pulled me along faster and faster. Got the tail up and easy back on the stick and we were up and away. It was a wizard feeling being all alone and floating through the air, but I stuck to instructions and kept climbing straight ahead until I was well over Cambridge looking lovely in the bright sunshine. At 1,000 feet levelled off and made a rather wobbly turn left. Went along a bit to enjoy my first flight before getting back into the circuit and made ready to land. I flew along until I was level with the middle of the drome, it did not look so large from up there, then turned dead into wind and cut the throttle to 1200 revs and speed to 70 mph, which brought us down steadily. I levelled off correctly at about 30 feet, cut the throttle completely and then just kept her straight until she was nearly on the grass; then a gentle pull back on the stick and we were down to an almost perfect landing, easy as pie. Actually it wasn't too bad – said the Instructor.

Then we kept practising turns of all sorts, climbing, level, and gliding also stalls and spins, incipient and otherwise.

Aerobatting was next on the list and this I really enjoyed – at least most of it. Loops were easy and good fun if done properly. Slow rolls are quite another kettle of fish. It is a highly disconcerting feeling, in those open planes, hanging upside down with nothing to stop you hurtling down to earth but two web straps. On such occasions, any loose change was likely to be lost and all the dirt in the cockpit went whizzing down to earth.

Discovered that it takes quite a lot of concentrated effort to fly a plane revolving around its axis. The control surfaces keep changing functions. The rudder acts as an elevator when the plane is on its side and the elevators as a rudder. Likewise the rudder steers the opposite way when upside down. Also great care must be taken to fly reasonably level. Any tendency to rise, so dropping flying speed, is particularly dangerous as a plane has a high stalling speed when upside-down and is then sure to go into a spin with tricky, back to front, recovery procedure. Difficult to say the least, especially for us beginners.

I remember very clearly the day I dared take the Tiger up to 5,000 feet and indulge in some spinning all on my own. It was another clear Spring day with good visibility and few clouds. I put her nose up until she started to wallow and then kicked the rudder sharp left. The plane promptly responded and slid sideways and down in a sickening lurch and in no time we were pointing straight down and revolving fast with the earth whizzing round. As a matter of fact the sensation is more that of falling straight with the earth revolving. Let it whizz by three times then pressed opposite rudder and was glad when it took effect and the turning ceased. Then, eased back on the stick until the nose hit the horizon. Then I went up to 5,000 feet once again and did it all over again. Must admit it took quite a bit of nerve to give that decisive kick to the rudder that would start this sickening whirl through space.

Early on in our training we were flown under a hood, that is with outward visibility cut off obliging us to fly entirely by instrument. This procedure was fairly difficult until one became trained to ignore instinct and believe blindly in what the instruments indicated. This is more difficult than it sounds and some of the boys simply could not force their wills to do this and were turned down.

The Instructors would enjoy themselves at our expense and go through a series of weird manoeuvres and, when the plane was in some impossible angle, would tell us to take over the controls. However, provided one stuck rigidly to the rules and took no notice of instinct, which invariably was in error, recovery was easy. For example, if the air speed was piling up meant we were diving. If the turn and bank needle was over to the left, we were lying on that side. If all needles were stuck on the right, we were spinning that way.

Spinning under the hood was particularly sickening and most of the chaps headed for the bucket and mop on landing. I was lucky in that, at most, I got really giddy.

Soon we were doing aerobatics all on our own and that was fun, except when things did not go quite right and fright set in. I used to try and climb high above the clouds, but always over a clear spot as I was scared of finding myself in the middle of cloud at that stage of my training. Then I would plan a series of aerobatics to do one after the other, tumbling down in breath-taking swoops with the pretty green earth, blue sky and white clouds appearing in most unlikely places. Being all on one's own up there with a really nimble plane like the Tiger Moth was a marvellous sensation and one which I had dreamed of since boyhood.

It is a well known fact about flying that brand new pilots go through periods of super confidence, until something happens that makes them realize that they have yet much to learn. During one of those super periods, when I had all of 43 hours flying time to my credit, I went up high above the clouds on a sunny afternoon and decided to do two loops in succession then come out in a half roll when I was upside-down on the top of the second loop. Nosing down a little to pick up speed, pulled back fairly quickly on the stick and up we went in a graceful arc. When I saw the horizon appear from behind my neck and draw level with the top wing, all nice and level (not always the case) throttled back and went swooshing down towards the earth and up again for my second loop. When the horizon again appeared level with the top wing (now bottom) I levelled off, which meant that I was hanging up-side-down from my straps, always an uncertain moment. Then stick hard over to the left as I commenced to roll the plane. But things started to go wrong. Guess I did not have enough speed for the ailerons to act decisively and the plane wallowed sideways and the nose dropped in a stall but luckily not in a spin. It was obvious that the plane was not going to roll and my only hope of recovering from this awkward position was to gain flying speed.

And there I was hanging from my straps with the plane plummeting down half upside-down and on its side. The plane kept gathering speed in an increasingly steep inverted dive. Now there was a little notice in red letters stuck on the dashboard which said "DO NOT EXCEED 160 mph." By the time I got her under control, by then diving nearly straight down, the ASI [*Air Speed Indicator*] needle was walking past the 150 mph mark. Had a parachute but we were not supposed to bail out at high speed. The tail would have knocked my block off for sure. The motor was throttled back and backfiring badly, but all was fairly silent and I could hear the wind whistling through the wire rigging which, by then, was twanging like cello strings with the strain. I glanced at the wing tips and shuddered when I saw they were flapping. Any brusque manoeuvre at that time would certainly have been disastrous. Gently I pulled back on the stick and wondered whether I had sufficient space for the gradual pull-out if the wings didn't fall off before then. The altimeter needle was going round and round, but I was gaining confidence as everything stuck together and the angle of descent gradually decreased, and with it the speed. At last we managed to level off at just over 1,000 ft having dropped some 4,000 feet during this episode.

Then I climbed up again above the clouds and indulged in a few gentle loops but this time without attempting any frills.

Being at Cambridge I was near Way's estate at Brinkley and went out to stay with him on several occasions. We were also nearish to London and could run in for a weekend and do the town.

Cambridge itself in Spring was delightful and thoroughly enjoyed my stay there. Even went punting on the Cam, a most awkward form of water transport, though punts were just the job for a lazy afternoon. Pubs were good and plentiful and many crawls were done.

Cross country navigational trips were part of our curriculum and many of these were undertaken successfully. These would take us away across superb country and we invariably picked a good drome with first class grub laid on for our stopping points.

A Spot of Night Flying

We had of course, to learn night flying, and this we did when we had an average of 50 hours flying time all told.

Flying at night during civilized times with lights all over the landscape is easy, but it is quite another proposition to sail up into velvety nothingness with nary a glimmer to steer by. If the sky is clear after a while the horizon can be discerned but if at all cloudy it is difficult to keep the plane straight and level unless, of course, one resorts to instruments. However, to duck one's head into the cockpit and not keep an eye skinned for anything stirring in the outer darkness, took some doing.

After three short hops dual I was sent off on my first night solo. It was an eerie sensation but not unpleasant. There were no bumps and flying was smooth and gentle.

For fear of Jerry night raiders the landing strip lights were dim and could not be seen over 1,000 ft, so it was quite possible to lose sight of the aerodrome and lose oneself. Searchlights were scanning the skies in the distance and gave me a reference point to fly by. They also meant that raiders were somewhere about. In this case, should they approach too near, our landing strip lights would be doused and we were supposed to make our way, via a given compass bearing, to a lit up satellite drome away from any town.

Gingerly I did my circuit and came round for the landing run with the line of landing lights straight ahead and glide indicator showing amber. This latter gadget consists of a half cylinder shaped reflector placed horizontally to the ground and shining up at an angle equivalent to our best gliding angle. Horizontally placed coloured strips of glass divided the wide beam into three. The topmost one showed "amber", the middle "green" for safety and lowest "red" for danger. This was set alongside the landing strip round about where we were supposed to touch down. The procedure was to come in high on "amber" descend more steeply than normal until "green" appeared and so down to a perfect landing. If one dropped too steeply "red" would appear and a touch of throttle would flatten the descent back into green. Quite simple and effective. Thereafter one just let the plane sink down until it hit the ground in a two point landing. Here again a certain amount of restraint was required as we were accustomed to three point landings and many tried to do just that to find that their three pointer was done perfectly but ten feet up. Distances are deceptive at night.

Lt Melley, one of the Course boys had done a couple of circuits of the drome instead of the usual single and was coming in to land quite happily on the "green" area. He hadn't seen the "amber" to start off with and it all seemed a bit too easy. He thought he was coming down pretty fast but no "red" appeared and, of course, we had to obey our instruments blindly. Then suddenly "red" came on and he pushed on throttle gently, then not so gently and he could not get back into the "green." Then he found himself skimming thirty feet up over the marshalling yards of Cambridge station and the signal he had so faithfully obeyed turned back to "green." That shook him somewhat.

My First Prang

So far I hadn't even dented a tail skid, but of course, there is always a first time.

One fine day Sgt. Eric Hall, my favourite instructor and good friend, decided that a really lengthy cross country flight would improve my education and that a weekend trip to Chester would be just the job. Keen types we were.

And so it came about that early after lunch on the 29th day of May 1943 we set sail in our best Tiger Moth. I acted as navigator and successfully directed Eric practically right across England until, after a two hour uneventful flight, we landed at the Fleet Air Arm drome near Sealand just in time for tea. Hitch-hiked into Chester and put up at the Blossom's Hotel where Eric had friends. Explored that most interesting town, oozing with ancient atmosphere, and sampled the good beer at diverse antique pubs, finishing up for dinner at the Royal Oak.

We were up bright and early the next morn and caught the 8·35 train for Sealand. The weather report was good – SE winds, ceiling 2,000 feet. After duly checking our plane we set sail round about half past nine on a bright Sunday morning.

Again I was acting as navigator and flying in the rear cockpit. We were well on course at Crewe but after that the clouds came down. By then we were over hilly country and the hills were getting higher, according to the map. Rather than descend, and having in mind the favourable weather report, Eric decided to carry straight on through the clouds, a good experience for me. However, after about a quarter of an hour of gloomy travel, when we were considering turning back, I suddenly saw trees looming ahead and not far below us either. Eric had spotted them at the same time and took appropriate action, and as we flew over them saw that they evidently

50   Warlike Sketches

Uttoxeter plane crash.
We join the Highly Derogatory Order of the Irremovable Finger.

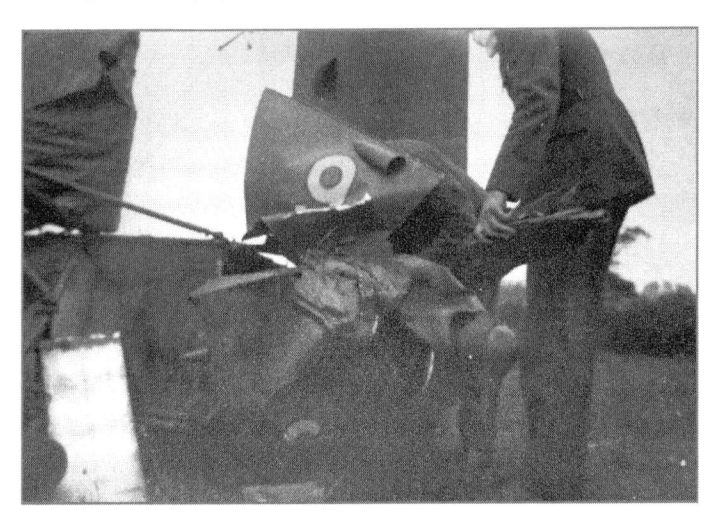

Uttoxeter plane crash. Picking up the pieces

lined a fairly large field. Eric was a skilful pilot and, there being not much future in low flying in cloud, decided to land there and then. By wriggling the plane around and side-slipping over the trees we landed fine and found we were right in the middle of the Uttoxeter racecourse, now a RASC [*Royal Army Service Corps*] Depot. These good folk discovered us and invited us in for a cup of tea. They also promised to keep an eye on the plane whilst we walked into the village to find a friendly pub in which to while away the time until the fog lifted. The "Black Hart" proved just the right place and the beer was good.

The fog appeared to be lifting as we walked back to the plane shortly after noon and we decided to continue on our journey to Cambridge. Eric swung the prop whilst I wiggled the switches and soon she was roaring comfortably. The field was big enough and Eric taxied up and down to check for possible holes. There was not a breath of wind so he chose a take-off patch in the longest stretch that faced a thicket hedge with a wooden gate in the middle.

We started off normally at full throttle and went roaring tail up gathering speed. I leaned down to collect my maps feeling all was well, when suddenly Eric yelled over the intercom "We've had it chum." And sure enough, when I popped my head out of the cockpit there was the hedge and gate approaching at a good rate of knots and we were still on the ground. Eric tried to lift her over but she was flying about three feet up when we hit. The under-cart smashed against the gate and the left wing hit the higher hedge. The plane rose a little then came crashing down on one wing and started to cartwheel until the motor hit the ground with a crunch and the fuselage slammed sideways against the ground completely demolishing what was left of the wing on that side. Destruction was thorough so much so that I found myself with one elbow resting on the damp earth.

The petrol tank, placed in the centre section of the top wing, and just over my head, had burst and that highly inflammable stuff was pouring out onto the ground and soaking my flying suit. Very alive to the danger of fire I then noticed an ominous spiral of black smoke arising from the engine cowling. We were undoubtedly on fire and a large flash could be expected at any moment. Not wishing to be cremated at such an early stage, I took immediate action as per Fire Drill and leaning down tugged at a lever under my seat which was supposed to spray foamite over the engine – but nothing happened. Eric had, by then, nipped smartly out of his cockpit. I was wearing a zipped on flying suit which by then was nicely soaked in high octane petrol and very difficult to get out of, so I made all haste to follow suit and seek safety.

The flash did not materialize, goodness knows why, it should have, and the fire remained localized in the engine, obviously the carburettor. I remembered a trick from old Corrientes days, when the "Surubi" had often caught fire in the same spot. Without wasting time I wrenched off the cowling, gathered up some mud of which there was a plentiful supply, hurled it at the source of the fire, and soon had it out. There again I was darn lucky that my suit didn't catch fire, which would have been most awkward.

Eric got a scare when he saw me as my face was streaming blood and I looked a gory mess. However, on checking I found that I was leaking from a cut lip and chin which had been split open when my face smashed against the cockpit cowling. A loud clanging noise announced the arrival of the village fire-engine and right behind came an ambulance with a lady Doctor inside. We walked over to the RASC Mess carrying our suitcases and parachutes. There Dr Parry-Evans, a pleasant female, did some fancy stitching on my face. Very neatly done it was, and hardly shows today. She then bandaged me up as though I had a toothache and checked us both for further damage. Eric had acquired a bloody nose and naught else and I had bruised knees, destined to suffer likewise every time I crashed in future due to my unauthorised height.

The really tragic event occurred after we had made our way back to the Black Hart and the good lady there invited us into her private parlour where she promptly prepared a lovely large *bife* [steak], the first one I had seen since I landed, and this she handed to Eric. All I could tackle with my sewn up mouth was a bowl of horrible mush. However, I made up for it partly by imbibing a couple of double scotches on the house in view of the increase in customers due to our notorious presence.

Eric proceeded to make all the necessary phone calls and reported the event to the police. We went with a Sergeant to have a look at the crash, a real beauty it was, and rescued the clock and part of the splintered prop which I kept as a souvenir. Highly against regs. The

Sergeant took some photos which he later sent on to me to use as evidence for this line-shoot. He also arranged for us to stay at the local inn, The Three Tuns.

Cambridge refused to send a rescue plane and we were told to make our own way back. Next morning caught an early train for Derby, there caught connection to Bedford where we had to change stations. We were quite an intriguing sight and most puzzling to fellow travellers who just could not make us out at all. There we were, an Artillery Officer in Service Dress carrying a parachute and a flying suit with his face cut up, accompanied by an RAF Sergeant Pilot also with a parachute over his arm, and we were travelling by train. We had time enough at Bedford to do a brisk pub crawl and then on to Cambridge arriving around tea time.

The Chief Flying Instructor flew down to the scene of the crash and confirmed that the field was more than ample for a safe take-off. No satisfactory explanation was ever given for the accident and we can only presume that a sudden gust of following wind, at the critical moment, was the cause. One of the unsolved mysteries of the War! Anyway, Eric got away with it at the Court of Enquiry.

We were kept busy flying and studying until tests commenced. As a result four more of the chaps didn't make the grade and were sent down. I was pleased as punch when I was passed "above average" on the rigorous flying CFI [*Chief Flying Instructor*] exam, mostly tricky aerobatics and under the hood work. And now only 9 of the original Larkhill Course were left to go on to the more difficult next step which was to be flying and gunnery combined. However, nobody seemed to worry much about the future at that time.

We Meet the Ubiquitous Auster

A slight regression to meet the famous Auster, the wee plane we were to fly in battle. Shortly before we left Marshall's, three arrived. They were small high winged planes comfortably cabined and we could therefore fly in relative comfort. The RAF types had never seen them before, and of course had never flown one. We would watch them trying to come in to land at Tiger Moth speed, about

54   Warlike Sketches

"The Ubiquitous Auster"

60 mph, and go floating practically right across the large landing ground before the Auster deigned to land at 28 MPH precisely, her designed landing speed.

It was strange, at first, flying the plane sitting low down on the left, but we soon got the hang of it.

Aerobatics in the Auster was forbidden. They weren't built strong enough for rough handling and whenever possible I took up a Tiger Moth to pile my aerobatic hours and enjoy the thrill of tumbling all over the sky.

We went on many navigational cross country flights, a really necessary part of our training and most enjoyable. Thus I slowly got to know more and more of this beautiful country, enhanced by perfect Spring weather and seen from above.

Exploring Cambridge and surroundings, weekend trips to London and to stay with Way and his beloved horses, not to mention many hours swotting for our final exams, kept me happy and busy.

It all ended, but not before we had spent three wizard months in Cambridge, and then we were given another week's leave before reporting for our final and most critical period of training.

At Ancient Old Sarum

After getting to know London and suburbs a bit better, entrained for Salisbury. Met some of the lads on board and on arrival made our way to Old Sarum, site of an ancient Roman Camp, now turned into a sizable aerodrome and for years home of the Army Co-Operation Flight.

The weekend was upon us before we could do any flying and took advantage to explore Southampton and Winchester.

An Auster III had to be modified to fit me and then we started to pile up the hours to become accustomed to the planes and to learn how to land really short – very important for our work

Then we commenced doing Field Exercises. Several suitable fields would be picked out by the instructors, a series of map references given, and off we would go at suitable intervals. At first locating the individual fields, identified only by a landing 'T' which also indicated wind direction, was difficult, but practice eventually made us near perfect. Getting into them was quite another matter. Invariably the fields were tree lined and never too large. Many a time we just didn't dare get in. On one memorable occasion two of the boys pranged. One dropped too quickly and broke his undercart, and the other overshot and hit the far hedge breaking his prop. And then the Instructor, who flew in bringing spares, also pranged. This pleased the rest of us who had used this particular field with impunity. We were becoming pretty hot pilots.

We were encouraged to fly low and land in any field we considered suitable. Then early morning mushroom hunts became popular as also landing beside a farm with chickens visible, and buying rationed eggs off the astonished farmer.

I thoroughly enjoyed this sort of flying and soon became proficient. So much so that I sailed through all tests with flying colours. Others weren't so fortunate and two more of the lads were RTU'd [*Returned to Unit, failed*].

Towards the end of July carried out my very first live shoot from a plane and managed to get a B. The next day, however, just as I commenced my shoot a whole bevy of Whitleys towing gliders came overhead and let them loose. I became so preoccupied dodging these, as well as the tow cables hanging down from the bombers that I did not do so well with my shoot and only got a D.

At that time Air OP was in its infancy. Our operational procedure was based on what meagre experience had been gained during the North African campaign and as there the fighting was most unorthodox the lessons learnt proved quite erroneous when applied to the more conventional Italian campaign.

The pre-Dunkirk experience was not taken into account as the larger and more powerful but less manoeuvrable Lysanders used there were shot out of the sky with ease by the Luftwaffe.

At that time we were supposed to operate at a maximum altitude of 600 feet. As soon as the target was identified we were to dive down to the deck, and hide behind trees or in valleys thus keeping out of danger while the guns were getting ready, then up again to observe the shot and back down to cover. After a maximum of twenty minutes, the time the enemy was supposed to take to have a fighter up and at us, we were to be back at our landing strip and under camouflage. As we were flying so low, parachutes were considered superfluous and not carried.

The highlight of our final Course was a two day scheme which had us jumping from field to field, the final one for the evening conveniently beside an inn near the small village of Hungerford. It was a lovely mild evening. All the villagers turned out to greet us, and buy us beers, and, wonder of wonders, a barbecue was prepared in the courtyard and fair sized *bifes* turned out.

The 18th of August 1943 was a proud day for us all as we were officially presented with our coveted wings, which we proudly put up on our Service Dress. Gathering up the CO and the Adjutant off we all went to celebrate at the Cathedral Arms at Salisbury, which we did in grand style.

Air OP was a most select unit. There were only about 80 of us pilots at that time in the whole of the British Army. I was certainly proud of having wriggled through, where so many had failed. And I had attained my lifelong ambition – to fly. Unfortunately, I could not write home about it all because of the unfriendly censor, and could only hint in my letters home that my life was now airborne.

Awaiting the Call to Arms

Another ten days leave spent in London and then [*28 Aug 1943*] I found myself travelling to York with four old friends from the Course where we were to join 659 Air OP Squadron whilst awaiting a definite posting.

We soon settled down to a quiet life at Clifton aerodrome just outside York. Enjoyed exploring that beautiful city and the magnificent York Minster. Not really belonging to the Squadron we had scant duties and we did our best to pile up as many hours as possible in borrowed Austers. A lone Tiger Moth gave me the opportunity of indulging in aerobatics for the last time.

I volunteered to fetch a Humber Staff car from Leicester and this allowed me to see another little bit of fair England. On the way back stopped at Chilwell to look up Amalia Dennis, an old family friend, and there had a good tea.

On another occasion went along with a bunch of pilots to fetch a convoy of eighteen aeroplane carriers. These were Bedford 3 tonners, enormous contraptions as they had been enlarged to carry an Auster each.

We travelled to Lancaster by train arriving in time to attend a Home Guard Ball held at the City Hall. A very enjoyable affair. The lorries weren't ready until after noon the following day. We set off rather late in the afternoon. In a lengthy convoy we wound our way steadily east and by dusk were climbing up and onto Ilkley Moor where half of the lorries got lost in that featureless expanse. A few of us managed to keep to the route and arrived at Ilkley village for a late dinner. It was good and dark by then but we decided to carry on and try to make York by midnight. The rest of the journey was uneventful but I enjoyed the trip.

Cathie and the twins were staying at a farm not far from York and I landed many times on their not too large field in time for elevenses.

Life was rather quiet and I wasn't doing anything important, so I wangled another fortnight's leave which I spent at Grove Park.

In which I join the PBI [Poor Bloody Infantry]

It was decided, and quite rightly too, that if we were to co-operate efficiently with other arms we should have some firsthand knowledge of how they operate. It was for this reason that I suddenly found myself attached to the 2nd Battalion Glasgow Highlanders, then under intensive training on the moors near Bingley.

Was pleased to find that their Padre was Capt. Taylor, ex Buenos Aires and an old friend of the family. He was destined to die in battle a short time later.

Got down to learning all about Bren guns, grenades, carriers, mortars and sundry other odd weapons and, what was most interesting, fooled around with demolition charges and produced some lovely bangs.

Mess life was really *pukka* with all the trimmings. I was awed with the ceremonies carried out on guest nights. This included pipers stamping round and round the small dining room producing a mighty volume of sound, and I was thrilled to the core of my Scotch blood.

The highlight of this fortnight was a night cross-country navigational scheme when, in pairs, we were supposed to find our way from point A to point B, distant some five miles. This to be accomplished over the featureless moors with the aid of a prismatic compass. I was paired off with Major Hall, a pleasant type, and after much stumbling around, climbing over umpteen stone walls and wallowing over much swampy peatland, we managed to find our way to point B. Then a fog clamped down and it took us hours to find our way home in the lorries.

After an extremely interesting stay with the PBI and rolling my rrr's a wee, we made our way back to York via Leeds, which we explored briefly.

In which I join the Elite Lancers

A few more weeks of flying whenever possible at York, and then I was sent off to Bridlington to learn something about tanks and how they work.

The 8th November found three of us reporting to Major Sir John Gilmore, OC 'B' Squadron the 2nd Fife & Forfar Yeomanry RAC [*Royal Armoured Corps*]. During the week we were with them we learnt a lot about their tactics and this was to come in useful later. We also learnt how to drive tanks. These were Shermans but because of the diesel engine shortage, they were powered by a monstrous engine composed of five Chrysler motor car eight-cylinder engines welded together. When one pressed the starter button no less than 40 cylinders sprang to life with an ominous roar. Pity the poor mechanic who had to look for a faulty spark plug or a leaky water pump in that conglomeration of moving parts.

Found it rather a tight squeeze to slip through the manhole and into the driver's seat, but I managed it. I was pretty good at driving a lorry and had mastered the art of double declutching and such, but it was quite a different matter trying to shift a tank from 1st to 2nd gear without stalling, as full speed in 1st was about 5 mph. However, it was great fun driving the brutes over obstacles, and enjoyed smashing through hedges and over ditches, the tank roaring mightily and taking them in its stride. Far from being a hot job the task of driving proved the reverse as a large aeroplane type prop, placed just behind the driver, drew air in huge quantities through the hatch cover, if open, and via the unfortunate driver to a substantial radiator cooling the massive engine. It was November and the wind whistling by was frigid.

A week later we joined the posh Mess of the 24th Lancers and managed to put in some more hours driving Shermans and learning more about their tactics in battle.

Made friends with some Air Sea Rescue lads and one Saturday they invited me out for a spin in their boat. It was a lovely sunny day, if cold, and we were to do a two hour routine patrol. The pilot was a Canadian and we had two WAAF Officers on board, highly illegal, quite a picnic in fact. We kept in touch with the mainland by W/T in case any rescue work should come our way and off we sped. The two Rolls Royce engines pushed us at a great speed over the waves. Whilst I was up front in the cockpit trying my hand at steering, one of the WAAF's brought me a mug of tea. The boat was jumping from wave to wave and rising and falling in quick time. The content of the mug was doing likewise and if an accident was to be averted the mug's movement had to be closely synchronized with that of the tea and I had a heck of a time just preventing it spilling, let alone drinking it. In fact it was a good leg pull. They took pity on me eventually and told me to go to the stern, which was much steadier, and there I was able to enjoy my cuppa without peril.

Life at the 24th Lancers Mess was decidedly stuffy. The Officers were practically all of the nobility and very much the supercilious type, though there were exceptions. Mess customs were rigidly upheld and, for the first time ran into Mess Dress – a far cry from easy Air OP habits.

Recently I had positively answered a War Office signal requesting volunteers for overseas duty and the result caught up with me whilst I was yet with the Lancers, and I had to pack up and head back to York.   I enjoyed the experience and getting to know the tanks and the men that drove them as also exploring that pretty seaside resort, but I cannot say I enjoyed the rather enforced social life in the Mess.

After being duly inoculated and having said cheerio to my 659 Squadron pals, I entrained for London on the 15th November on embarcation leave.

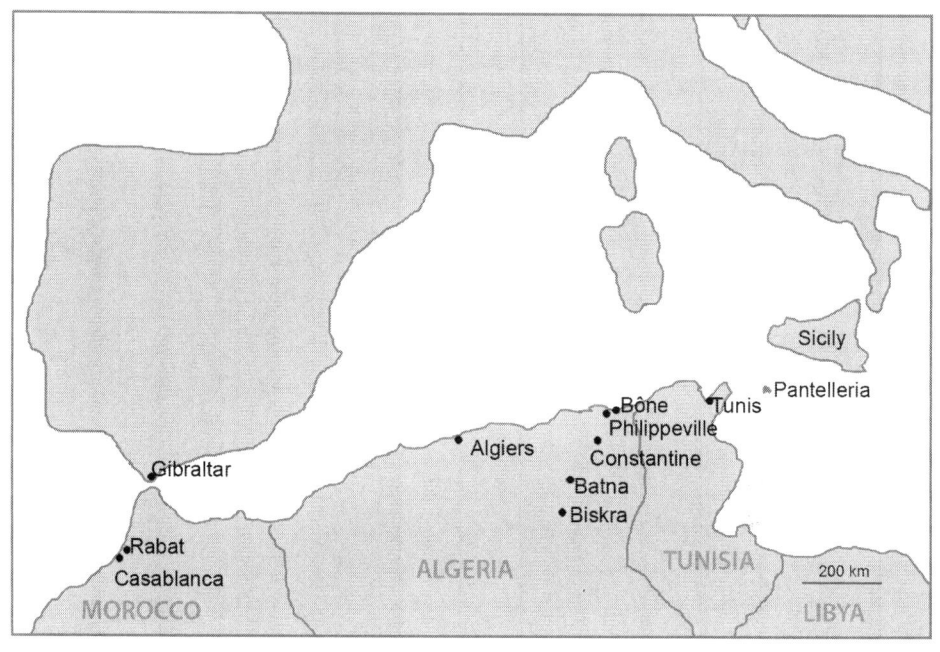

Sketch Map of North Africa

To North Africa to join 657 Air OP Squadron RAF

Off to War at Last

Our valuable presence was required with such urgency at the front that the six pilots involved in this move, to wit, Gander, Hall, Buchanan, Mickleborough, Martin and myself, were to fly post haste by British Overseas Airways to North Africa.

After another grand leave we made our way to Woolwich Arsenal where we were issued with Tropical Kit. We were allowed 44 lbs but invoking our pilot category, were allowed a further 41 lbs for flying kit. The remaining equipment and valise with camp bed etc. was sent on by sea to Algiers.

The 28th November 1943 found us all aboard the 10 am train from Paddington. Right from the start we were treated with BOAC [*British Overseas Airways Corporation*] courtesy. We travelled in a reserved compartment and enjoyed a free lunch on board. By late afternoon we arrived on Bristol Drome and there boarded a Dakota which took off but landed soon after at Newquay to top up with petrol and await darkness as Jerry planes were doing their best to disrupt this air service. Recently they had shot down a plane believing Churchill was on board but, instead, bagged Leslie Howard who was returning from Gibraltar.

An elegant dinner was served us at an American mess and we were shown a film which helped while away the time before take-off, round about midnight. The plane was full. Among the passengers was a War Correspondent by name Talbot, later to become famous for his coverage of the Yugoslav partisan front, and several French diplomats with their much guarded attaché cases. We headed straight out to sea, on our long lap to Gibraltar. The night was pitch black and nothing could be seen through the windows. The steady droning of the motors soon put us to sleep and it was 7.50 am when the steward woke us up to partake of a picnic breakfast. We were still flying over the sea and there was no sight of land. Our destination had been changed, enemy planes around no doubt, and we were heading straight for the African Continent. About an hour later land appeared and a little while later we landed on a sandy aerodrome with palm trees around. This we later found to be Rabat.

We were led to another breakfast, this time with orange juice and eggs, both highly rationed in the UK and a while later we took off once more and flew due east parallel to the majestic Atlas mountains. The day was clear and sunny and we enjoyed the scenery.

15.30 hours found us landing at Maison Blanche [*Algiers airport, now Houari Boumediene Airport*] and nobody was expecting us, and nobody could tell us where we were supposed to report. The RTO arranged for us to go to the RA [*Royal Artillery*] transit camp at Cape Matafou [*Matifou*], a few miles along the coast from Algiers and there we arrived by lorry in time for tea. We were assigned a tent pitched by the shore of the very blue Mediterranean – very romantic – and there we made ourselves comfortable. The weather was mild and nights pleasant, ideal camping conditions.

No one knew anything about us at Africa Force HQ and didn't much care. It was only by chance that we eventually bumped into a chap sporting Air OP wings during one of our wanderings through interesting Algiers. He turned out to be G3 Air and the one man who did know something about our problems, and was able to give us our final destinations.

Whilst at the St. George Hotel, then AF HQ saw a big shot arrive. They told me he was a chap called Eisenhower and I wondered who he was.

Gander and Buchanan left the following day and were flown straight to Italy. Hall and myself, after nine days of leisurely living at Cape Matafou, during which we spent many hours exploring Algiers, entrained for Constantine and Philippeville.

I catch up with my Squadron

Travelling by rail was a slow business in those days especially as the French rail workers were hostile and deliberately slowed things down. We were each given four days rations and had to fend for ourselves during the laborious, winding trip through the wild mountains common to these parts. We were six to a compartment for eight and therefore were reasonably comfortable. On the other hand the troops were 25 to a cattle-truck and not so well off. We cooked on the floor on Tommy cookers and had plenty of time to think up and produce some weird, but mostly reasonably tasty, meals.

Three days and not many miles later, arrived late one evening at Constantine. With Lt Pitts, a co-passenger who was also changing there, walked from the station towards the centre of the town. It was a bright moonlight night as we wended our way over the long suspension bridge that spans a seemingly bottomless gorge that had defended Constantine from attack for many centuries. It was an impressive sight. We made our way to a swanky casino and after a much needed wash, the first we had had for days, we sat down to enjoy a first class dinner with all the trimmings, including soft music from an orchestra.

At 2 am [*9 January 1944*] of a freezing night found us on the last lap of our train journey and sitting shivering in a 2nd class carriage without windows. It was still dark when we puffed into Philippeville [*now Skikda*] station. We did not stir until the sun came up and then made for the nearest Officer's Club for breakfast. We then made our individual ways to our respective units. I reported to HQ 657 Air OP Squadron then occupying a farmhouse in an orange grove. Major Ingram was the CO and he made me welcome. I was to remain with this mob throughout the rest of the War.

The three Flights were scattered around, one even occupied a lighthouse in a most pleasant spot, and all used the main Philippeville aerodrome for what little flying was carried out. Planes were being received in crates and our Erks [*AC or aircraftman*] were busy putting them together. I was promptly nominated "test pilot" and had to take them up and chuck them around a bit to see that the wings were properly stuck on, and also report on any rigging defects. We did not carry parachutes; needless to say found that all the wings were properly stuck on.

A Spot of Larceny and a Murder

Practically the first serious job I was given on joining was to carry out an investigation regarding a charge of robbery brought against 'A' Flight by the Civil Authorities. That kept me busy for a while and I found myself up against real experts in the art of scrounging and could prove nothing. I knew darn well that the lads had swiped the wood to keep themselves warm. Much later I discovered how the dirty deed was done as one of the suspects became my driver and told me all about it.

One evening accompanied Major Ingram to the local Cinema to see Abbot and Costello in *Who Done It*. In the middle of this mystery a shot was heard coming from outside and there was a bit of a scuffle somewhere near the entrance. A moment later the lights went up and MP's arrived. The ticket booth had been held up and the manager shot dead. The murderer was seen to escape into the cinema. Bullets were found near the stage where they had evidently rolled, and then everybody was searched. The MP's soon had an inkling of who had done it, several soldiers having reported hearing the bullets being dropped, and then they found him. He was a

Canadian soldier, one of the tough ones.

We were warned to walk in pairs and armed, as there were many Arabs, as also some Frenchmen, who were decidedly unfriendly.

We move to Châdeaudun-du-Rhumel

On the 9th January 1944 we moved to the centre of a large bleak aerodrome at Châteaudun [*now Teleghma Airfield*] which we were to share with a Free French Squadron flying Marauders.

We sited our camp plumb in the middle of this drome hoping that by so doing, we might be able to defend ourselves from the petty pilfering for which the local Arabs were notorious. Maybe we did manage to cut it down but despite all precautions, such as double sentries armed with tommy-guns and with Aldis lamps mounted on lorries with which to sweep the barren surface of the drome, things disappeared.

Our fifteen planes were lined up close together and at night they were covered over with a light canvas cover tied to the fuselage by about a dozen tapes. On no less than three occasions Arabs succeeded in stealing several of these canvas covers. To accomplish this they had to crawl unobserved across a large expanse of bare ground which was swept at frequent intervals by the powerful beam of the Aldis Lamp. On reaching the plane they then had to cut through the tapes, remove the cover stealthily from off the fuselage and wings and fold it up carefully into an unobtrusive bundle, meanwhile the sentry was pacing up and down but a few yards away. Then, handicapped by a bulky bundle, they made their unobserved getaway. After the first cover disappeared sentries got trigger happy and would spray any imaginary shadow with their tommy-guns. The canvas screen around the "bogs" acquired several bullet holes, this was the only bit of real cover near our camp. One unfortunate man in a hurry in the middle of the night acted with even greater promptitude when a string of bullets whizzed by.

We complained to the French Authorities about the robberies and a few days later, were told that the thieves had been caught. I was the Officer to go along and identify the covers. When I arrived at the local police station was told that a certain small village was responsible and two men had been arrested and had confessed. However the covers had not been found and, it was only too obvious by the battered appearance of the prisoners, just why they had confessed. I promptly dropped the charges, much to the Frenchmen's disgust. Thereafter we refrained from denouncing robberies.

The Arab is a weird character. Whenever a family would amble by the old man would be first astride a diminutive donkey, his feet nearly trailing in the dust. Then would come the wife, probably carrying a bundle on her head and in line astern, the children in order of seniority.

Coming from egg starved England we were always eager to acquire extra ones to supplement our diet and the Arabs knew that we were willing to pay fairly handsomely for them. A shilling an egg was the current price but they were not averse to quoting more favourable terms if an old pair of army boots were offered in lieu of legal tender. And many a boot went missing about that time.

Cruising along in our Jeep we would come across an Arab standing silent by the roadside covered in his sheet. We would stop and by sign language plus atrocious French would ask him where we could buy eggs. How many he would ask, and no matter how many were required, he would have them on him. Digging deep under their voluminous clothes they would produce all the eggs needed and even a chicken or two if requested. They must have worn pretty deep bloomers.

Our bathing facilities were not up to much, the usual open air shower arrangement, and Bamford and self made frequent use of the local village baths which, twice a week, allowed infidels to make use of their facilities.

The bath house itself was really ancient, built of sandstone and with a flat roof. It had a central courtyard with a beautiful *aljibe* and a shaded veranda affair where patrons could take it easy after a bath. They had a series of changing rooms and the bath itself consisted of a large gloomy room lit by a vent-come-chimney in the roof. It was steaming hot from the vapours off a large open cauldron set over a wood fire. The cauldron let off quantious steam, and in that atmosphere one started to perspire freely. A "slave" in a loin cloth would slide rope handled wooden buckets over the greasy floor with piping hot water and, on request, would hurl a bucket of cold water over one which he raised from a well in the corner of this room. Shadows came and went in that gloomy interior but not a word was spoken, all very mysterious. After about half an hour of sweating and rubbing in pretty good palm oil and being doused with cold water one felt good and clean.

Very few of the other fellows dared make use of this Turkish bath and it was there, whilst drip drying in the courtyard, that we met some of the Free French pilots who were on the other side of our aerodrome and flying Marauders. We were invited to their Club in the village and there had many pleasant evenings with them imbibing *vin rosé* and *brændi* and helping out with the inevitable chorus of *Alouette* plus many tuneful but less decorous songs.

An Unexpected Cold Clime

I am always accused of gross exaggeration when I tell people of the weather we had up there in Châteaudun-du-Rhumel. We were in legendary torrid North Africa but here, at an altitude of 3,000 feet, although days were decidedly hot, nights were decidedly cold. And furthermore we were living in tents. Every night, the blanket near my face would acquire a thick layer of ice as would also the tent roof sloping overhead as my breath froze. Bottled beer kept for safety under my bed, despite its alcoholic content, would also freeze.

Washing outside in the morning, before the sun rose, was an ordeal. I can certify, really, that if I wet my hair it would freeze before I could pass my comb through it. The best Ripley line, however, was that if I wet my finger and then touched my safety razor, I could pick it up as the water froze instantly.

We had fun and games inventing, building, and operating diverse clandestine stoves to keep our tents warm during the long evenings. Several went up in smoke after a violent explosion was heard, luckily nobody was hurt but it was no joke being left homeless in the middle of a freezing night.

My invention consisted of a mud oven cum stove affair that soon turned to brick. This contraption stuck out of the back of the tent and the tin chimney was well clear of the tent wall and relatively safe. It operated with paraffin which dripped onto a hot plate. The regulating valve consisted of a screw that, when turned, flattened a bit of rubber piping.

It wasn't very accurate but it worked fine. Other chaps devised pressure jobs that were more efficient but were highly dangerous and would blow up with fair regularity covering all with soot.

Some Pleasant Trips

As MT Officer, I was that too, it was my job to collect vehicles of which we were well under strength. This took me out several times to Bône [*now Annaba*] and the Ouid Farara Vehicle Dump where I had to wheedle and lie like a trooper to obtain our much needed trucks and jeeps; picked up several TCV's (Troop Carrying Vehicles) which were to be converted to Plane Carriers, also small and large trucks and on one memorable occasion a fleet of twelve Jeeps.

Set off early one morning driving a TCV with a dozen drivers on board and arrived in Bône in time for lunch. It took me a long time to pick out the dozen Jeeps that met my fancy. They were all very much second hand and evidently had seen much rough action in the desert. It was after five when we were all ready and lined up to go. Did not wish to stay there for the night and decided to try and make it through the mountain pass in the dark, hoping that drivers and vehicles would behave. Picked the least trustworthy looking of the Jeeps for my steed, one which had Paratroop markings and I suspected that, on more than one occasion, it had been dropped without the parachute opening. As Elsie this sturdy vehicle was to serve me faithfully throughout the Italian campaign and through into Germany.

The Sergeant set off leading the convoy whilst I hung around the rear shepherding my flock. Right at the start two remained behind and I had to chase back and rescue them. They had slight mechanical trouble quickly fixed and we had to drive hell for leather to catch up with the remainder. Once they had settled down I ordered a halt for a quick brew up, then started off again with me in the lead and the Sergeant bringing up the rear.

The winding road led us over a pass in high mountains that were snow capped and the bright moonlight lent enchantment to the scene. It was bitterly cold and Jeeps are draughty jobs. Looking back saw the dozen double sets of headlights winding along behind like a following luminous necklace. It was easy to check. We wended our way steadily along winding roads and over the highest part of the pass and then started to descend and right away came in sight of Constantine glittering in the distance.

A while later we approached this romantic city and rumbled over the fantastic hanging bridge over the famous gorge and on to Châteaudun.

A Spot of Live Shooting

On the 22nd January 1944 the official notification arrived announcing that I was now a fully fledged Captain RA. Very pleased with myself, I laboriously sewed on my third pip. Four days later the BBC announced that the Argentine had, at long last, broken with the Axis and I felt justified in sewing my Argentina flash on my Service Dress uniform.

Flights were busy doing movement exercises which entailed plenty of flying but we in Squadron HQ were lagging behind in this respect. Major Ingram, however, managed to organise some live shoots with a nearby Regiment that had 25 pounder guns and agreed to cooperate.

The target area chosen was far more interesting than featureless Salisbury Plain and reference points were easy to identify. Our tactics were still the same. That is, flying at a maximum of 600 feet and carrying out the entire shoot in under twenty minutes.

I accompanied the Major to his ground Observation Post on several occasions to watch the others doing their stuff, and learnt what not to do.

I was given the opportunity of carrying out five live shoots from a plane. They went fairly smoothly and I gained quite a bit of confidence.

Our target area was an area of ground about a square mile in extent, reasonably far away from civilization but, as was inevitable in this place where every square yard of ground is cultivated, we were firing into ground worked by someone. Although the Arabs were given due warning to stay clear, being Arabs they were apt to ignore such warnings. On one of my shoots the chosen target was an outcrop of dark rock half way up a gentle hill. A couple of rounds had already fallen in the area when I observed through my binoculars that an Arab was busy ploughing a field that extended over the top of this hill, and not far distant from my target. I had already given a plus 400 yard order to the guns and next time I observed the farmer had disappeared. The chaps in the ground OP had witnessed the disappearing act. When my plus round had landed pretty close to the ploughed land, the donkey towing the plough had taken off at high speed, the plough bouncing behind. The Arab went chasing off behind until both disappeared over the horizon.

On one occasion Major Ingram was returning from one of these shoots and flying on the deck, as was our wont and pleasure, he did not notice some high tension wires strung from pylons and he hit them dead on. He was extremely lucky and hit the cable with his propeller boss and the propeller, turning at high speed, managed to cut through it before the balance of the plane was affected. He managed to carry on and land at our aerodrome. On inspecting the aircraft the leading edge of one plane [*wing*] was found full of small holes where electrical sparks had penetrated. He was lucky to get away with it as usually these accidents are fatal.

Crazy Radcliffe, doing a spot of night flying, misjudged distances and landed too soon, or rather tried to, and hit a telegraph post writing off his plane. He ended up in hospital but the only damage, as far as he was concerned, was a cut face and tongue, and he was soon back but wasn't able to brag for some days. His plane was a write-off. We all indulged in a modicum of night flying, and I enjoyed my share of flying in the silky smooth night air. We used rather dim hurricane lanterns to light the strip, and had to do without a Glide Indicator, but we managed fine. This training was to come in useful when we became operational in Italy.

Here my tin trunk and valise, sent on from Woolwich, caught up with me. As I had already acquired a second lot of camp kit, on the strength that the first lot had been lost, I now had a double issue, the second one free.

The Desert and a Dicey Do

This tale, under the more austere title of *A Flying Visit to the Sahara* has been published by the British Legion in their Bulletin and it will save me some trouble if I just copy the article as printed.

We were awaiting our cue to join the Eighth Army in Italy [29 January 1944], and being somewhat bored, we hinted that Flights were enjoying life going on schemes that invariably had as final objectives such places as Algiers and Tunis. Our CO caught on quick and gave orders that 657 Air OP Squadron HQ would carry out a movement exercise travelling from Châteaudun, a small village not far from Constantine, to the romantic town of Biskra that lay on the edge of the Sahara Desert.

There were two Auster III planes on Squadron HQ strength and Capt. Bamford and myself were detailed to fly these during the exercise, the remainder of the party was to travel by road. We were to rendezvous at a place called Batna, not quite half way to Biskra, to refuel our planes as they could not fly direct with any safety.

Bam and I saw the road party off at 9·00 hours and having lots of time to spare I flew off and landed at a nearbFy RATD [*Royal Artillery Training Depot*] camp for a haircut and a cup of tea at their canteen. Bam joined me there and we took off again at 11·30 which allowed us plenty of time to reach Batna for lunch.

I should mention that there was a scarcity of maps of this general area and we had but one available. We tossed for it and Bam won so, therefore, I had to follow his lead from then on.

It was a grand day when we set off, clear and fresh. Having been to Batna before I did not have to rely entirely on Bam's doubtful navigation. Got there without trouble and came in to a cautious landing as the wind was rather gusty and the field tree-lined.

Shortly after landing the convoy turned up, and it didn't take long to refuel our planes and eat a haversack lunch. By 13:30 we were off again on what was supposed to be a direct hop to Biskra. Therefore, instead of following the valley that carried the main road, which would have been a safer but longer route, Bam headed straight for that place on a compass course, ignoring contemptuously the 8,000 ft high mountains that lay in between.

On this flight I certainly could not afford to lose sight of my leader. The planes we were flying had an official endurance of but one hour and 10 minutes, and that did not allow one much time to look around for landmarks if one went astray. To force land in that mountainous region of tumbling rocks, deep narrow valleys and precipices, without making a mess of things, was next to impossible. The only likely rescuers were wild Arabs of doubtful friendliness. As usually happens under such circumstances my little puny four cylinder engine developed an ominous rattle, entirely imaginary no doubt, but very real to me at the time.

We climbed steadily into the sky to get over those harsh looking mountains. Our rate of climb forced us to wriggle through the valleys and we were never able to rise much above the rocks and consequently we were caught and buffeted by every gust and eddy of wind that whizzed around those draughty crags. At last we rose above the highest ridge and over, with the rocks leaping down and away from us; down to narrow valleys with tortuous streams winding far below, and went sailing on free of the earth at last. From that height one could see for miles and the view was superb. In the distance the mountains dwindled away and the vast expanse of nothingness that is the Sahara, began.

Beneath us the mountains gave way to a wide valley with a narrow road winding along beside a fair sized river. Small specks were to be seen moving along this road and then I felt much safer as the valley afforded a reasonable landing place and civilized help was at hand.

We came upon a weird freak of nature. Right across this valley, straight and towering like a wall, ran a high narrow ridge of pink and grey rock that was easily 1,000 feet high. A deep cleft that reached down to its base allowed the river and accompanying road to creep through and the whole affect was unnatural and weird.

Still flying on a compass course, we came upon a railway line that edged the desert, with a station and a cluster of houses. This place was not Biskra and if we kept on flying there was no doubt but that we would head straight into the middle of the Sahara. Bam decided quite sensibly against doing anything of the sort, and after circling the village a couple of times, landed in a nearby field. With only about 15 minutes supply of petrol left I promptly followed suit and switched off.

As I suspected, Bam hadn't a clue as to our whereabouts and had landed to ask his way of the local tribe. Arabs young and old swarmed around in no time at all and there was Bam endeavouring to find out where Biskra was without much success, as brown arms kept pointing all around the compass. Just then the familiar sound of Spanish being spoken reached my ears and looking towards its

Bamford landed beside a station to ask the way to Biskra

source I discovered that the station master's wife and small daughter had arrived on the scene. Found out that they hailed from Barcelona and that Biskra was about 15 kilometres to our east.

We had just enough petrol to make Biskra in comfort and after a short flight sighted that romantic place shining white in the sun. We landed on a huge dusty aerodrome that was a half-way stop for transport planes on their way to Cairo and the Middle East.

The road party arrived at 17·30 and packing everything into an empty hangar, including the two planes, we got things ship-shape for a two day stay. It was warm. A pleasant change from the sub-zero temperature of Châteaudun.

Next day with Bam, our Adj and a Jeep we set off to explore Biskra. Found it a sultry sandy place of white Moorish buildings, shady palm-lined streets, Foreign Legion Officers gaudy in their red lined cloaks and, of course, mysterious veiled Arab girls swathed in sheets. We had wizard meals at the "Glacier" and "Oasis" hotels and sampled plenty of their various wines and other less benign drinks and generally made the most of our two-day stay in this quaint place.

On the third day the Squadron upped sticks and went, leaving Bam and myself to our own resources. No sooner had the last truck disappeared in a cloud of dust than the stiff breeze that had been blowing all morning strengthened into a veritable *Mistral* creating a fair sized sand-storm. It then occurred to us, still slightly EFTS [*Elementary Flying Training School*] conscious, that it would be a good, idea to check up on our weather and we set off on a long trek across this vast drome to where an RAF unit was encamped beside the control tower. The news they gave us was not at all cheering. In fact we were properly shaken as the weather report read "Wind gusty 30/40 mph – Snowing." It seemed it was snowing all along our chosen route. We walked back to our planes in silence feeling somewhat despondent. It was an uncomfortable walk as the flying wind stung our bare parts and we were wearing shorts.

There didn't seem to be much future sitting in that empty aerodrome. Not having anything better to do we decided to have a try. To make matters more interesting Bam had told the CO that we could get back in one hop to the RATD camp that was some 20 miles nearer than Châteaudun, and had therefore not arranged any refuelling rendezvous. This meant that we just had to go over the top of the mountain range and could not take the much safer route following the road.

Our first problem was how to take off by ourselves. The wind velocity was by then considerably higher than our take-off speed and therefore we would be airborne before we could start our engines. Quite a problem. Despite RAF rules and regs. we pushed our planes as far back into the hangar as possible and there started them up. The slip stream added more dust to that already in the atmosphere and one could hardly see, let alone breathe. Bam went off first and disappeared into the maelstrom of dust and I followed suit. Jamming on the throttle the plane commenced to move into that mess. As soon as we cleared the shelter of the hangar the cross winds caught us and whisked us away up into the air with a sickening force, but I kept on going up like a lift to meet Bam circling around in the clear air above.

Biskra is below sea level and the 8,000 ft high mountains that lay across our course were, in fact, really higher than that and looked huge and foreboding, heightened to the very heavens by a towering pile of dirty black clouds that appeared solid and impenetrable. Our chances of survival seemed slim. Our little flimsy planes, made of piping and cloth, were not built to do battle with the violent air currents common to Nimbo Cumulus clouds. Our lack of any but elementary instruments called for good visibility for map reading; a condition hardly to be encountered in a raging blizzard. This latter detail did not worry me unduly as, in any case, I did not have a map. Also it would be difficult to keep my trusty Pathfinder in sight under these climatic conditions. But there again there really didn't seem to be much object in so doing as he was almost sure to get lost anyway.

With such reassuring thoughts to comfort me we climbed steadily towards the enemy. It was an awe inspiring sight to see the clouds shunning the desert, not daring to overfly their fixed limits nor let drop the lightest rain-drop to ease its dryness, keeping just over the mountains as if kept in place by a gigantic sheet of glass.

Soon we left the bright sunlight and slid under the layer of cloud and into bumpy undercurrents and we approached the place where the mountain side disappeared into the swirling mist. There was no future in carrying on straight ahead, Bam wisely turned off course hoping to find some way over and flew parallel to the mountainside in a most disconcerting manner as violent vertical draughts flung his plane away over the top of mine and, the next minute, he would go plummeting down to whizz past my nose, the while his wings wobbled erratically.

I was doing much the same and my head kept hitting the perspex roof with monotonous regularity. Eventually Bam discovered a likely dip in the crest that with luck might let us through to the next valley. This small valley was barely below the general ceiling and rifts of wind-rent clouds came tumbling through. There was no option but to make use of this escape route, Bam headed in and, for safety, climbed a bit. I saw him disappear into the murky mass overhead. I promptly followed suit hastily setting a rough course on my compass. Flying blind was far from easy as the instruments behaved crazily, the compass acting like a merry-go-round. Dropped my speed to about 65 mph – actually our optimum rate of climb – hoping that this would give me a slight chance should a rock turn up unexpectedly. We crept along for a lengthy sixty seconds or so then descended cautiously at about the same speed with flaps down. Luckily nothing ominous loomed ahead and we dropped down into clear air, still all in one piece. I even was pleased to see Bam's plane flying erratically across the valley towards another range of mountains with their tops obscured in black clouds.

Between scared periods found time to enjoy the marvellous, if eerie, scenery, now ghostly white but still grand and ruthless. It had evidently just stopped snowing and I dreaded to think what would have happened if we had dropped down into a raging blizzard instead of clear air. We would have been trapped in that valley for sure as it was only by luck that we found a narrow cloud-free pass that took us through this highest crest.

This time we descended from the clouds to find ourselves flying over a wide valley and the next range was well beneath the cloud ceiling. After that it was all plain sailing except that I suddenly became acutely conscious that the blob, stuck on the end of a piece of wire attached to a cork that floated in our petrol tank, placed just in front of us, which constituted our petrol gauge, was bobbing far too low in its metred tin guide; and we still had far to go.

I knew that Bam's plan was to head straight for Batna and from there, as we could not set a direct course for home because of the high mountains in our way, follow the valleys running east to a road junction then taking the road North to the RATD camp. We reached the first valley and duly turned east and overflew a large town which I took to be Batna. We came to the road junction and, instead of turning North he flew straight on. It must be remembered that I did not have a map. Recalling our trip out, my faith in my leaders ability to navigate with any accuracy was at a low ebb and there and then I became obsessed with the certainty that we were hopelessly lost and were heading into the blue without any hope of reaching anywhere in particular before our petrol ran out. I began to fret and fume at his utter incompetence, stupidity, craziness, etc. and looked forward glumly to a day of trouble and discomfort, if nothing worse.

Reluctantly followed on and a short while later another large town appeared astride the valley. Hopeful doubts assailed me then which turned to certainty when another road junction appeared and Bam turned North as if he knew where he was going. I forgave him then and took back all my evil thoughts.

By now the blob was bobbing about just visible above the bottom of the gauge. I flew as high as possible and kept choosing likely landing places as we flew along. It was somewhat like playing musical chairs as one felt reluctant to let a good spot slide by underneath in case no other appeared in time.

The heavy snow fall had covered the whole countryside and the road was hardly discernible as it was only hedged in places. This made a forced landing doubly hazardous there was no means of knowing what unpleasant obstacle lurked under the pretty white mantle.

The blob was now bumping jarringly on the bottom, not surprising considering that we had already been flying for 1 hour 25 minutes which was well over the planes official endurance. Then away in the distance I saw row upon row of tiny white tents that could only be our destination – and I forgave Bam his sins. Then began a race against time to see if we could reach this haven of safety before the petrol gave out.

The landing ground at the camp was a *pukka* two runway affair with deep ditches either side of these. Once again I started to worry as ditches, runways and all was covered in an unbroken blanket of snow. A plane parked, presumably with wings parallel to a runway gave some indication as to their probable position. Bam, who was below and a couple of hundred yards ahead, guessed right and ploughed his way through snow without tippling over, and I came down practically on his tail.

We both crawled out feeling very pleased with ourselves and life in general and strolled across to the canteen to have a cup of tea.

The Erk told me later, that there was but half a gallon of petrol left in the tank when I landed, which was cutting things rather fine.

Before lunch it began snowing again and it came down thick, so much so that we were not able to fly the remaining twenty miles to Châteaudun until evening. Our timing had been fortunate,

When we eventually did get through to our base we spent the rest of the evening shovelling snow to clear a space for our tent. Brrrr.

Route from Châteaudun to Naples in the Auster III, Feb 21-27, 1944

FLIGHT FROM ALGERIA TO ITALY

The Squadron Moves to War – Leisurely

The long awaited order arrived at last. 657 Air OP Squadron RAF was to proceed by air and sea to join up with the Eighth Army and go into battle somewhere in Italy. But the order came through whilst a snowstorm was at its height and had been raging for days and "sparrows walking" was chalked up on the Met. Board.

Preparatory to the move all Flights had congregated on the large Châteaudun aerodrome, some 30 miles west of Constantine, and all planes, vehicles and equipment had been thoroughly checked and rechecked. Wireless sets, mounted beside the pilot, where the passenger seat should be, were taken out to lighten the load and allow the carrying of spare petrol and the pilot's kit. Also several

The Auster Mark III that I flew from Africa when the Squadron moved into battle

Erks were to accompany the planes to carry out maintenance and generally help out.

By now we had our full complement of 15 Auster III's four to each Flight and three spares in Squadron HQ. The latter were to be flown on the long flight by the CO, Bamford and myself.

There was no hope of getting off for at least a couple of days. I was MT Officer, as well as many other things at the time and my mechanics reported having discovered several duff parts in our secondhand vehicles, most of which had seen rough action in the desert, and spares were needed urgently if we were to carry out this important move with any efficiency. Prompt action was called for, so picking a reliable utility – they had nice enclosed bodies, preferable to draughty Jeeps, and with my "Tiffy" Sergeant, set off for El Khroub to scrounge for sundry pieces of hardware. The trip was interesting, to say the least, and surprisingly no avalanches nor unsurmountable snowdrifts were encountered on the mountain roads. We moved fast and were back just after dark.

The storm was so severe that one of our Sergeants, returning to camp in a Jeep after midnight, got lost within the aerodrome's perimeter and just could not find our large and extended camp that sprawled in the middle. He eventually gave up the attempt and waited coldly for dawn, when he crawled in sheepishly for breakfast.

The next morning was also hopeless with scattered rain and very low clouds scudding along and these we disliked intensely. So we lounged around with ants in our pants waiting for a favourable change in the weather. The CO was far from happy as we were supposed to reach Tunis that day.

By midday [*16 February 1944*] there had been no improvement and it seemed we were not to get away that day. However, around four o'clock, there seemed to be a slight improvement and it was then the CO gave his famous movement order that was to move his squadron into the bloody fray. "Squadron HQ is going to have a crack at it."

As can be imagined, Flights were not going to permit Squadron HQ to get away with it and soon props were being wound up all over the landscape, and cold motors reluctantly rattled into life.

We were a rather happy-go-lucky crowd, there was not much discipline amongst the pilots and we took off whenever we felt like it without any previously planned sequence.

It did not take me long to chuck my kit into the back of the plane and I was one of the first to head up into the turbulent air and set course for Bône [*now Annaba*], where we were to refuel on our trip to Tunis. The first lap was easy, our course taking us straight up the valley to Constantine. After passing that city high mountains stood in our way. I started to climb to meet them but while yet not high enough to get over them I found myself flying into thick clouds of such a turbulent nature that it played havoc with my instruments and I had the unpleasant sensation of not knowing whether the plane was flying straight and level or upside down. There was certainly no future in that sort of flying. Besides, I was scared stiff and, as soon as I caught sight of a piece of *terra firma* in an unexpected quarter but at a safe distance, I dove down and headed back to El Khroub, our alternative landing place. Several of the others had already decided for safety and were circling around preparatory to landing. Someone had already done so and had hit something hidden in the snow and his plane was upended. I waited for somebody else to go in and followed in his wheel marks. It is a nice sensation landing in soft snow.

All the others came in except Bamford and, believe it or not, that chap went over the top on instruments and made Bône safely. Once we had picketed our planes we made our way into Constantine and put up at the swell Transit Hotel. Then off to the casino for a quick one and a civilized dinner with sweet music in the background.

The stormy weather persisted well into the following day. It was only after lunch that we considered it possible to take off. We Bradshawed[1] our way to Bône, not over the cloud covered mountains but the long way, following the road, and once there made our way to the RAF Mess. It was obviously impossible to carry on to Tunis that day.

And it rained and snowed steadily for three more days.

We received news that one of Squadron HQ aircraft-carrying lorries had broken down in Philippeville. It was still my responsibility to keep them going so I chased over to Khroub in a borrowed truck and was able to send along the vital spare.

We discovered an Officers Club tucked away in a wooden shack that had a first class cook, an ex French Chef in fact, and there did enjoy many a wizard meal plus the proper liquids.

On Monday the 21st February, though the storm had hardly abated, the CO decided to try and reach Tunis. The overall distance was too far to do it in one hop and arrangements had been made to have lorries with petrol waiting for us in a field about half way there. Without any difficulty found Souk-el-Khemis and the nearby field and landed to load on petrol from Jerrycans. This trip was particularly interesting as it took us over the recent grim battlefields where the Afrika Corps had made their last stand and many burnt-out tanks were to be seen.

---

[1] Bradshawing was RAF slang for navigating by following railway lines. Bradshaw's were a series of railway timetables and travel guides published from 1839-1961. Thanks to Vic Flintham and Wikipeida for this clarification.

Having sufficient petrol in my tank I decided to have a good look at this interesting part of the world before landing and was able to discover and examine the ancient aqueduct and see the even older city of Carthage.

With Bill Bolam of 'A' Flight we drove into Tunis and were put up in an elegant flat by an Italian couple who looked after us well. Again we were able to indulge in elegant eating at the Majestic Hotel and later carried on with the boys at Max's Club, a lowly but fashionable dive, until It was time for bed.

Flight to Sicily

Another day was lost in Tunis as the weather continued foul and too dangerous to attempt the crossing of the Mediterranean in our flimsy kites. This gave us an opportunity of getting to know another North African city.

The next day, 23rd February 1944, the weather report was slightly better and it was decided to attempt the crossing to Sicily. Due to Luftwaffe activity we were to have fighter cover to be supplied by the US Air Force with some Airacobras, and an anti-ditching patrol by means of a Walrus amphibian. In the event of such a happening, our high wing monoplanes would go right into the drink and float for a little while with the fuselage, and us, under water. For this trip, the port door hinges were modified so that a pull at a cable would jettison them and allow us to escape quickly. We were also supplied with Mae Wests and felt reasonably safe.

Trucks collected us and transported us to the aerodrome after 9 and soon we were ready to fly.

The distance to Sicily's nearest shore, about 170 miles, was too great for Austers with a range of some 90 miles and we were to use Pantelleria as a stepping stone. From Tunis to this island was 90 miles, again a bit far for safety, and we had arranged to be refuelled in a field near the tip of Cape Bon.

I was one of the first to take off and headed for this field, near Korba, and there landed and filled up from the trucks. The chaps there were Yanks, very hospitable, and they invited us to have a cup of pretty good coffee whilst they topped up our planes. Then took off and headed on a course into the blue of the sea. The small island was not visible and although I was not unduly worried I was glad when Pantelleria appeared over the horizon. Flew over the little town of that name as I came in to land. It was in one hell of a mess having withstood a whale of a pasting from naval guns and a trigger happy crew.

This place was also run by Yanks and here we had a snack lunch and took time off to explore the famous underground hangars, and some of the remains of the Italian Air force. We took off for Sicily in groups of four, so that we could report any ditching. The Airacobras were flying around but at such speed that I doubt if they could have spotted a downed plane. There was no sign of the Walrus.

As soon as I was airborne and on the correct compass course I observed a tremendous pile of cumulus cloud, obviously covering Sicily. On approach could see that the cloud completely obscured the land and, seemingly, was right down on the deck leaving no space underneath for us to sneak in. Should this be so our range would not allow us to return to Pantelleria and it seemed likely we would have to land on the beach, foaming white with breakers. However, at the last minute a space did appear between land and clouds, but it was not much. My course was dead on and I sailed over Cape Granitola lighthouse. A few minutes later discerned Campobello village to my right and then came a larger town, Castel Vetrano, with the aerodrome sitting alongside.

I refuelled quickly out of Jerrycans, doing the job myself, as also starting up, and took off without wasting time for our next stop Ponte Olivo – 90 miles away along the coast.

Relieved at having arrived safely over dry land again, enjoyed that flight over different country. It was overcast but quite bright. Forced to fly low by the meagre ceiling I was able to see the countryside more closely. Very green and cultivated with pretty little villages perched atop hills. The map was accurate and the correct reference points passed at the right time. My navigation was on the dot and hit Ponte Olivo on the nose and landed on the drome in good order [*in 2016 - Ponte Olivo is listed as an abandoned WWII airfield north of Greda*].

The next lap was short, 65 miles as the crow flies; I navigated pleasantly along until the large city of Catania loomed ahead. Yanks were very much in evidence and they even allowed me to put my plane inside a hangar after having it refuelled, and made ready for an early start the next day.

Catania

The boys drifted in one by one and when a goodly bunch had collected a bus took us into town and to a US Officers Hotel. As could be expected it was the best in town, and there we made ourselves very comfortable. Even had a hot bath.

The town itself was first class and we were surprised by the window displays full of good things, even watches, fountain pens, and such, all decidedly unprocurable in austere England.

Made pigs of ourselves at wayside kiosks selling orange juice and nuts. To this we added the good grub turned out by the Yanks, who certainly knew how to look after themselves and imported all sorts of delicacies all the way from the States for their soldier boys.

We were up early next morning, but our departure was once again postponed due to stormy weather. Attempted a real USA breakfast. Tomato juice, then corn flakes, then sausages generously covered in maple syrup plus gallons of good coffee and bread and butter and marmalade. Few copied me.

The weather remained foul for three more days, days spent in seeing the sights and doing flicks and theatres. The highlight of our stay, as far as I was concerned, was seeing *Rigoletto* at the Opera House. This was the most delightful theatre I had ever seen. It was not very large but beautifully proportioned outside and in. It possessed a marvellous domed ceiling painted with a scene showing the gods standing upright on the columns that held up this dome. The perspective was so perfect that it seemed as if the figures were really standing upright, and the colours were superb and fresh. The building was not ancient but quite modern and, it seemed, Italian art had certainly not died. The Opera itself was first class and an orchestra of about fifty made plenty of stirring noises.

In which we Creep up the Soft Underbelly

Sunday the 27th February 1944 found us once more out at Catania aerodrome, hanging around waiting for the weather report. This reported foul weather all along our projected route. We were many days behind our schedule and, despite the dubious met report which assured us stormy weather all the way, Major Ingram, fed up with waiting, decided to take a chance and gave the order to "Get weaving."

Our plan was to attempt to reach Naples in four hops, and we were given three map references of fields, or abandoned aerodromes, where somebody would meet us with petrol.

It was about 10 am when we started taking off individually and I was among the first and set course north up the coast. Was very disappointed that Etna was completely covered in cloud. In fact we never once set eyes on that volcano. We followed the coast and the coastal road watching the wild breakers dashing themselves against the cliffs. Came up to the town of Messina and then turned sharply east to cross the Straights and set course to hit the mainland, some 30 miles away and unseen due to bad visibility. Once over land again set course 40° and sailed out to sea in order to cut across the Gulf of Gioia. Our first filling up point was 90 miles from Catania and therefore at the very limit of our range and not quite if we had to fight head winds.

The weather was grim, scudding dirty clouds overhead and a grey, heaving, nasty, cold looking sea underneath. I was glad when we reached the shore and were over dry land. Right away picked out the town of San Fernando. We were dead on course. I had by then been flying nearly an hour which left me just a quarter of an hour before my petrol ran out. This was cutting it rather fine. What if I couldn't find the abandoned drome! However, the terrain underneath unfolded correctly – as per the map – and just before reaching Vibo Valentia an aerodrome appeared looking very much the worse for wear. Landed near a large completely wrecked hangar where I could see some activity and there found U.S. Army lorries with fuel aboard. The Yanks filled my plane up and gave me another Compo Ration box.

As soon as we were ready a GI swung my prop and away we went on the next leg, which would take us to Scalea, a small town on the coast, and 85 miles away as the crow flies. But the crow would fly straight across the Gulf of Sant'Eufemia and I did not relish the idea of flying so long over that dirty, hungry sea. Decided, therefore, to make a slight dog leg, stretching my distance to dangerous limits, but preferring the devil to the deep blue sea. Even so had to do quite a bit over the ocean with land just discernible through the rain that was then falling, thanks to the fleecy white line of breakers. The weather grew worse. It was a real wintry storm we were battling through and the wind was off the land and rough, as it came tumbling off the mountains.

The little plane was being buffeted up and down violently and my heavy valise kept hitting the perspex roof and the back of my neck and I worried should it break either. As my course was now slightly west of north the wind was no better than neutral but we had to crab sideways to keep on course. Started worrying again as visibility became really bad. With no windscreen wipers, the pouring rain made it hard to see ahead.

After some forty minutes flying my course took me over land, parallel to the coast. According to the map the drome was just north of a fair sized river, but rivers are highly misleading. However, I could be sure there would be plenty of water pouring down this one. The hour was nearly up when through the rain I vaguely discerned a river and a rail and road bridge which checked with the map. Sure enough, just the other side there appeared another bedraggled aerodrome. I came in to land and splashed soggily onto the grass field raising a wave like a speedboat. This time found a couple of Brazilians awaiting us with a pile of Jerrycans. Had a chat in Spanish with one who was from São Paulo and he gave me some Spam and bread to eat plus a mug of coffee. I was pretty hungry by then it being after 1 pm and dicey flying always gave me an appetite. They say that an hour of nervous flying is equivalent to eight hours of manual labour, and they are not far wrong. By not lingering much at each place I was getting ahead of the gaggle. With me at Scalea were Bill Bolam, "Crazy" Radcliffe and Bamford. A couple of fellows were coming in to land when the four of us started to take off. Some of the others had already abandoned the trip.

The next hop was another long 90 miles but with a more westerly course we could expect some help from the violent east wind. Again the compass course took us out to sea, over the Golfo Policastro, as we dared not cut corners. By then I was getting accustomed to this type of ropey flying, or cared less for my skin, so I blew up my Mae West and headed out to sea. The low ceiling kept me down and I was scared of hitting the waves which seemed to be no distance at all underneath. Flying low over water when everything is grey with no horizon visible is highly disconcerting. I was mighty glad when a quarter of an hour later a line of white foam appeared and I rose up and over the cliffs to safety. Then moved inland and flew over some hills that got higher and higher and it was touch and go whether we could sneak under the ceiling. However, all went well and there was just enough space for my small plane to sneak over the highest ridge and down to the coast again near Salerno, of recent fame, and down to a small grass drome at Gaudo near Agropoli. The other three also made it. Nobody else caught up with us. We had a confab as things looked pretty grim. The next lap was to Naples, journey's end, about 80 miles away in a straight line but we had the Sorrento Peninsula with highish mountains, astride our Course. I was for forging ahead. The others were doubtful. I opined we would lose nothing having a try and could always turn back should Sorrento prove unhealthy. Besides, that particular drome we were on looked decidedly uncomfortable and civilized Naples sounded most desirable. It was decided to have a go and the four of us left, one after the other, me last of all.

The last lap – Hostile Balloons

Splashed my way across the grass, made a soggy take-off and rose into the hard driving rain. By then it was 4 pm and tea time – and no tea – and it would be getting dark around 5 pm. In other words, we could be certain that visibility would be practically non-existent around the time we were approaching Naples. We had been flying

Naples. ... balloon after balloon loomed overhead...

and refuelling without stop since 10:30 that morning and were feeling pretty tired and somewhat miserable by then. The planes we were flying, Auster III's, lacked any form of heating. Obliged to keep the side window open to be able to see anything in that rain, the cockpit was draughty and my feet were cold. I could not fly in boots as the only way I could use the rudder bar was by ankle movement, my knees being jammed tight against the instrument panel of those too small planes.

A short time after take-off a solid mass of towering land appeared ahead, all covered in black clouds. A plane flying ahead, it must have been Bill Bolam's, wheeled round and sailed by me going back. I thought I would carry on a little further. There was still time to turn back if necessary.

Obviously I could not cut directly across Sorrento so turned west and followed the coast for a while. Going all the way round was also risky as too much distance was added. I came upon a valley that would take me through the Peninsula and turned in. Five minutes or so later the valley rose steeply going to meet the murky stuff overhead. Tried to escape up a valley that branched off to the west but this one also rose and, furthermore, became increasingly narrow and I barely had space to turn around and get out. So it was back to the coast for me. It had stopped raining by now and this encouraged me to go on. Following the breakers was easy and could see across the many bays and was able to steer from point to point saving some precious distance. And so I went past my point of no return.

I did not know quite where I was, all the bays seemed alike. The compass was pretty useless. The violent movements of the plane kept it spinning. I managed to see a large island to my left, obviously Capri, and this gave me a fix. And then it started to rain again and it was getting dark.

By then I had crept round to the North side of Sorrento but dared not cut across the Bay of Naples in case I should miss the beginning of the Port area which I had to find in order to make my way to Capodichino aerodrome. Eventually I managed to see Vesuvius and could cut across what remained of the Bay, thus saving time and, more important, petrol. Hit the coast again which I followed seeking the Port. Suddenly I received a terrific shock when balloon after balloon loomed overhead and I realised I was in the midst of the port aircraft defence system. Every balloon carried a trailing wire, just the job to hack off one's wing, and some had explosive charges attached to send one to Kingdom Come, and there I was without a parachute. How on earth I was able to weave my way through that barrage I do not know to this day. There's a saying of course! Virtually shut my eyes and hoped for the best.

Once clear and in the dimming light I looked for the railway station near the port. With the low ceiling and bad visibility I was, by then, flying at roof top height and trusted there were no high steeples around. Found the station at last, it was a large one thank goodness, and I headed inland following the railway lines. A little later, as the map had predicted, a large open space appeared to my right and there was Capodichino aerodrome. It was so dark by then that I could not make out the runway nor could I see the control tower, so I explored its large expanse, flying just off the grass, and was lucky to find an Auster and I landed right beside it to find Crazy picketing his kite.

Some Ities with a Yank in charge turned up and helped us tuck our planes away for the night. We hung around a while to see if anybody else made it, but nobody did. Two Austers did arrive, but they were chaps from another Squadron who had turned back on their way to Anzio bridgehead. They could not afford to fly along the coast, as we had, on account of Jerry occupying all the surrounding areas.

This was a lucky encounter as they knew the ropes and took us to their Hotel, the Patria on via San Felipe, and Crazy and I managed to book a swell room.

We had a splendid dinner with plenty of good *vino* and then right upstairs to a steaming bath and to sleep the sleep of the just feeling mighty thankful to be snug and warm and alive.

One of the Air OP boys who had befriended us was shot down and killed two days later when two Messerschmitts pounced on him when he was carrying out a shoot over Anzio. It seemd we were in for an interesting time,

Exploring Naples and Surroundings

The next day [28 Feb 1944] Crazy and I, after a leisurely breakfast, made our way by bus to Capodichino drome to find out if any of the others had turned up. The weather had improved considerably and the sun shone fitfully. It was after lunch that we heard the first Auster rattle across the sky and come in to land. By tea time all were accounted for. We learnt that Bill Bolam had returned to Gauda where he spent an uncomfortable night. Bamford, somewhat shaken when he ran into a balloon barrage in the mist before reaching Sorrento (I missed that one), had turned back and landed in the grounds of the 103 British General Hospital, to the delight of all the nurses – so he said!

This large mob was shepherded into a RAF Transit Camp. Crazy and I forgot to report the arrival of our parent unit to the Town Major, and remained in our very comfortable room at the Patria.

That evening we dined in style at the ex Royal Palace, now an Officers' Club. The next evening we saw *Madame Butterfly* at the famous and impressive San Carlos Opera House. Quite a show.

The weather deteriorated to standard and to our delight, we were stuck in Naples for several days. Our next move was to take us right across the Apennines to the shore of the Adriatic and the weather had to be fairly stable if we were to get across in safety.

Impatient to get on with the job Major Ingram and his Flight Commanders set off by road to Vasto to report to Corps HQ. At that time the Adriatic front was stabilized along the Arielli river, some thirty miles to the NW of this town. The Squadron had been ordered to relieve 651 Squadron who were supporting the 1st Canadian Corps then holding the right hand corner of the Front.
'A' Flight was to support 1st Canadian AGRA, 'B' Flight 5th Canadian Armoured Division (and later 8 Indian Division) and 'C' Flight 1st Canadian Infantry.

And so we remained static for the next five days and made the most of them to explore Naples and surroundings..

Crazy and I went out to have a look at the ancient ruins of Pompeii, which could hardly compete in grandeur with the modern ruins of Naples waterfront efficiently blown up by Jerry prior to retreating.

I managed to get in touch with Fred Bonner, now a Major looking after an Ammo dump at Nola, not far from Naples. He met me at the station and we drove to the monastery cum school where he had his HQ, for lunch. The monks were very strict with their pupils and we watched some of the young lads, they must have been about 15 years old at most, during one of their study periods. Dressed up in cassocks, they walked forward and backwards in a straight line, eyes to book and without saying a word. When they went backwards, they literally walked that way. Indeed it was a strange sight.

We had time to explore all the swell grub joints and night clubs, all very much under military surveillance, and Naples in general, before the weather cleared enough for us to attempt the hop across to the Adriatic where the Eighth Army was anxiously awaiting our arrival in order to hurl us forthwith into battle – or so we imagined. They were, in fact, properly bogged down by the foul weather and the raging Sangro River, not to mention the enemy sitting pretty on the other side.

The Pass over the Apennines

At long last, on the 5th March 1944, the met. report improved and the Squadron set sail, in its usual dribs and drabs way, heading first for the flat lands around Foggia and then North to our final destination – Vasto. This roundabout way was necessary as Jerry was very much in "them thar hills."
There were so many aerodromes around Foggia that I had to beat up three before I found the one I was looking for. Then up the coast to Vasto where we landed on the sands, just beside the breakers. The whole trip took but two hours flying time and nothing happened worth mentioning

The Case of the Missing Squadron

While we were in Naples we had received nary a word regarding the whereabouts of the rest of the squadron which we knew had departed on schedule from Philippeville heading, so we believed, for Bari. But no news had come of them and they were long overdue. At last the CO decided to start investigating off his own bat and sent me off on a secret mission to Bari to find out where the hell our spare shirts had got to. No Nylons in those days.

And so it came about that one day, at a reasonable hour of the morning, I roared tail up along the sands of Vasto and into the cold air, heading for Bari. Intended putting in at Foggia to refuel but discovered that, with a strong tail wind blowing, I came abrest of Foggia in just half an hour and I decided to carry straight on. This was a mistake of course as the total distance was far too much for our restricted range. As could be expected, the wind abated and my ground speed dropped. An hour passed and with some 15 minutes flying time left we were still miles away from our destination. However, to cut a short story shorter, by judicious wiggling of the engine controls, managed to eke out the petrol supply until the wheels touched down on the grass at Bari's aerodrome.

There I luckily bumped into Mickleburgh, an old pal from Cambridge days, who helped me put the plane away. Then we

Sketch map showing Arrol's travels in search of the
missing squadron and other trips. March 5 to 27, 1944

hitch-hiked into town for a really grand lunch at the swanky Hotel Majestic. There ran into Johnny Walker, another Course pal, who possessed a much coveted room at this hotel. As he was leaving that night I silently took possession without advising the desk. After lunch, strolled around to the Desert Air Force HQ but they knew nothing at all about our ground party. However, they promised to try and find out and meanwhile I just had to stick around until news came through. Returned to the Majestic for an elegant tea with music, a much needed hot bath, then a walk on the prom to work up an appetite to tackle a quantious dinner.

Here I was lucky in making friends in the Bar with a Polish General and his Aide and we dined together. They were good company and we discussed horses, the Argentine, the Russians (hatefully) and the Curzon Line (more so). They also regaled me with tales of the Yugoslav guerrillas, with whom they had been fighting. We carried on at the Bar for a while and then off to bed.

By next day DAF HQ [*Desert Air Force HQ*] were able to tell me that the squadron was not coming into Bari at all but had been diverted to Naples.

It seemed that the vehicles sailed from Bône and the men from Philippeville all heading for Bari but, en route, the convoy was split and the men found themselves sailing into beautiful Naples Bay three days later. For the next few days frantic efforts were made to locate the transport party which, of course, had not arrived in Naples. On 10th March news was received that the MT [*Motor Transport*] had been unloaded at Taranto, nearly 200 miles away.

I returned to Vasto that same day, but not before partaking of a wizard lunch at the Hotel Majestic with friend Walker. This time landed at Foggia to refuel and carried on carefree to land safely on the sands.

Two days later the major sent me on another mission, this time to Naples, to find out "what the hell had happened to the ground party" as no further news had been received. So away I went looking forward to the marvellous trip across the beautiful Apennines now bedecked in snow.

Again put into Foggia to refuel before braving the high mountain passes. There was a bit of panic on board when a strong unsuspected cross wind drove my plane off course and I lost my bearings. However, by then I was experienced enough to guess what had happened and I changed my compass course. A little while later we were back on track. Vesuvius came into view and it was plain sailing making Capodichino.

Hitchhiked to the RAF Transit Camp near Pompeii and there found the Adj. who was able to inform me that only the day before they had been informed of the whereabouts of the lost vehicles. He had promptly sent off a batch of drivers to bring them along to Naples.

Was able to locate my tin trunk and rescue some clean clothes. Did not care much for the Transit Camp so, making use of my contacts at the Albergo Patria, managed to find a room there without having to register with the Town Major. Thus spent two pleasant and comfortable days further exploring Naples and doing the odd flick, theatre and night club, and pestering the Africa Force HQ for latest news of the ground party coming up from Taranto.

As soon as the first vehicle turned up and we had a clear picture of the position, I reluctantly made my way to Capodichino and headed back home.

Strong head winds delayed me somewhat. Reaching Foggia shook the Yanks there by landing the Auster across the runway right beside a damaged Flying Fortress where some Erks were able to catch hold of the wing struts and prevent the plane being blown away by the strong wind. Saw her picketed down and had a good lunch at the US Canteen. Managed a tricky take-off and proceeded, crab wise up the coast until I reached Vasto and softly sank into the sand.

Bamford Does it Again

Learnt that the day before Bam and Tanner, returning from Foggia in two Austers with a good tail wind pushing them along, had inadvertently passed Vasto without recognising the village and gone sailing along, quite happily, until Tanner suddenly saw men rushing out to man an AA gun. It dawned on him then that he had gone a bit too far up the coast and he wisely turned out to sea. Bam, however, was then a bit inland and when the penny dropped he also turned towards the sea but this took him, flying at around 400 feet, right over the AA gun then firing at Tanner. They were both chased by tracer bullets coming up from several sources and they were lucky to escape unscathed.

The MT party eventually arrived at Vasto on March 17th and Flights quickly sorted themselves out and took over ALG's from 651 Squadron. The take over was officially completed by the 20th.

Squadron HQ was established near 1st Canadian Corps at Paglieta on the high ground south of the Sangro. Our landing ground was a bull-dozed strip of earth which during the first week or so was a sea of mud owing to the persistent rain.

Conditions were more or less the same at Flights but, nevertheless, they managed to become operational. There wasn't much to do as ammunition was severely rationed. However, this proved advantageous as it allowed an easy breaking in period for green pilots.

I was kept busy doing odd jobs around Squadron HQ and ferrying planes to and from Flights. Despite the duff weather I enjoyed flying over such pretty country and meeting the local Ities, all very friendly and genuinely so.

In which I do some Demonstration Shoots

On the 27th March 1944 I took off for Benevento, about an hour's flight away, there to be attached for a few days to the 2nd Regiment of the elite Royal Horse Artillery for the purpose of carrying out demonstration shoots and teaching them how we worked and how best they could cooperate with us during battle.

Reported on arrival to Colonel Welsh, their CO and was soon settled in their Mess and putting them back with the boys.

The next day was too windy to attempt any shoots and, instead, went up to 1 Battery HQ and watched them carry out a live shoot.

The grub was good and beer better and had a pleasant quiet day. The next day proved favourable and went up and did a demonstration dummy shoot with the RHA [*Royal Horse Artillery*] and pupils from Central Med. Training School watching. Carried out the official drill, in other words observed a shot, then dove down to the deck and hid behind trees until the next shot was ready. It was mountainous country and, in fact, I would disappear from view from the spectators by diving into a valley and this impressed them no end.

Next day gave them a lecture on Air OP procedure and how our work tied in with the Army in general. The following did a live shoot. The RHA boys had already zeroed in on the target I was to be given but, deliberately, shot a reasonable distance away with the first round. By giving the obvious corrections I soon had the shells right on target – a perfect shoot in fact! Was congratulated by the CO who admitted he never realized how efficient an air observed shoot could be!

I think, all in all, my visit there did our cause quite a bit of good. The instructors, usually with little faith in anything new-fangled, now could boost our methods with some authority and belief.

On the way back ran into a stiff head wind, nothing unusual around there, with scudding low clouds. Just managed to sneak over the last high mountain ahead of the clouds and dove down and followed the Trigno Valley until I sighted the Adriatic. This detour had taken me off course and lengthened the distance flown and I was obliged to land at Trigno aerodrome for petrol and lunch. The storm was right overhead and pretty rough but thought that I would chance the trip up the coast. It was not very far to Paglietta and it shouldn't take more than half an hour. However, when I had my kite wound up I found a bad magneto drop and that added a handicap that made the flight rather hazardous.

By the time they had managed to find out what was wrong with the ignition, the wind force had increased to 30 mph. The Austers land at under that figure and, therefore, theoretically we would have to land flying backwards at some 2 mph. Too dicey for me so decided to wait the storm out. It kept on and on without any signs of abating. The 1st South African Air Force Squadron was using that drome with their Mustang fighter-bombers and they kindly offered to put me up for the night. They were a goodly crowd and had an interesting and enjoyable evening yarning with the lads.

Next morning came bright and clear and took off just after 9 for a pleasant trip through brilliant sunlight and clean air to land eventually at Paglietta. Found I had a job awaiting me and soon I was off again with my little plane for Biferno there to pick up a party of Staff Officers. I on-loaded Brig. General Audland, CBE, MC and brought him back to Paglietta.

The Squadron Heads for Bloody Battle

The battlefront on the Sangro had proved disappointing. There was virtually no troop movement and flying was, after the novelty had worn off, rather boring and very few shoots were carried out on account of the ammunition shortage.

Pilots were therefore pleased when we were told to get ready to move over to the Cassino Front; this time to take part in a concentrated attempt by Eighth Army to get through that, so far invincible, barrier.

On the 3rd April 1944, Flights started to move over to the new Front and I ferried a plane across to the primary drome at Presenzano a town some 15 miles S.E. of Cassino and where we were to wait quietly until we were ready to move up to our battle ALG's.

Next day I headed back for the Adriatic in a Troop Carrying Vehicle, a huge Bedford lorry, together with Bdr. Barnett. They had come a long way round along a flatter route. On the return journey, as we were travelling empty, I decided to risk the more direct route through the mountains.

After going through Isernia, we hit the high mountains and had to grind along slowly over winding lonely roads. Then we began to have qualms about the advisability of travelling alone through that particular territory as it had never been captured properly and Jerry could well be hiding there. Got out our tommy gun and kept it at the ready and drove keeping a sharp lookout. Stopped briefly to brew up a cup of tea and eat our sandwiches. Nothing happened and by evening we were safely back at Paglietta.

Two days later the CO, Bam and self in the three remaining Austers started off at crack of dawn for Presenzano. I managed to get lost on my way over. Carelessness I suppose. I certainly was not following Bam and after some casting around, while my petrol gauge dropped lower and lower, located the place at last with some five minutes flying time left.

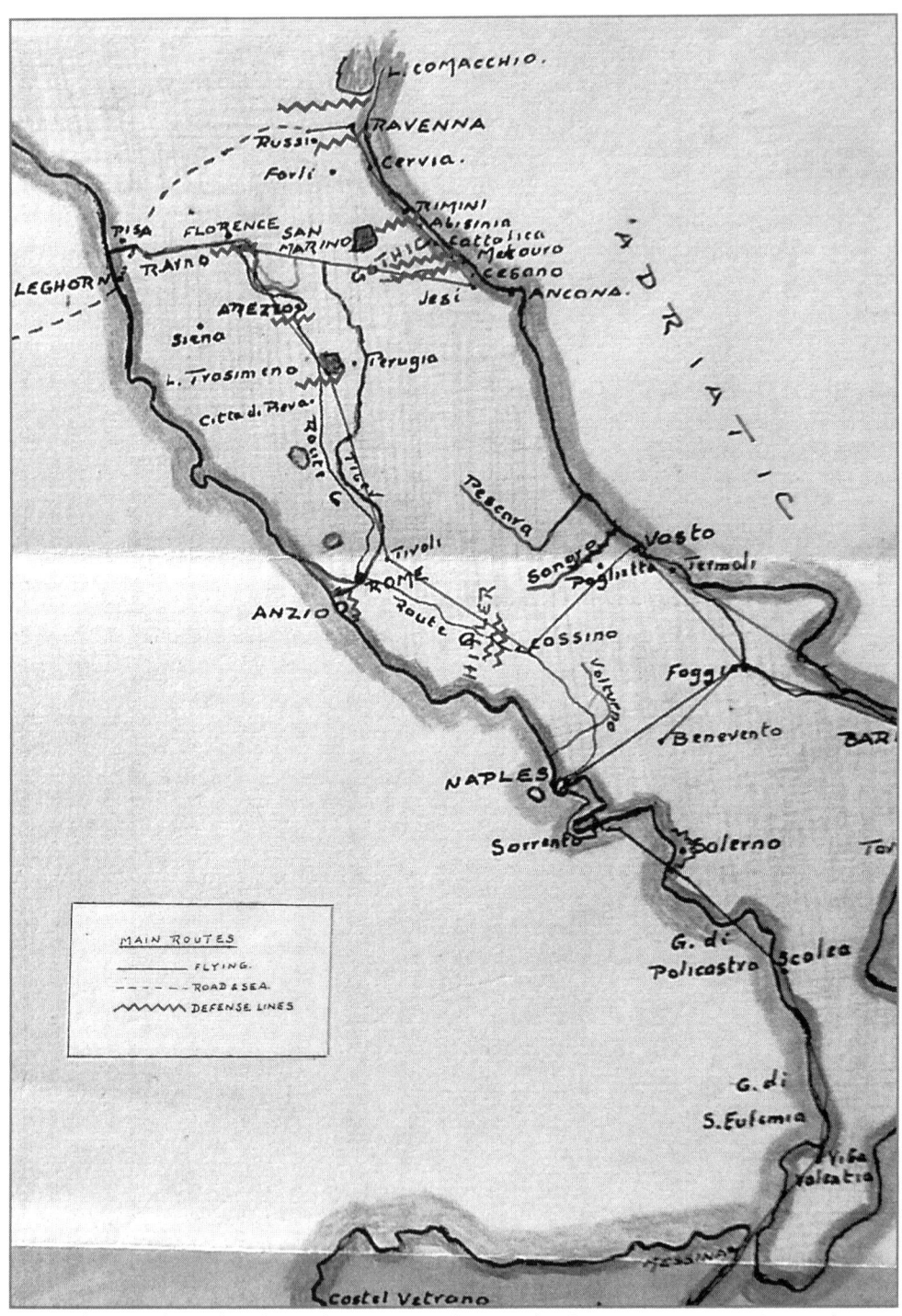

In this map the author shows the successive fronts as the Germans went retreating northwards, the Cassino Battle and Hitler lines, then Arezzo, followed by the capture of Florence. After that Arrol plus the rest of the 8th Army crossed the Apennines and fought their way through the Gothic Line, the Rimini Front and on to the Ravenna Front. See the coloured map on the back cover.

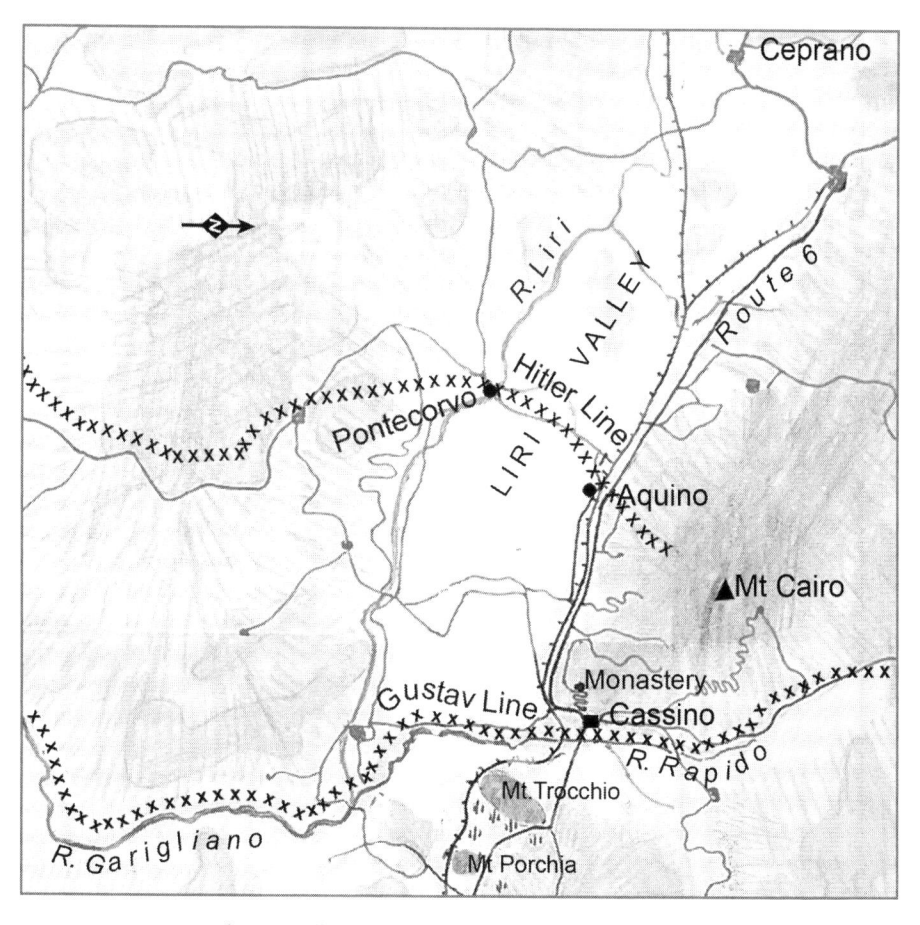

The Liri Valley before the Cassino Battles

The Battles for Cassino

Here a few words about the now famous battles for Cassino might make the picture clearer for readers.

Whilst the Eighth Army and we were held up by the Sangro River, the Fifth Army, mostly American, were getting a bloody nose trying to cross the Rapido, a river only 60 yards wide and a natural obstacle defending the Liri Valley beyond, dominated by the Cassino Monastery and Mount Cairo. These features have been for centuries the vital defence point on the road to Rome and had been chosen again, for the same purpose, by the Germans to build their Gustav Line.

First Battle

This started on the night of January 17th 1944 and the Rapido crossing was attempted by the 36th Texan Division and 2nd US Division but the attack was so badly handled that the two attacking regiments lost more than 1,600 men in two days.

The Anzio landing was about to go in and it was considered imperative to continue the attack on Cassino to keep the Germans occupied and prevent troops being made available to repel the landing. Fresh attacks were hurriedly and prematurely set going with further disastrous results, although some managed to get up the hills and remain dug in and miserable on the slopes of Mount Belvedere. It was raining and snowing continually.

Towards the end of January General Alexander transferred the 2nd New Zealand and 4th Indian Divisions from the Eighth Army in an attempt to stiffen the attacking forces, but the terrible weather and exhaustion won out and the attack slowed to a stop.

Second Battle

This was preceded by an event that caused consternation throughout the World. The famous Monastery founded by St. Benedict in 529 AD was smashed into rubble by 250 Allied bombers that dropped 576 tons of bombs on that tough building that really had never been occupied by the enemy.

The main attack went through along the causeway and railway leading into Cassino village but Jerry was far from dead and came up out of holes in the ground in strong defence. Bloody bayonet and grenade fighting lasted throughout that day with terrible casualties on both sides. The rain that fell next day was the last straw as the holes dug by the bombs filled with water and tracked vehicles could not get across to support the infantry.

On the slopes of Mount Belvedere the troops held – but barely – and grenades were lobbed wholesale. The Allied troops, scantily supplied by mule trains, could not retaliate against the rain of mortar shells coming over from the enemy, and they held on by sheer grit.

Three days later the attack again ground to a standstill.

Third Battle

This one commenced on March 15th 1944 and lasted for seven days. It was touched off by a 500 plus bomber raid with the Cassino village and the enemy-held banks of the Rapido for a target. Bombing was so close that the Allied forward troops withdrew leaving a few suicide snipers to keep the rate of fire to hoodwink the enemy.

The bombing was far from accurate and one lot of bombers mistook Venafro, a town a good thirty miles away from Cassino, for the target and dropped their bombs there to the consternation of our 'A' Flight who had just moved across from the Adriatic. General Oliver Leese's (our General Officer Commanding) caravan was destroyed. Luckily, he wasn't in it at the time.

There were too few of our infantry to go into the attack and too many Jerries survived. As before, our tanks bogged down thanks to the numerous fresh bomb craters. Dogged by bad luck, rain came down heavily the following day when Jerry put in a strong counter attack and recaptured Castle Hill. However, we had gained and held a lodging in the Station which was across the Rapido.

Fourth Battle

Obviously something had to be done to get by the Gustav Line and on to Rome and all points North, so General Alexander ordered the Eighth Army and, of course 657 Air OP Squadron, to come across and get the job done. And so it was to be.

The decisive battle commenced on the 11th May. The 2nd Division of the famous XIII Corps was successful in forcing a way across the Rapido, breeching the strong Gustav Line that had already successfully held against three attacks. The Poles, starting from the bridgehead so painfully gained on Mount Belvedere, were to go up and over the hills and down to meet Route 6 in the Liri Valley.

At the start of this battle the Eighth Army had massed 1,000 guns, 2,000 tanks and had 3,000 aircraft in support. The enemy had

4 Divisions defending Cassino. There were enough belligerents and hardware in this arena to make a first class rumpus.

Bailey bridges were built across the Rapido and the famous 78th (Battleaxe) Division, which had never known defeat, went through the bridgehead to push ahead and they kept going until they reached the Hitler Line, six miles behind the Gustav Line, now hastily renamed Dora, where they got stuck meeting extremely stiff opposition from well prepared positions bristling with high velocity anti-tank and 88 mm guns in concrete emplacements.

On the 23rd May the 1st Canadian Division made a main attack on Dora (ex Hitler) Line and by the following day had breached that supposedly impregnable line and their 5th Canadian Division poured through.

On the 25th *"Viva la Patria"* advance guards of the Eighth Army contacted the Anzio people who had only then broken out.

Then General Mark Clark, evidently fearful lest the British Army should beat him into Rome, instead of cutting straight across Route 6 and catching all the retreating German troops in a watertight trap, ordered his Fifth Army up the coast straight towards Rome. By so doing he allowed 4 German Divisions to escape and fight another day. This silly decision, taken contrary to the established overall plan, definitely prolonged the war in Italy.

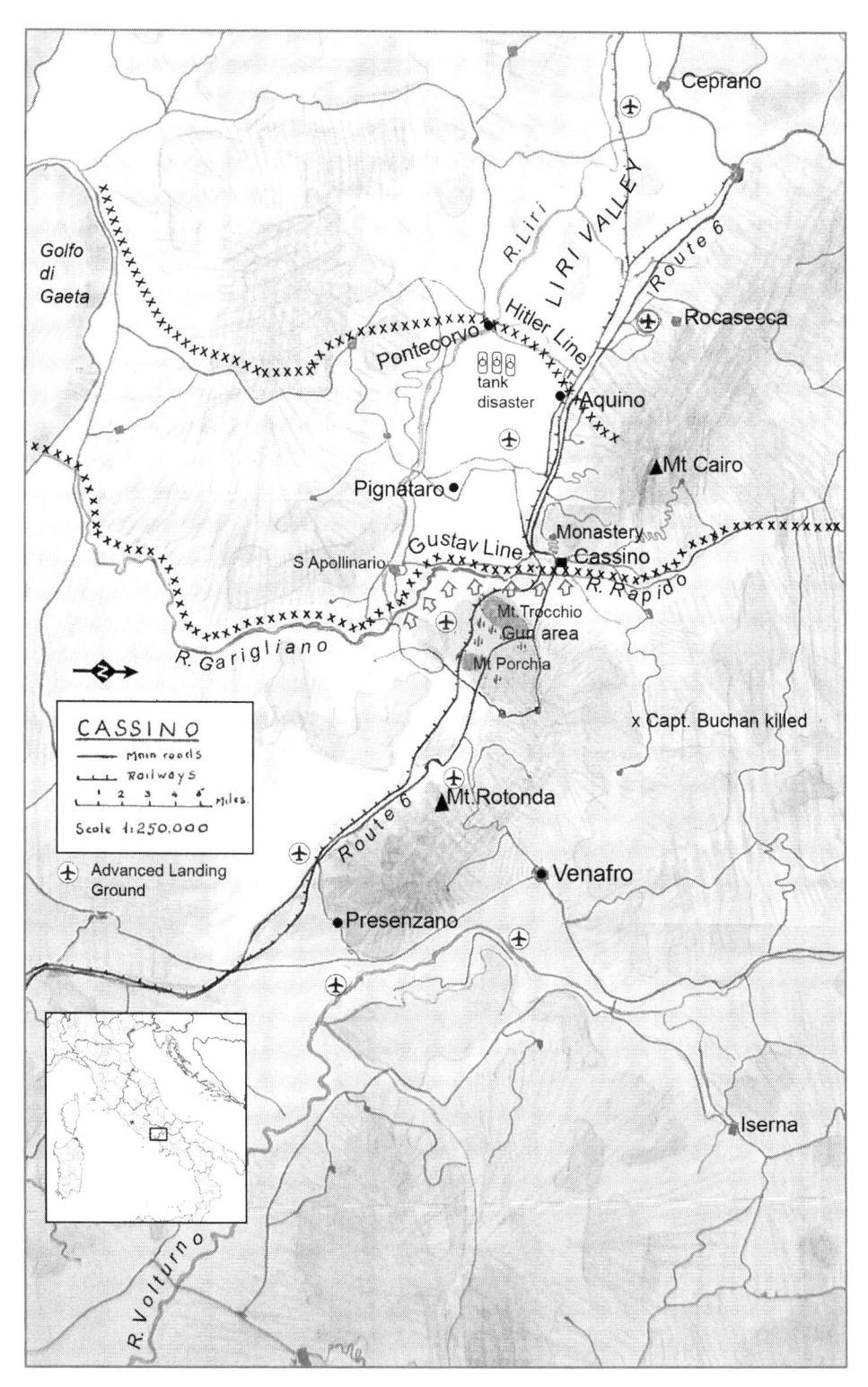

The Gustav and Hitler Lines

INTO ACTION AT CASSINO

Into Action

While events as related were leading up to the last and successful battle for the small village of Cassino, and the more important commanding hill surmounted by the famous Monastery, I was still attached to Squadron HQ doing odd-jobs and anxiously awaiting our first casualty which would allow me to take over a Section, and so see something more of this War I had travelled so far to get into.

Our three Flights were scattered around strategically, all well within ten minutes flying from Cassino. In the lull before the battle our planes were kept busy observing for enemy movements and getting the lie of the land, very important from our point of view, where split second recognition of a target on the map could save lives.

The doubtful honour of being the first pilot to be shot down by the enemy fell to Captain Durrant of 'A' Flight [*10 April 1944*]. His Flight was stationed at Venafro and, to save time, they would sneak up a valley leading straight to their observation area, instead of climbing over the top of the hills. He had probably been shot at umpteen times but did not know it. Returning from a sortie a burst from a machine-gun fired from a hilltop, knocked his prop off, wounding him in the arm. He managed, somehow, to glide in the right direction and crash landed pretty successfully under the circumstances, within fifty yards of our troops. Tommies rushed out to the rescue and he had the presence of mind to carry away his map, codes, etc. Durrant spent many months in hospital but never regained the use of his right arm, so could not return to Air OP where two arms are far too few.

His bad luck gave me the opportunity I was waiting for and I took over his Section. This consisted of four men and three vehicles. One aircraft, one 3 tonner lorry to carry spares, kit, cooking things etc. and one Jeep. Of the men two were Army and two RAF. Of the former one acted as my batman and drove the Jeep, the other looked

Into Action at Cassino 107

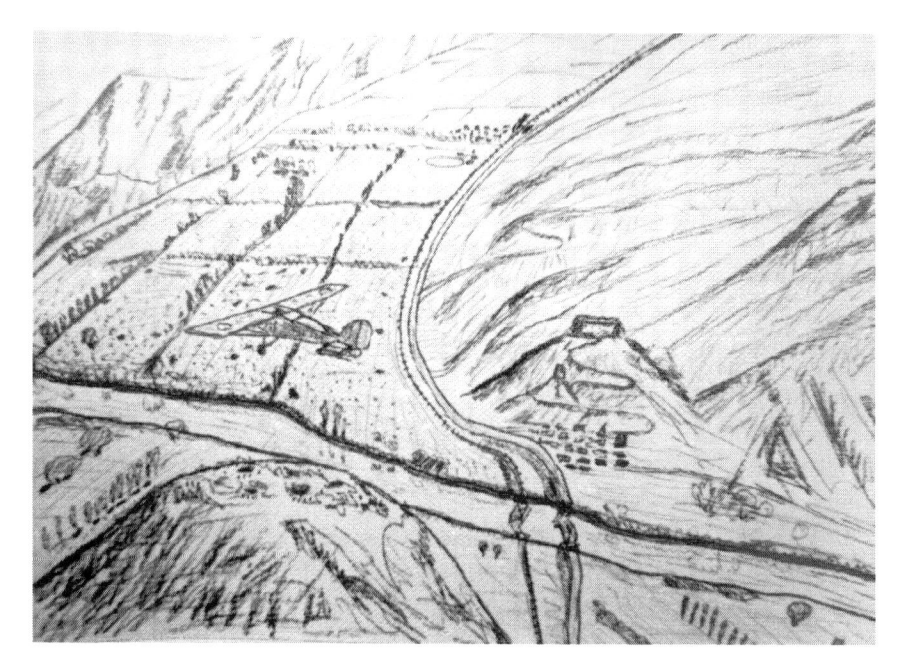

Observing the Battle Scene – Mount Trocchio in the foreground. The Rapido and the Liri Valley beyond. Aquino, Route 6 and the Monastery on the top of the hill.

A view of Cassino, taken from Trocchio.
New Zealand. Department of Internal Affairs. War History Branch:Photographs relating to World War 1939-1945,. Ref: DA-09505-F. Alexander Turnbull Library, Wellington, New Zealand.
http://natlib.govt.nz/records/23065351

after all the wireless equipment and drove the 3 tonner. One RAF man was a fitter and looked after the engine of my plane, and the other was a rigger and looked after the airframe, putting on patches when necessary.

Next day bright and early found Johnny Buchan of 'A' Section and myself flying up the valley in his plane to have a dekko at the Front. Yes, it was the same valley and the same thought occurred to me. However, we sailed over safely into the Liri Valley then filled with low lying smoke screens as both sides tried to hide from the other, what mischief they were up to.

At this time things were reasonably quiet as we were marking time, preparatory to the big push.

Whereas we had got through safely, Aubrey Young, the next pilot up, got it going and coming luckily missing both times. There isn't much one can do flying up a narrowish valley in these puny kites that only do 100 mph all out, and we know what ducks must feel when flying past a shooting box.

To add insult to injury, not only did they shoot at poor Aubrey but somehow they got onto his wireless frequency and told him to "Go away you are not doing any good" in somewhat guttural English. They certainly were keeping a good eye, and an ear too, on Air OP activities.

Johnny Buchan Killed

Johnny Buchan of 'A' Section and a really decent chap, took off the next day at 16:30 hours on a routine flight to the Front [*12 April 1944*]. This time luck was against him and he died horribly but quickly, hit by one of our own large shells as he sailed over a crest just as the gun was fired. The plane was smashed to smithereens and fire consumed what little remained.

At the ALG we carried on as usual, listening in occasionally at the Control Set which was in permanent touch with any plane flying. As little was happening it was not unusual that calls were not coming through. However, when an hour passed and there was still no sound of Johnny returning we became anxious and tried to contact him but without success.

Just then a phone call, from the Royal Artillery Regiment stationed up the valley, reported that they had hit a plane which had crashed in flames. There was no doubt that Johnny had had it.

Bob Barrass and Aubrey Young were very cut up and I have never seen such grim despondency amongst the men. The fact that he left a wife and small child made it worse.

Archie Cowan, who was up with the RA Regiment, rang up later and gave us details. It was his sad job to collect and identify what was left, and next afternoon he turned up in a Jeep bearing a sandbag with the remains. The Padre had already arrived and a burial party went off to the Presenzano Military Cemetery to render last honours to a brave chap.

With two casualties in three days it seemed as if this racket wasn't very healthy; and to think I had left a jolly cushy job with the ATS for this.

And so I moved up one again and took over Johnny's Section consisting of Green [RAF], Wilson [RAF], Hilton [RA] and Powell [RA], who were to remain with me right through the Italian campaign, on to the Dutch Front and, eventually, into Germany.

My First Shoot

A few days later [17 Apr 1944], with rumours of a big battle pending, 'A' Flight moved to an ALG, in another wider valley, nearer to Cassino itself. Here I took over the Air OP commitments of 132nd Field Regiment RA from Rodger Barham of 'B' Flight who was also to meet a messy death a few days later.

Running up the road in "Elsie" the Jeep, with Powell at the wheel, we were in full view from the Monastery for many a mile and the drill was to batt along as fast as possible to discourage Jerry putting a round at the odd cross-roads to which they knew the range to within a yard. Luckily they did not bother much about a solitary Jeep, although they stonked that road pretty frequently at odd moments. So far we hadn't been shelled. We had yet to learn a lot in that respect.

Found the guns I was to shoot dug in on a hillside and met the usual run of decent RA types in their Command Post, a hole in the mountain side. Things were easy and they weren't firing much, and Jerry wasn't doing much mischief either.

Returned to camp, had my plane readied and took off to look into likely target areas. As can be imagined, these little sorties were very interesting and rather pleasant if the atmosphere was peaceful.

April 19th was a real red letter day for me as it was on that day after a long wait, that I was able to get in my first blow against the enemy.

I was ordered to take on a registration shoot against a cross road. Sent plenty of shells across no-mans-land into Jerry territory, and saw them burst beautifully in the area, which must have shaken somebody. Once registered accurately, the cross-road could be engaged at any time, preferably at night, when transport is most likely to be using the road.

Maybe I should explain that we were using ordinary ground wireless sets, covered with many knobs and dials, and tuning in was quite a problem. The set was placed sideways on what should have been the passenger seat and, consequently, all the knobs were difficult to get at when we were safely strapped in with a Sutton harness. Added to that, we were busy flying the plane, map reading and observing all at the same time. To tune in we had to be in the air, as our aerials were not good enough for ground reception.

At a predetermined time the control set would send out a tuning call for one minute. This consisted of a code signal. This simple procedure didn't always work and the amount of cursing that went over the ether, on a wrong frequency, is nobody's business.

At this time I was on the same net, and could talk to the flight Control Set, the guns that I was firing direct and their Regimental Command Post. Later on I could call up five Regiments as also Brigade HQ but that was when they realized that us Air OP chaps knew a lot of tricks and literally controlled the battles for them.

On the 21st April 1944 engaged a Jerry mortar position that was firing from a tree-encircled hollow a couple of hundred yards south of the Monastery and splashed shells in and around the position where they did most good. It was on such targets, impossible to

A half covered Auster in front of Monte Cassino.
Museum of Army Flying, Middle Wallop Stockbridge, Hampshire,

observe by any other means, that the Air OP was invaluable. What surprised me was that Jerry failed to take any efficient action to knock us out of the sky, which should have been easy with a couple of M.E.'s instead of just potting at us with small arms fire.

The following day Aubrey pranged coming into land, doing so on one wing tip and one wheel. Bob Barrass followed suit a few moments later overrunning the runway and going over a slit trench, leaving his under-cart behind.

Intent on doing the hat trick, Aubrey wrote off most of another kite the following day making a ropey landing in a strong wind, collapsing his under-cart and, of course, writing off his prop.

Bad weather stopped flying for a time and, in any case, we weren't supposed to fly too much, not to give the show away.

Took off in Holy Smoke II (thus I had christened my cannon

firing war-kite in honour of a famous boat) just after lunch on the 25th April and went sailing over Mount Trocchio to take on a cross-road target SW of the Monastery. Visibility was poor and I failed to observe the first ranging round from a 25 pounder gun that should have burst somewhere around the target. This was always an awkward moment when something unforeseen happens to break the even sequence of a good shoot. 25 pounder shell bursts are rather white but, if the ground is misty, they are difficult to see. Also in hilly country it was quite likely that the shell went sailing over a crest and burst in a valley a good distance away from where it was expected. To be on the safe side ordered "smoke" which simply, cannot be missed as they let off a good smoke screen. Now, knowing where to look, switched back to HE and had the satisfaction of seeing a plus round hit a house beside the cross-road sending brick dust and mortar flying. One always hoped, on these occasions, that some Jerries were having a quiet *siesta* inside.

Having reached a verified short bracket registered the target for future stonking and, with the job accomplished, climbed higher into the sky to have a relatively safe view of the Rapido River that formed the boundary between the enemy and ourselves. This was for future reference as split second recognition of the terrain was of primary importance to our job.

Hitherto we had been operating on the accepted principle that, for safety, we had to fly our unarmed planes at a very low height, maximum 600 feet, and for not longer than 20 minutes. In the Cassino area this low flying business was ridiculous as the Monastery Hill and most of our targets were far higher than 600 feet. Besides, low flying was just asking for trouble from the many machine guns and chaps with rifles who lurked underneath and did not think kindly of us. As we were still according to the text book flying low, parachutes were supposedly unusable and we carried none.

During this particular shoot I had already climbed pretty high and went up to 4,000 ft to cruise up the Rapido. Away up there I felt positively giddy and light headed at such an unaccustomed altitude. Also started to brood on what would happen should a shell – and there were plenty around as the bumps and eddies that

Cassino Battle - RAF photo.
Pignataro in Liri Valley before the monster shoot.

buffeted the plane showed only too plainly – just damage the plane sufficiently to send it spinning to the ground out of control, and I without an umbrella. Was thankful when I had followed the Rapido right across the Liri Valley and my conscience allowed me to turn and dive towards Mount Trocchio and the safe area behind. Leapfrogged over the guns and sailed down to a gentle landing in time for tea.

That was to be my last operational flight until after the big attack. Taking advantage of the lull, Archie Cowan, our flight CO, George Riley of 'C' Flight and myself got hold of a utility and headed for Naples and Sorrento beyond. There we had a wizard four day leave living in Cucumella Hotel and roaming around that lovely place, exploring beaches, mysterious caverns and sailing on the clear blue waters of the bay. That was to be Archie's last holiday on this earth.

The Decisive Cassino Battle

All during April the Eighth Army had been preparing to wage a decisive battle to dislodge the enemy from the perfect defensive position astride the Liri Valley, watched over by Monastery Hill and towering Mount Cairo behind.

The rushing waters of the Rapido were a nasty obstacle to overcome. We knew, from air photos, that the enemy had deep defensive systems with many concrete pillboxes and enlacements culminating in the famous Hitler Line which pivoted on Aquino. If it bore that illustrious name it could be taken for granted that Jerry considered it impregnable.

A force of Artillery mightier even than that which started the Eighth Army rolling forward at El Alamein was slowly massing behind Mount Trocchio and Mount Porchia, two pimple hills that directly faced the Liri Valley and afforded the gunners an excellent platform for their "ground" OP's. The decided disadvantage for the gunners was that most shells from the guns hiding behind these hills perforce had to whizz over them and the odd shell that didn't quite make it would burst amongst them causing much consternation and alarm.

Furthermore, these OP's were not high enough to see into the Monastery and surrounding hillside, valleys and woods, all cluttered up with hostile bodies, and these areas were, therefore, our happy hunting grounds.

For the impending battle the Squadron was attached to XIII Corps and 'A' Flight to the crack 75th Division that had been in practically continuous action since El Alamein. To break it down still further I was detailed to look after the air observation and shoot of 132 Field Regiment with 25 pounders.

On the eve of the attack, never having seen a real battle, I became rather apprehensive regarding what would happen on the morrow when I would have to fly flimsy Holy Smoke II right into the thick of it all. With the biggest concentration of guns the World had ever seen firing from one side and goodness knows how many firing from the other, there was sure to be an impressive amount of airborne hardware making use of the same bit of sky as myself.

That evening Bob and self went along to see *Pistol Packing Mama* given on a nearby hillside with the screen visible for miles around, should Jerry have wished to drop a card. The film was somewhat spoilt towards the end as at 23·00 hours, the guns all around commenced firing the softening barrage, the prelude to the infantry crossing the Rapido; and we could not hear the sound track properly.

The scene was quite Dantesque. The continuous gun flashes lighting the valley in bright flickers and those beyond causing the trees momentarily to be silhouetted against the sky, all in a hotch-potch of vivid hot colours.

By dawn of the 12th May 1944 the infantry was reported across the Rapido – but at a price.

My Regiment was fully occupied with barrages and predicted shoots and had nothing for me. However, in an emergency I could call on them to take on a special target, such as guns firing and causing damage to our forward troops. In order to add my penny's worth to the proceedings, I took off to have my very first look at a first class fight. By dodging guns firing all around our take off area, and skidding round fast to the lee side of Mount Trocchio, I was able to do some observing in relative safety. The scene below was disappointing. Infantry on the ground is difficult to see especially if they are moving cautiously and are well camouflaged, as in this case, and besides, they were putting down smoke screens. Tanks operating are far more interesting as they certainly can be seen without trouble, but none had crossed over yet. Eventually returned to the ALG with nothing to report.

That same day we moved to the first of a succession of difficult ALG's most of which would have been considered suicidal in "civvy street." This particular landing ground was a small field just north of Hill Rotonda and Highway 6 and was a lovely spot, very like a rock garden with a stream running through.

Scottie, a newcomer to the Flight, somehow or other damaged one plane on take off and Aubrey pranged his on landing, leaving us with only two serviceable planes; Bob's and mine.

We were well within range of Jerry guns and clearly visible from their OP's on Mount Cairo and we could just imagine them working out the range and bearing to such an inviting target. We made haste to dig convenient slit trenches and camouflage our kites. Sure enough, the odd shell was soon crumping around, but none came too close.

So far I personally had lived rather a quiet life, apart from the occasional bomb dropped nearby in England, and the whine and crump of a real live shell was somewhat of a novelty; but just a mild sample of what was in store for us later on, as 'A' Flight was invariably right bang up with the guns and, on one memorable occasion, ahead of them.

Although I did no shooting whilst my Regiment was busy putting down barrages, I carried out quite a few information sorties over the front, some just routine and others to check up on information received by Corps HQ. These flips were really interesting.

As already mentioned, flying over the front was precarious work and the skies were thick with shells most of the time during the main attack. Just to look back and see hundreds of jabs of flame, each one representing a shell leaving the muzzle of a gun aimed in ones general direction, made one feel apprehensive for one's immediate future. As each shell caused a violent displacement of air throughout its trajectory, which persisted for quite a while like an express train going through a station, the air just over the front through which we had to fly was in a continuous turmoil. The violent jolts the planes received were added reminders that a shell had just passed that way. One or two of the lads swore they had actually seen shells receding away from them. This is quite possible but somewhat dubious.

Of course, on top of this we were still flying without parachutes the which did not add to our peace of mind. In fact, I was worried stiff whenever I was floating up there amongst all that hardware. We were also informed that Jerry often had a go at us with machine guns and rifle fire but we were too preoccupied to give thought to such a trifling matter as that.

It was round about this time that Capt. Rodger Barham of 'B' Flight wasn't so lucky and his plane was seen to explode in the air over the front line, presumably hit by one of our own shells. Some days later, whilst roaming around the Liri Valley in my Jeep, I came across what looked like the remains of an Auster. Wary of mines I entered the field in which it lay and scouting around found a freshly dug grave just under a tree in a quiet sheltered place. A rude cross was set on top and his name stencilled on. He was a funny chap, too old for this game, dour but kind; and he also got left behind.

On the 18th May 1944 we moved on to a new ALG, to keep up with the advancing front line. Our camp, on this occasion, was sited in a dreary dusty wood that had been thoroughly bombed the night before and the people in it at the time had been rather unlucky.

Our landing strip was a ten yard wide path bulldozed through a field of standing wheat with highish trees not far from either end. This called for some tricky flying to get in and out all in one piece. Such RAF dogma as "always land into wind" and "landing strips must be free of obstructions for at least 600 yards" had been left way behind, and we now flew trusting in the Lord and by the seat of our pants.

We were to spend some time at this ALG in fact, until the Hitler Line had been breached.

The next day was pleased as punch as I was given no less than three targets to engage in the Aquino area. However, just as I was sitting pretty right over the target area, and getting ready to have some fun, something happened and the shoot was cancelled by Control.

I meet Mrs. Finnigan

On the 20th May, things being quiet, got hold of Elsie and went off to visit my Regiment now across the Rapido. Several Bailey Bridges were spanning this river, sufficiently strong to take tanks. The other bank had been heavily mined and the Sappers were still looking for these horrible things. One of them had not managed to spot a booby trap in time and they were carrying away what remained as we passed, not a pleasant sight. Cleared paths were marked by white tapes and we took great care to keep within their borders. The sickly smell of "good Jerries" was rather overpowering. This particular spot had been the scene of very bitter fighting, the enemy was doing everything in their power to retain what had been for many months a stable front. Jerry was a pretty good fighter and their best troops had lined the Rapido; consequently many bods had been dragged into ditches and bulldozed over.

Following the "132 Field Regiment" sign-posts along narrow tracks and new bull-dozed dust roads pushed straight through fields and over hedges until we came to the HQ Command Post in a farm house. We had only just arrived and were having a friendly chat in what had been a large living-cum-dining room, when Jerry started putting down a real good "stonk" on the area. We made haste to reach the relative safety of the cellar. While this show was at its height with shells screeching and crumping all around, there came a tap at the door and in did come Mrs. Finnigan accompanied by the Padre carrying a large tea urn between them, and the inseparable basket of "wads."

Mrs. Finnigan was certainly a character. Her husband had been killed in action earlier on and she had joined the YWCA. After a lot of string pulling she succeeded in obtaining permission to work with 78 Division and wasn't happy unless she was away up front taking tea to the boys. She had a special canteen lorry to carry her Naafi wares but on this occasion, the large lorry being far too conspicuous to bring up the line, she had persuaded the Padre to let her come in his 15 cwt truck.

She soon set up business and handed round hot tea and buns to all, cheerfully and quite at ease despite the trouble she had just gone through.

Unfortunately the Padre had to do his stuff as word came through of casualties in 'C' Troop and their Sergeant Major had been killed. Mrs Finnigan left as soon as the firing petered out to keep on doing her good work. Her presence in the gun area was excellent for the morale of the lads under fire, and the tea was also welcome.

She followed 78 Division through many campaigns and did really noble work. Later we were transferred to the Canadian Corps and I never had the opportunity of seeing her again.

I Observe a Monster Shoot

Partisans had reported that Jerry was moving out of Pignataro, a village in the middle of the Liri Valley and I was ordered to check on this. Our guns were firing a great deal and I was careful to put Mount Trocchio behind me before heading my plane into the valley to get a close look at the roads leading out of this village. Unfortunately the main road heading NE was tree lined and I was obliged to shift my position in order to look straight up it, the only way to ascertain, with any certainty, if anything moved. This put me in line with all the shells that were heading for Pignataro, which I could see bursting merrily in and around the village, causing much havoc and flying brick dust. The air was decidedly bumpy, and not from meteorological causes either. Although I had nervously pushed the throttle to full speed and the ASI [*air speed indicator*] showed we were doing all of 100 mph, yet Holy Smoke just seemed to creep across that unpleasant area taking simply ages. After obtaining a good look straight up the road with my binoculars and could report accurately that not a vehicle or body was using it to escape, I turned tail and fled, still at full speed, to the shelter afforded by Mount Trocchio. This information was important and hurriedly made plans were altered.

That afternoon I was sent aloft again to observe a Regimental Shoot concentrated on Aquino, pivot of the strong Hitler Line. A Regimental shoot is some bang as all the guns in the Regiment fire in such a way that their shells hit the target at the same instant.

It was a clear sunny day as I climbed past friendly Mount Trocchio, waving to the odd OP chap up there, and sailing over and into the Liri Valley, taking care to position myself to a flank of the path the shells would soon take when the shoot began.

As always, had synchronized my watch and right on the dot the whole of Aquino erupted and boiled in black and red smoke and was blotted from view. The guns were firing well and no correction was necessary, it was a very impressive sight and I would have hated to have been in that village at 14·17 hours that day.

I had barely sent down my report on that shoot when Control

piped up and told me to stay around and observe a Divisional shoot, something every Artillery Officer dreams about and rarely sees, let alone controls.

Chances were extremely remote of that ever happening; and there was I not only seeing this stupendous shoot but in sole charge of correcting it if necessary. Did I feel important! Until I realized I couldn't possibly get out of the path of the shells coming, as they would, from all over the countryside and all at the same time. Maybe it would have been preferable to read about such a wizard shoot in a text book, rather than be conceded this privilege. But who was I to reason why.

As Jerry would surely have picked up this message given in clear, the shoot had to come pretty quickly before they could get word to their troops in Aquino. Something big must have happened to warrant such a drastic step being taken, obviously on the spur of the moment. Look as I might with my binoculars I could see nothing at all stirring in the target area which, meanwhile, had cleared of smoke, except for the odd building burning.

Was on pins and needles whilst I watched the second hand of my aircraft clock tick slowly round to zero hour, only about three minutes from the time the warning order had been given.

When the time came this super stonk topped anything I had ever seen, and have yet to see, even in the movies. The whole target area simply disappeared from sight beneath an instantaneous surge of boiling reddish smoke, as buildings were smashed to smithereens. Could report without any qualms that the shoot was effective, hardly any round going astray; should this have not been the case I would have estimated the centre of destruction and given a correction to bring it onto the centre of the target area.

An Absentminded Waltz with Holy

The following day I was up in Holy Smoke looking into the Liri Valley battle seeking trouble and anti-tank guns firing from Aquino. Signalling was lousy and the 132 Field Regiment went off the air just when I needed them and no amount of knob twiddling did any good. Flew over their HQ and beat them up hoping that "Pronto" (code for Signalling Officer), would get his finger out and give me a tuning call; but nothing happened.

In desperation, decided to land, and did so after having a look at a nearby field, devoid of any suspicious looking round marks. Sliding over some highish trees I sat down gently and switched off.

Pronto saw me land and came chasing over the field in his Jeep and was most apologetic. When I told him my trouble he chased back to his control set to send me the required tuning call.

No sooner was everything fixed up than Control reported an anti-tank gun being a real nuisance and, no doubt, playing havoc with our tanks. I could imagine what that meant to the chaps inside.

The plane's engine had to be started and I was alone and in a hell of a hurry. Needless to say solo starting is contrary to all sorts of RAF rules and regulations, and it is somewhat tricky.

The brakes were fully on. Checked that ignition switches were OFF and gave the prop a few turns. Switched ON and swung hard and, of course, instead of behaving decently and commencing to purr as normal Holy decided to act stubborn. After a couple of minutes of frantic swinging it was obvious she was not going to start that way.

Under the circumstances the next step was to Blow Out all the duff mixture. To do this switched OFF again, pushed the throttle fully OPEN, petrol OFF, all in the approved manner, and turned the prop anti-clockwise 16 times. Now she was supposed to be clean as a whistle and ready to start first go.

Time was flying and that anti-tank gun was still being a nuisance. Ran round to the cabin, snipped the two mag switches to ON and then gave the prop a good swing, She started first go all right – and how! With a terrific roar that shook me rigid Holy started coming towards me and a madly spinning prop is mighty dangerous. Of course I had absent-mindedly forgotten to close the throttle, still fully OPEN.

The brakes could not hold the pull of 128 horses and Holy kept moving forward, though they restrained her sufficiently to cause the tail to rise and, if nothing was done very quickly, the prop would hit the ground and then there would be hell to pay all round.

All this happened in split seconds. Without considering consequences I jumped sideways and caught hold of one of the side struts. This had the effect of changing the line of advance from a straight line to an arc of a circle and there we were, clinging together waltzing around and around and covering quite a bit of ground. My partner did not seem to enjoy it a bit and was kicking up an awful din. My eyes were glued to her tail, hardly correct etiquette, but the higher it went the nearer to sudden destruction went the prop. The higher it went the more I would push, and the faster we'd go round. It was quite a to-do.

This was becoming decidedly monotonous, and I'm not a keen dancer in any case. Thought I'd take a chance, a decision influenced by the fact that all this waltzing around was drawing us nigh some trees. Dropped the strut and made a wild lunge for the cabin door clawed it open against the violent buffeting of the slip stream, sprawled across the seat and slammed down the throttle lever. The tail, away up in the air by then, subsided with a bump. Was I thankful!

Shakily I clambered in, buckled on the Sutton harness, put on the headphones and laringa-phones and was all set and sitting pretty. I released the brakes and eased on the throttle to commence taxiing when the engine spluttered, coughed and the prop windmilled to a stop. A glance at the dash and I knew the worst. I had absentmindedly forgotten to switch the petrol to ON.

And so I had to start from scratch again. Luckily, however, Holy started first go, evidently being ashamed of her recent behaviour. By taxiing right up against the trees at the far end of the not too large field, managed to rise above the trees and soon we were out of that place and raining down HE shells in the neighbourhood of that gun firing at our tanks. And then some people wonder why we got 2 shillings extra flying pay.

Telling of a Day of Close Shaves

May 22nd 1944 proved to be a pretty hectic day and rather unhealthy for Holy Smoke and myself. We simply could not keep out of trouble; which rarely comes singly.

Our first job was to carry out the preparations for a fake barrage, a good bit north of the real attack line on the Hitler Defences astride the Liri Valley. As soon as Holy Smoke was warmed up we chased down the narrow strip stirring up the standing wheat on either side, heading for the tall trees at the end. With my weight up there was always a doubt whether we would make it and hence these take-offs were always "interesting."

We were so near the front line that five or six minutes flying was all that was required to get us well into position to observe. This time however, no sooner was I looking into my target area than the wireless packed up and no amount of knob twirling helped. Therefore, had to wend my way back with my mission unaccomplished.

Things were brewing those days and Jerry was expected to launch a pretty stiff counter attack at any moment. No sooner had Hilton repaired the wireless than a tank scare had me scampering up again and careering over the front looking eagerly for those monsters; but nothing stirred and I was able to allay that scary report.

Just before tea time took off on another sortie, this time to do the fake barrage registration shoot, and was soon sitting pretty over the target area, wheeling and wriggling around, as we always flew to make it more difficult for the chaps on the ground who could be expected to have several pot shots at us. Was all set to commence sending down orders when strips of tracers went whizzing past my nose, the which shook me no end. Strips of five tracers meant Bofors were firing and they were coming from our side of the lines. That struck a chord and remembered that was a signal to us that enemy fighters were approaching. I glanced up through the perspex roof and saw that the sky was liberally covered in woolly AA bursts aimed at four Jerry fighters coming in fast. Did a quick half roll and dived down to relative safety, relative in that of course, I had to take care to miss flying into the nasty stuff being pumped up by our lads. And it must be remembered – I did – that all the ironmongery sent up was coming down fast in smaller pieces, to which must be added all the stuff travelling through the air in a horizontal plane.

Upstairs wasn't too healthy with four "Bandits" fooling around and therefore decided to carry on with the shoot at a low altitude, but this obliged me to keep too darn near to the Hitler line for comfort. On two occasions the plane was badly shaken by the blast of four large calibre HE shells bursting right underneath. It may have been a coincidence but several other pilots had also reported a like occurrence. It seemed that Jerry tried to dissuade us by aiming a troop of guns at a point just beneath us in the hopes of blasting us out of the sky.

The barrage detail was lengthy. Six points had to be accurately registered, and I had to return for more petrol in order to finish. Filled up quickly and took off for my forth sortie that day.

Directing a shoot from a plane keeps one pretty busy especially towards sundown when static adds to our troubles by making it extremely difficult to get wireless messages through. After my recent experience, decided a medium height would be best for all concerned; as the daylight dwindled, I became very much aware of a detail I had hitherto blissfully ignored. Streams of tracers evidently from machine guns, were arcing their way gracefully towards us. It was fascinating watching them rising slowly, to accelerate suddenly, and whizz by in a wicked flash. Very pretty, undoubtedly, but not at all funny.

The darkness also intensified the flashes of our own guns firing – an awesome sight especially for one sitting in their direct line of fire. Was glad when the last point was duly registered and we could head for home as fast as our four cylinders could take us.

Our troubles were not yet over. One more narrow escape lay ahead. Little did we know that another lone soul was winging his way home through the dusk, hoping to land safely in 651 Squadron's air strip that was sited in the next field to ours but placed at right

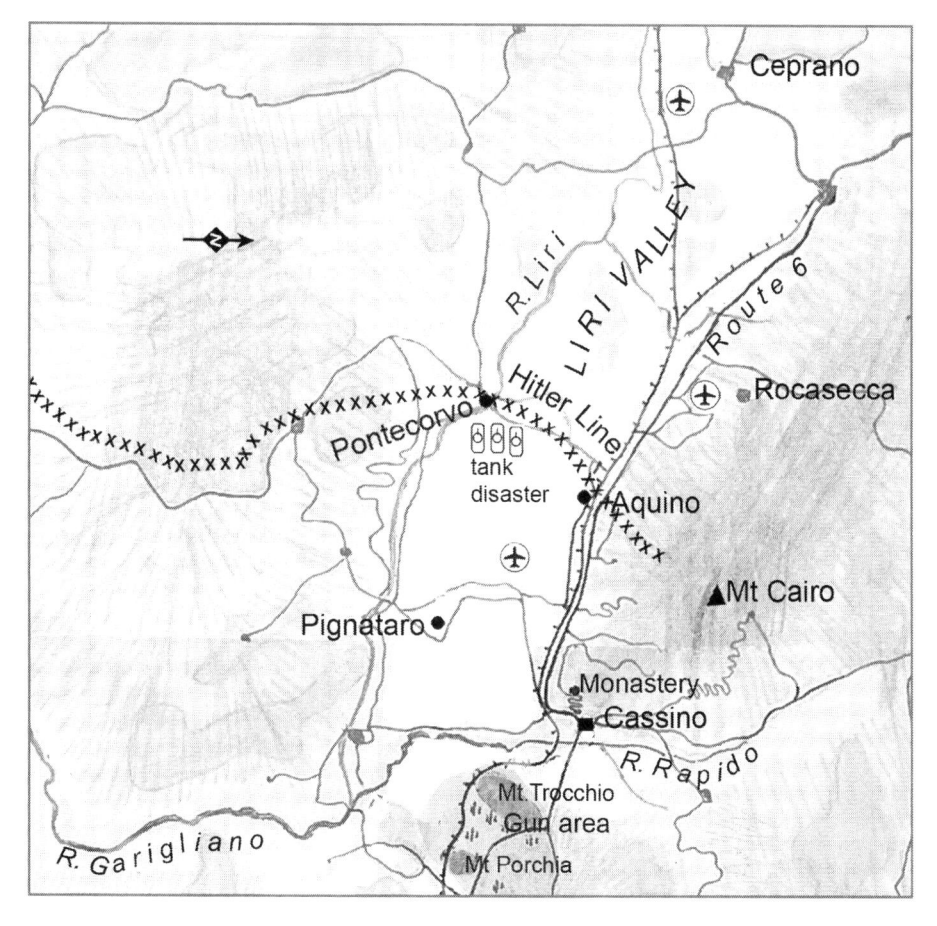

Hitler line Battle

angles, with ends adjoining thus forming a letter L. As he was heading in to land from the left, up the short arm, and I was coming in making for the bottom of the long arm, if timed correctly we were bound to meet some 50 feet up, just over the boundary trees. And so it happened. There was I crawling towards the trees with landing flaps down and next to nothing on the clock, a hair's breadth from stalling, when a large shadow loomed out of the gloaming right in front of our noses. Was feeling pretty tired after four nerve wrenching trips and was all keyed up for a difficult landing into a narrow and short strip. We had no landing lights or flares to help us out, and it was already too dark to see properly. It was only by instinct that I reacted instantaneously and pulled back on the stick and jammed on full throttle. We staggered over the other plane, missing it by inches, then went into a stall just over the trees. Missed them too, dropped like a lift, and I just managed to catch Holy before she hit the ground with a wallop. We did a mighty short landing but we were all in one piece.

That night I slept the sleep of the just despite the noise of battle going on all around.

Went along to 651 Squadron the following day to check up with the other pilot in this little drama; he never noticed a thing so intent was he in piloting his plane in to a safe landing under these adverse conditions plus darkness.

FROM CASSINO TO THE AREZZO FRONT

My First Little Prang

With our lads pushing, the Jerries were pulling out their soft skinned vehicles from Pontecorvo and surrounding area and taking them to safety behind the Hitler Line defences. Our forward troops had reached the vicinity of Aquino, a very important point forming the northern pivot of this defence line, and they were bashing it as much as they could, but were meeting strong resistance, as was to be expected. It was up to us chaps in the flying contraptions to sit right over the trouble and try and locate and neutralise the enemy fire. This was a somewhat hectic job but mighty interesting and one felt that one was doing something useful for the war effort; though digging a nice Victory garden also has its good points.

In order to give maximum support to our chaps, who were being given hell by the enemy comfortably entrenched behind concrete pillboxes and emplacements, I had planned to take off at first light and land beside Regimental HQ where I could be accurately briefed and be up and in action without loss of time. This plan was not very popular with the RA people as they feared that my landing there would attract enemy fire. However they were being shelled intermittently anyway and, in the end, they agreed to my making use of a suitable field some 100 yards away from their Control Set.

Therefore, at about 5:50 am on the morning of the 24th May 1944, when I could just discern the trees at the end of the runway, Holy Smoke nobly did her stuff and pulled me over the trees with feet to spare.

When I reached the Liri Valley a thick morning mist covered everything and only the tops of the high trees could be seen.

I was fairly familiar with the lie of the land by that time and a bit of scouting around brought me to some trees I recognised, and I was able to pin point the chosen field. Then I made several attempts to get in but without success. Flying my approach in the clear air above I would sink down into that cotton woolly stuff and then would start

"Marion" in the Liri Valley, the Monastery can be seen on the near hill.

a blind nerve- wracking glide into nothingness. I could not get rid of the impression that we were veering although the steady compass belied this, and quite wrongly corrected knowing this was wrong. Trees were, I knew too darn well, all around and only split second piloting could save me from disaster. My nerves just could not stand the strain and each time I would push on full throttle and stagger out of the mist, zig-zagging to miss the higher trees.

Each time I circled around a bit to recover my nerve before making another attempt. After the third try decided to give up. Then I realised that the mist was extending and an easterly wind was pushing it towards our landing strip and this gave me something else to worry about as we sped back hell for leather. Sure enough, the mist was billowing over the end of our small landing strip and had to land in a hurry. To make matters worse, the east wind forced me to land straight into the rising sun which blinded me completely and could not see ahead through the scratched perspex. I manoeuvred into the correct line of approach, just cleared the boundary trees and guessed the rest. I wasn't far wrong, in fact did pretty well considering, landed a bit short and slightly off for line. Unluckily my left wheel hit a small mound of earth which skewed the plane round sufficient to send us off the narrow 10 foot wide runway. And there we went tearing through the tall standing wheat in a shower of straw and grain. Had switched off as soon as I felt her hit and the prop was safe. Unfortunately our erratic course took us over a deep hole and this bowed the under-cart; this was the very first damage ever inflicted on a RAF plane by me.

Meanwhile the battle was raging and three anti-tank guns were giving our troops hell, firing from Aquino. I was ordered to take them on and knock them out if possible. With my plane out of action, borrowed Scotty's. By this time the rising sun had done its work and the mist had lifted sufficiently to allow me to land as originally intended beside Regimental HQ. Colonel Nichols wasted no time in pointing out where tanks were being held up and the reported position of the guns then firing.

"Pronto" whizzed me up to my plane in his Jeep and within minutes was floating over Aquino and peering down into the target area partly obscured by the smoke of shells bursting. There was a good old shindy going on below and was mighty glad to be sitting pretty, in comfort, way above.

All this smoke made ranging difficult and was only able to take on one target smashing shells into and around the house hiding the anti-tank guns, with good effect; I hoped.

Things were really sticky on the ground and I saw five of our tanks brewing up. They were Shermans and this usually meant that most of the crew was sizzling inside.

Later on I was to witness, in one pretty green field in this same area, no less than 18 of our bigger tanks, Churchill's and Sherman's, all knocked askew and burning bright, hit by high velocity guns firing mercilessly from invulnerable concrete emplacements from across a shallow valley. This horrible slaughter, which I saw, was one of the major tank disasters of that campaign, and we were powerless to do anything, our shells just bounced off the tough gun turrets and thick cement walls. Later I was to accomplish the impossible during the Gothic Line battle by putting one of these turrets out of action with a 4.5 inch shell; but that is another story.

Returning to this one, the other two guns had yet to be silenced. Chased back to our ALG, loaded up with more petrol and was soon roaring tail up along the runway and soaring over the trees. Must admit there was a feeling of adventure in the air those days and one lived keyed up and in a mood to do deeds of daring. Should really have been on a trusty steed charging towards battle with a sword in my hand; but must admit that old Holy was much more comfortable and could always get back for my cup of tea; or run away from trouble in double quick time.

When I came over Aquino again the smoke had cleared sufficiently to commence firing and in three minutes, normal time for quick ranging if the guns behave, the shells were falling nicely in the target area and giving the Jerries something to think about.

Meanwhile a message came over the blower to the effect that a Jerry convoy was moving along Route 6. As soon as I had finished with the anti-tank guns went north until I was in line with that highway but a good look with binoculars did not reveal any movement of vehicles.

After that Flight called it a day. The nervous excitement gets one pretty tired.

A Memorable Birthday Party

May the 25th 1944 –"*Dia de la Patria*" and my 33rd birthday; and what a way to spend it. Anyway there were plenty of *disparos de bombas* as my mother would say.

At crack of dawn, the four of us that comprised 'A' Flight, that is Bob, Aubrey, Scottie and myself, took off and landed in a slight ground mist right in the middle of the Liri Valley in a new bulldozed ALG that we were to share with 'C' Flight. Jerry was sitting atop Mount Cairo that towered above us to our north and could see exactly what we were doing. Can quite imagine them chuckling in glee at the sight of such a perfect target, eight beautiful shiny planes all stacked together in a small area.

From Cassino to the Arezzo Front 131

Remains of Holy Smoke II, Bob Barrass and self

Capt. Aubrey Young RA and the remains of his plane.

Here a slight regression might be in order to put the reader in the picture as to the enemy's sentiments towards us. Our watchful presence in the sky made it virtually impossible for Jerry to make any move whatsoever during the hours of daylight, they could not even have a hot meal anywhere near the front as the mere sight of smoke was instantly spotted by us and stonked. In consequence we were thoroughly detested and were always singled out for their particular brand of hate, getting more than our fair share of the shells that would whine mournfully across the lines during the hours of darkness when we were doing our best to sleep. The most nerve wracking part was when, at dead of night, a shell would whine over and "crump" just beyond where one lay in bed. A minute later another "crump" would seemingly land just short. Knowing the rules of the game we knew that the next one would be right in the middle and an eternity would pass whilst we waited for that one to come. Next morning we would find that the shells really landed a fair distance away, but around the camp somewhere.

Not for obvious reasons, but to find out what was happening as the situation was most confused, jumped into Elsie and headed west to locate the Colonel. It always surprised me that I was able to find these odd bods amongst the shambles of war but this was thanks to an efficient system of signposting. It was a sort of treasure hunt but one had to know the clues, or rather, code signs.

Roads in the flat Liri Valley presented no problem as they were quickly bull-dozed straight ahead, only bothering to miss the larger trees, not worrying overmuch about the odd house that may have been in the way.

Mines were all over the place. Jerry had had plenty of time to plant them. As usual he was extremely thorough. Great care had to be taken not to drive over the white tapes that denoted swept areas. The smell of good Jeries was pretty powerful and some were still lying around, and where buried weren't buried very deep.

On the way up passed a Sherman burning furiously with three of the crew still in. They had taken a short cut through a hedge and had the bad luck of choosing the precise spot where a pile of Teller mines, just cleared, had been placed in a ditch.

A little further on an RE Officer or what was left of him, was being carted off. They certainly were expendable. He had been clearing mines and evidently had come across a new trick. As tricks were discovered they were immediately passed on to every unit, but the unfortunate discoverer paid the penalty.

The Teller anti-tank mine, for example, was normally placed just beneath the surface and the weight of a vehicle on the pressure plate sets it off. To prevent it being lifted out too easily Jerry would place a pull detonator underneath, tied with a wire to a stick buried deeper. When the mine was lifted it would explode. The sappers soon found this out and would carefully snip the wire underneath before lifting the mine. The next step was to place a push-pull detonator under some so that the action of snipping the wire would also make the mine go up. Exit many sappers. The next step was to place another mine under the first; and many other fiendish varieties of sudden death.

To be on the safe side my Jeep had a sandbag under my feet and I sat on another thus, theoretically saving my legs and other useful parts from being blown off, should we go over the wrong spot.

Caught up with the Colonel, who was with the East Surreys, whom he was supporting. They did not know what was going on, the battle was raging fiercely and was extremely fluid; I volunteered to nip up in old Holy Smoke and have a dekko. Chased back to the landing strip and was soon careering tail up along the runway and over the trees, and in no time was sitting in my ring side seat viewing the battle which, incidentally was being followed by the whole World, as the breaking of the "impregnable" Hitler Line (hurriedly renamed Dora) could well be the decisive turning point of our fortunes in Italy. Subsequent events, in fact, proved it so.

Was pleased as punch when I skidded over Aquino, moving fast and zig-zagging just in case, to see our chaps mopping up in the streets of that town. This meant that we had flanked the famous fortified line and the Eighth Army had done it again.

As usual, nothing moved on the enemy side of the line but on our side every road was steaming dust as tanks, guns and all sorts of vehicles moved forward towards success.

Did not waste time up and on my return rang up the colonel and gave him a detailed account of our troops advances; and was he pleased to receive the good news!

Evening came and Jerry had not yet taken steps to deal with us; the which got us wondering. 'C' Flight planes were all in a nice neat row along both sides of the runway, facing in and not camouflaged. We had taken the sensible precaution of dispersing ours throughout the field, not too large, and covered them with camouflage nets which, at least, prevented them from shining and certainly made the planes less conspicuous.

Marion, my caravan, was some thirty yards in from the strip and Powell had dug me a handy slit trench ready for eventualities.

Hit the hay early and was sound asleep when the fun started round about midnight. A flight of Jerry fighter-bombers attacked us and for half an hour they gave us a real pasting, dive bombing and letting go stacks of anti-personnel bombs that kicked up a hell of a noise as they burst in their hundreds, scattering whining splinters and shrapnel throughout the camp. The noise of the planes zooming down on us with machine guns chattering and then climbing on full throttle, was enough to scare one stiff, and that blanket I had over my head seemed mighty thin. As usual was too lazy to crawl out of my warm bed to make use of the slit trench, and hoped one wouldn't come through the canvas roof of the lorry and that Marion's steely sides might stop the odd splinter.

At half time stuck my head out to see what was cooking, and obviously something was, by the glare and noise of crackling. Discovered it was poor old Holy Smoke II going up like a fireworks display, lightening up the whole countryside, just dandy for Jerry to come back for flood-lit repeat performance.

We all crawled out of our pits and gathered around the bonfire where it was nice and warm. This was a foolish thing to do. We checked up on events and found that Holy was our only casualty which was a miracle considering the amount of hate put down. 'C' Flight fared worse as they deserved to, but even so they were lucky in having only three planes riddled with splinters and two chaps wounded, but not seriously.

Just up the road, a convoy, moving by night, got it really bad, losing five lorries and many men.

One thing and another it was quite an eventful birthday, but I had to mourn the loss of my first war-plane Holy Smoke II, the second of a lengthy dynasty, and not a bad kite.

Jerries on The Run

Nothing much happened the next few days. Our chaps had chased through the Hitler Line so fast that they had out distanced the artillery which was now out of range and, therefore, we were un-operational.

On the 29th May 1944 we moved to a new ALG just below Roccasecca, tucked into the mountain to the north, too near for comfort as Jerry was in them thar hills with nothing to prevent him from sending along a small Commando unit to jump us.

Luckily we did not remain there long. We jumped forward the very next day to a flat field near Ceprano, not far from the river, occupying what had been a Jerry 88 mm AA Battery gun site. Had my caravan driven into an abandoned gun-pit and my merry men erected a lean-to alongside. We flung a camouflage net over the lot and felt snug and safe whenever the odd shell came moaning over to crump nearby.

A Canadian War Artist [*Captain Lawren P. Harris*] joined us here. He took stacks of photos of our activities and did a jolly good crayon drawing of a plane taking off on a sortie.

It was the end of May and we were having lovely weather and we took full advantage of the nearby river to go swimming.

The Germans were retreating fast and we could not do much shooting but did help by flying over the fluid front reporting incidents and the position of our forward troops.

On the 1st June our Brigade was attacking past Frosinone, a town built on the very edge of a high plateau. Whilst cruising around aloft, enjoying the sunny weather and admiring the beautiful countryside, meanwhile keeping my eyes open for trouble of any sort, I suddenly saw, away down in the valley, two enormous explosions so large that

Watercolour by Lawren P. Harris. Air Observation Post ALG at Ceprano.
CWM 19710261-3634. Beaverbrook Collection of War Art. Canadian War Museum

they produced a visible shock wave and mushroom cloud, promptly reported this incident and giving map references of the spots as it was obvious the enemy was destroying ammo dumps prior to pulling out.

Control Set piped up reporting a gun firing from Veroli, one of those weird and wonderful typical Italian villages perched right on top of a pimple hill, a relic of the days gone by when robber barons roamed around and rolling rocks down a slope was as good a way as any of keeping them at a distance.

The gun, if still there, behaved while I was around and soon I saw our chaps swarming up the hill meeting no opposition. Left it at that and went home to tea.

The following day I was the first to take off and after completing my shoot, landed in the next ALG north of Frosinone which Archie had picked. It wasn't very easy to find a suitable landing ground in this intensely cultivated land, where literally every field, apart from

At Ceprano ALG, Scottie, Aubrey, Bob and self just back from a sortie

Aubrey, Bob and Arrol at Ceprano 1 Jun 1944.
Photo courtesy of the Estate of A. C. Young via VF..

138 *Warlike Sketches*

My "caravan" tucked into an ex-Jerry 88 mm gun pit. Ceprano

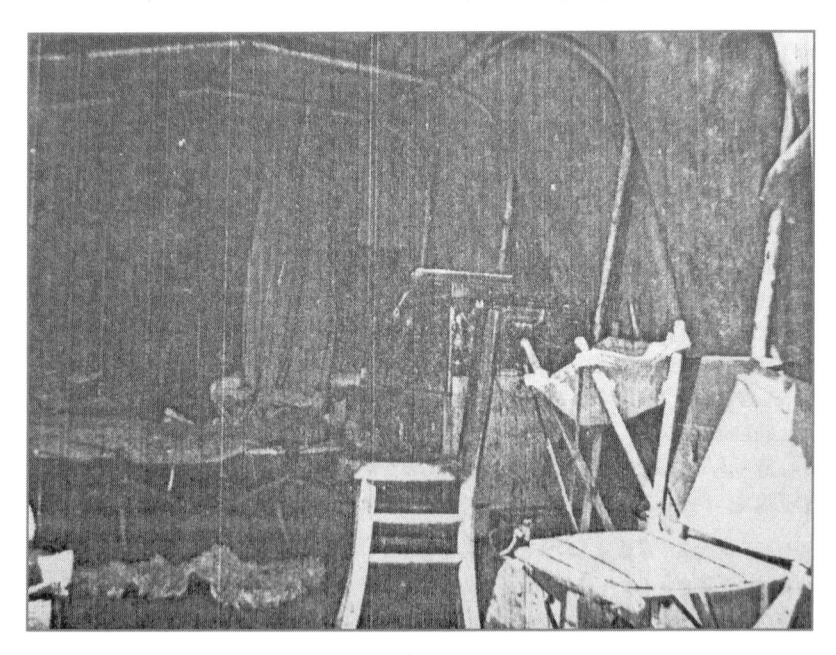

Interior of my caravan!

being small, was criss-crossed by trees on which were strung wires holding up grape vines. This time, however Archie had cut it rather too fine and though I came in with full flaps, nothing on the clock and maximum brakes yet I ran too far and tipped into a ditch at the far end. No damage as I had seen it coming and had switched off. Had the boys fill in the ditch as quickly as possible and this gave the other chaps another twenty yards or so more room to land on.

The front was only four miles away and I was soon up again to report on the fighting going on. Our troops should have been attacking Fumone by that time so gaily headed for that town and was flying over it when I realised that there was no sign of fighting down there and beat a hasty retreat.

Roaming around discovered some fighting in Alatri, a large town a few miles to the east, and saw our tanks cautiously creeping through the streets, blasting bits off suspicious buildings as they crept. Two of our Shermans were burning and Jerry was shelling the Cemetery on the north edge of this town where the Argyles were digging in, not too deeply I hoped.

More ammo dumps were going up and the scene was certainly warlike. We were still out of touch of our guns, or rather our guns were out of touch with us, as they lagged far behind and could not participate in the battle. I had to be content with sending messages back which often proved important to the HQ Formations.

The 66th Medium Regiment arrived nearby and came into action that evening and I was assigned to look after their shooting on the morrow. Went along with Archie Cowan to get acquainted and be briefed, found them in a farm house stinking to high heaven with the sweet sickly smell of polluting human flesh lying around in the woods. Met their Colonel a typical old regular with a fiery temper.

Bob Barrass does a Deed of Daring

Bob had been keeping a fatherly eye on our chaps advancing through Alatri and was swanning a bit ahead. Going over a wood at 100 feet he suddenly found himself flying over a clearing and right over the muzzles of four 88 mm guns.

He says that the Jerries got a bigger fright than he did and they scuttled for cover, little knowing that he was powerless and could not chuck anything at them at that moment. He retired a prudent distance away and soon had the 1st. RHA [*Royal Horse Artillery*] planting shells accurately amongst that outfit and was able to put them completely out of action. As these guns were dual purpose, and had a high muzzle velocity, they were deadly against tanks. He therefore did a jolly good job as they were obviously lying in wait for our Shermans to appear and undoubtedly would have accounted for quite a few. For this episode Bob was later awarded the DFC [*Distinguished Flying Cross*]. Brigadier Packard was so pleased with this that he ordered Aubrey to take him up to have a look at the clearing.

We Join the French Foreign Legion by Mistake

Great things were certainly happening. On the 5th June 1944 Rome fell. On the 6th news reached us of the Normandy landing and this meant that the Second Front, long awaited, was on its way.

With the fall of Rome the Jerries in front of us, who were blowing up their ammo dumps as fast as they could, disappeared in a cloud of smoke and our lads lost contact. As Air OP types were very rare, I mean scarce, the Army consequently had to get their money's worth out of the few of us. Whilst the units we had been supporting pulled out of the battle and retired to rest, we were ordered to fly on to a point as near to Rome as possible, and as close as convenient to the enemy, and keep on with the fight. No peace for the wicked so they say.

Two days after Rome fell 'A' Flight took off heading for a vague map reference in unknown territory. Archie had raced ahead the day before and reconnoitered an ALG but how he did so we never discovered, and had sent back the map reference. Bob Barrass had pranged a few days before and was sitting by his kite waiting for the fitters to arrive. This left Aubrey, Scottie and self to fly ahead into trouble. The other two headed straight for the ALG but as I had some business to attend to at Squadron HQ I landed there to follow on some time later.

Renewing my journey I stooged along and "Bradshawed" my way over the pretty, hilly countryside, taking time off to fly over and admire the beautiful City of Rome, before looking for the map reference given. Was surprised to find that the spot was plumb on top of a hill and there was nary a sign of a landing 'T' or any plane; although I did notice people standing around near a wood.

The battle was extremely fluid and considered it prudent to be cautious under the circumstances so I sat the plane down on a Piper Cub strip I had noticed in a nearby valley, and was assured by a friendly Yank that a couple of "Whizzers", though he did not use that name precisely, had landed up there a while back.

Taking off again I had another look at the hill and it did not look too good a place to land a plane on. The crest had a hedge running along its length and a cart track ran slantwise up towards a clump of trees on the summit. However, we were used to odd landing grounds by that time. Choosing the cart track, I came in mighty cautiously, making allowance for the cross wind and the ground slope, and brought the Auster down all askew but without incident, and she ran to a stop along the ruts.

Then and only then, did some Erks appear from under the trees and pushed the plane bodily under their shelter, hastily throwing a camouflage net over us before I had time to clamber out.

A quantity of tough looking bearded types were lolling around, all armed to the teeth and bedecked with hand-grenades, tommy guns and knives, and several fully manned heavy machine guns were ready for action with their snouts sticking through the hedge.

It so happened that these men belonged to a company of the French Foreign Legion and were then occupied in mopping up that particular area and had paused on this hill, which had been one of their objectives, to rest and feed, before advancing on the next hill feature.

They were rather surprised when our kites dropped in on them, but not half as surprised as we were when we realized we had inadvertently landed bang on the front line. A Yank amongst that motley crowd put us in the picture and treated us to some canned beer.

The first pilot in had already chased off in a Jeep to find a healthier spot and a while later we were careering diagonally down the hillside, taking no notice of an awkward cross wind, on a weird side-slip takeoff that certainly never figured in any book of words. We landed a few minutes later on a much healthier field, a large flat field just west of the famous town of Tivoli.

We Seek the Enemy

The next few days were spent mainly looking for the enemy in a very fluid front, and we hadn't a clue where he had stopped and dug in after his rapid retreat. We weren't too successful in this game of hide and seek and saw nary a sign of the beast from the air, but he evidently saw us all right as could be testified by the many small holes that appeared in our planes; and they weren't moths either.

An emergency call came for Aubrey late of an evening, he was not around at the time and I took on the commitment using his plane that was netted in to the guns that we were to engage. The job was to take on guns firing which had to be silenced at all costs and by the time I had completed this mission it was past 9 pm and getting really dark. We had no night landing instruments nor any strip lighting system and the field we were then using, though largeish by our standards, was really too small for this sort of thing. Flying back in the gathering dusk, not at all sure where I was, I became increasingly apprehensive for my immediate future and wasn't at all sure if I could find the landing strip; let alone land on it. My fright abated slightly when I observed two lines of flickering lights shining weakly from around the right place. My Erks, good types, had lit a series of jam tins partly filled with petrol and they were also jumping around waving white landing strips. With a modest show of skill and heaps of luck, came down nicely, missing the stone wall at either end, and no damage was done.

A couple of days later we continued on our way north to keep up with the running battle and Holy and I were the first to land on another new strip picked by Archie. It looked mighty small to me and I circled around prior to landing but, presuming that Archie had measured the darn thing, came in to land against my better judgement. Took all the precautions. Sneaked over the hedge with nothing on the clock and even though we landed with brakes on, a dangerous procedure, we went whizzing gaily along the full length of the strip, over a small ditch and thrashed our way into a field of ripe wheat. Undoubtedly it was too small. Before the rest of the Flight arrived I managed to find another, more generous field, and somehow Holy and I managed to stagger out of that pocket-handkerchief of a field and land in the new one.

Squadron HQ Receives a Pasting

As I already mentioned we were not at all sure where the enemy lines were and Squadron HQ, with rather too much confidence, had set up shop on top of a ridge [*10 June 1944*]. They had not had Flights' experience as regards periodic shellings, they usually encamped a prudent distance behind the front, and had become careless.

Their planes, including several in from Flights for repairs or routine inspection, were lined up beside the runway in a neat double row, visible for miles around. Jerry wasn't as far away as they thought and he promptly trundled up a hefty SP Gun (Self Propelled) hid it in a convenient wood and had a field day firing over open sights at these sitting birds.

It was around 15.00 hours on a bright sunny day when the shells commenced falling, creeping steadily along the runway systematically smashing up the planes. Scottie had gone to the Squadron HQ to collect his plane and was sitting in his cockpit with engine ticking over, all ready to take off, when the first shells fell. Without hesitation he jammed on throttle and went tearing down the runway and through the smoke of the shell bursts. He was lucky and he managed to time things nicely and nothing hit him. Once safely up he scouted around trying to locate the gun, but this is difficult on a bright day as the flash cannot be seen; and they were using smokeless charges besides.

These unexpected bricks coming down out of the blue caused much alarm and despondency on the ground and everyone took a

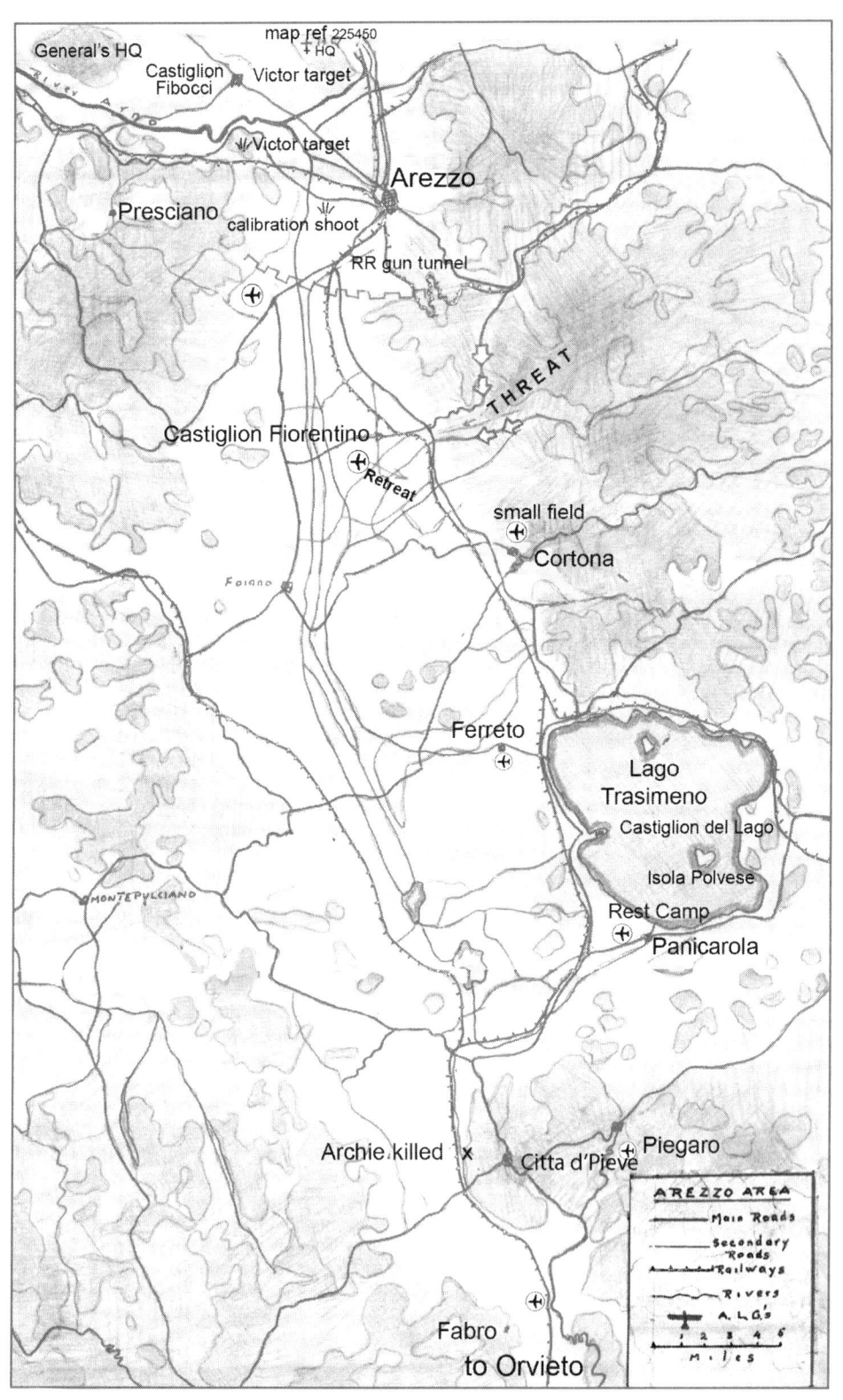

The Arezzo Front

running jump for a convenient deep ditch nearby. They were most unlucky. With uncanny accuracy, Jerry found the exact range to the ditch and pumped HE shells all along it, right amongst the lads. Bill Bolam and Ronny King, the latter from 'B' Flight had taken shelter together and two shells fell right beside them killing four of the men and wounding several others.

Bill and Ronny were lucky to get away with only splinter wounds and the former could not sit down for months.

Although the shelling made holes in most of the planes only three were write-offs.

Two days later they did the same thing to our ALG plastering us with shells; obviously firing over open sights by the accuracy and speed of the attack, although we were not on a crest. We were lucky in having no casualties, our lads were snug in their slit trenches, but the unit next door to us had several killed and wounded.

I missed the fun as I was airborne and carrying out a shoot at the time. Just as well as there is nothing more nerve-racking than the whine and vicious crump of lethal shells bursting near; we were receiving more than enough of these during the night as it was.

Round about that time I was doing plenty of shoots with the 66th Medium Regiment as their fiery Colonel had ordered me to have a crack at anything I considered suspicious; so gleefully plastered the countryside with the hefty shells they doled up which made a most satisfying splash when they hit, much better than the little 25 pounder ones I had been firing until then.

We found the natives in these parts most friendly and generous with their *vino*. Whenever they saw us lunching under the shade of a tree, as was our wont, they would come along and sling the tea out of our mugs, with expressions of disgust, and fill them up with the good stuff.

Archie Suffers a Tragic End

The 17th of June 1944 was one of those days when everything went wrong.

First of all we heard that Scottie had had a rather nasty crash whilst taking off from 'B' Flight strip. Something happened and his plane failed to get airborne in time and he hit the hedge and some trees making a mess of things. He got away lightly, considering, with only bruises and a cut forehead.

I was up as usual in Holy Smoke keeping a fatherly eye on our troops attacking Città della Pieve, a town built on top of a promontory overlooking the valley in which we had our ALG. While I watched I saw some guns firing furiously from the town, but wasn't allowed to engage because our troops were too near. Saw one of our tanks receive a direct hit, just beneath me, and it burst into flames, a most unpleasant sight when one is aware of the implications.

Archie Cowan had left that morning to locate another landing ground for our next advance. As Flight CO this was his responsibility and a fairly difficult one considering that suitable fields were virtually non-existent.

He took risks doing this job and his method for checking fields for mines was to run his Jeep up and down the landing path, a most direct method and certainly positive.

He had left early that morning and had picked up a REME [*Royal Electro Mechanical Engineers*] Officer before heading up the road that ran parallel to the railway line and headed up the valley south of Città della Pieve – still in enemy hands. They reached a clearing beside a wood and the REME chap had got off and entered the trees. Just then he heard a shot coming from the direction of the Jeep. It was obvious that an enemy patrol was around so he promptly took cover. When all was quiet, he made his way to an Infantry platoon nearby and reported the incident. They sent a rescue party but, though they found the Jeep untouched, there was no sign of Archie who had evidently been taken prisoner. We never heard of him again.

Months later, the Intelligence Corps people looking through a diary taken off the body of a German Officer in that area, found a reference made of a British Captain being captured and later dying of his wounds. I'm afraid that there is no doubt that that was the end of Archie Cowan.

Tricky Flying whilst Dithery

We had come to Orvieto, a lovely town with a view, set on top of a pimple hill, and our landing ground had been picked for us in the flats bordering a river, generously lined with tall elms, and banked on either side by hills. We were completely boxed in by the elms and the Sappers had cut gaps in them to let us in and out. Our wing span was 36 feet and a gap of 45 feet had been considered sufficient for our needs! Maybe this is a slight exaggeration but when one was careering towards the trees, or swishing in, side-slipping madly not to over-run, the gap looked more like 30 feet wide. It was a question of having faith and aiming at the middle.

Here it was that, for the first time in many years, I became ill with a touch of fever and somewhat light headed. As usual, and as it had been for nearly two months, we were flying continually from dawn to dusk. There were not enough Air OP pilots to go round and the artillery was depending on us more than ever to bring down effective fire on the enemy. And the infantry and tank boys were clamouring for us to get them out of tough spots.

There was nothing for it but to carry on, though flying light-headed gave me the horrible sensation that I might faint at any moment. This was something I had always dreaded, I don't know why, never having fainted in my life. Flying in and out through those gaps in the tall trees was a nightmare as I could not rely on my judgement. The slightest error in the line of flight was enough to put one wing into a tree with nasty consequences. We could not approach in a straight forward way because of the hills on either side and had to execute a tricky sharp banking turn. This had to be done fairly fast, otherwise we might go into a spin, and then we had to get rid of this extra speed, otherwise we would crash into the far end of the landing field. This meant going into a wild side-slip with full flaps and the plane, all askew, would sink like a lift in a most ungainly manner. All this called for split second timing, not easy under the circumstances when I could hardly concentrate.

To ginger me up a bit, the Jerries had a dual purpose 88 mm gun hidden somewhere around – I wished I knew where – and they would put up three or four quick rounds at me, causing lovely cotton-woolly bursts in the adjacent sky. Then they would close down for a while lest I should locate their gun flash. They never got close enough to do any damage, though they tried hard enough, but we always flew a zig-zag course and never in a straight line. This same gun would shell us all night long and was a darn nuisance.

We had been flying intensely and in the last thirty days I had done eighty operational sorties, enough to ruin anybody's nerves.

A couple of days later I was back to my normal health; and mighty thankful for that.

We Come Upon an Enchanted Lake

Bob Barrass was now OC [*Officer Commanding*] Flight and we leap-frogged once more to an ALG beside Piegaro, still in deep hilly country and very beautiful. Heavy rain and really duff weather had cut down our flying to a minimum.

It was therefore a pleasant surprise to climb away up, on the first sunny day we had had for a long time, and discover a beautiful milky blue lake with fairy like islands and a turreted castle built at the end of a quaint town that jutted into its waters.

The chaps down below must have sensed my attraction to this lake because I soon got the order to go ahead and reconnoitre the larger of the islands for signs of the enemy. Though undoubtedly a pleasant assignment, would have gladly forfeited the pleasure in the interests of security. It meant flying across some five miles of probably enemy held territory though, undoubtedly, the best way to find out if a place was hostile was to act the decoy, and run like hell once they commenced shooting.

Circled around to gain some height and when 3,000 feet up set a wiggly course for the island. It was such a beautiful day for a change, with the air washed clean and sparkling that it did not seem possible that anyone would act nasty. Could see for miles across beautiful green fields to blue hills in the distance, with the wizard milky blue lake spread out in the foreground. Was soon over the lake and it did not take long to cover the couple of miles to Isola Polvese. Kept my eyes skinned for the tell tale puff of smoke, but none came. Had a good look at the island, which could only boast a couple of houses. Nothing stirred and reported all quiet. Then returned to base; but slowly.

The next couple of days I did plenty of flying and shoots with the 66th Medium Regiment. A troop of Jerry 88 mm guns somewhere near the town of Castiglione, the one that jutted into the lake, persisted in having a crack at us whenever we were up, and some of the bits of cotton wool, with a dirty black core that spat steel, came rather close. We all tried to locate them but they were very well hidden and only fired when our backs were turned.

For some time the enemy had been employing Nebels [*Nebelwerfer*] that fired off eight whacking fat rockets that made an awful mess of quite a large area when they hit all together. They were causing a considerable amount of casualties amongst the foot-sloggers and consequently they became our favourite target. Whenever they fired the effect was akin to that of a minor firework display. The backlash of the eight powerful rockets taking off kicked up a considerable amount of dust and each one, as it whizzed through the air, let off a thick black stream of smoke. They were easy to see but, of course, we never knew when or where they were likely to go off. There was no difficulty in knowing when they had completed their trajectory as the blast was so powerful that we could feel the "bump" no matter how high we were flying. If we were lucky, and we had acquired a special instinct by then, we would spot the cloud of dust still in the air where they had been released. Needless to say that precise spot and surrounding area continued to be pretty dusty for some time from shells dropping around.

Nebels were Heath Robinsonish affairs, being somewhat like eight stovepipes mounted on a wheelbarrow. They were cheap to make and could be trundled around easily, and rarely fired twice from the same spot. One evening, some time later, I was to see no less than twelve Nebels firing simultaneously all concentrated on the small village of Santarcangelo at the time full of our lads, and what a mess they made, but that is another story.

A Town Surrenders to Aubrey

On the 24th June 1944, with the 66th Medium Regiment pulling out for a rest – but we just kept on forever – I went over to work for the 1st Royal Horse Artillery, a crack RA Regiment, that had Priest SP Guns [*105 mm Self Propelled Gun*] that were very accurate and, with these, did some jolly good Nebel hunts. We worked out a system and would yell "Murder Mike" over the wireless whenever we spotted Nebels firing and that meant as many rounds as we wanted from the whole Regiment. They fired extremely well and the targets were thoroughly plastered and we must have caught quite a few of these weapons and their personnel.

Was up doing a shoot, flying well over Lake Trasimeno to keep at a prudent distance from the 88 mm boys, when I saw a fighter plane approaching straight towards me from the enemy side. It was coming in low, a favourite trick to catch us silhouetted against the sky. We had developed an uncanny eyesight and could spot unbelievably small things out of the corner of our eye; provided they moved. Even though I was intent on carrying out a shoot in the other direction, I spotted that plane coming while it was still at a fair distance. Needless to say I was scared stiff and immediately went into a tight turn keeping my eyes glued on the approaching fighter trying to guess the instant the pilot would open fire with his multiple machine guns. Our only hope of survival was to nip aside smartly from the first hail of bullets. We had to leave the nipping to the last minute as, otherwise, the pilot could yet correct sufficiently to hit us. If he missed the first time, then we had a chance to get down close to the ground and out manoeuvre the fighter.

By that time was perspiring freely. The plane kept coming not deviating an inch from his course. Could imagine the pilot looking up at us, ready to pull the stick gently back at the right moment and spray us with lead. I kept flying in a steep left turn just to make it look easy, my muscles taut, all ready to slam the stick violently right and forward, the quickest way to change course. I was still expecting the worst when I recognised the plane as a Spitfire. A split second later it whizzed by pretty close in a real beat up. And then I carried on with the shoot.

A couple of days later [*29 Jun 1944*] Aubrey was up and flying over the lake when he noticed that there was a lot of movement in the streets of Castiglione, the town jutting into the lake. He flew closer and, sure enough, the Itie populace were jumping around and waving anything white they could lay their hands on. He was able to report to Brigade HQ that the town had surrendered to him. Jolly good for the Air OP, what?

Bob Bags Forty Vehicles via "Cab Rank"

As we were the only people who were sitting pretty over the battle front during all the hours of daylight – and had gained a reputation for seeing things – we got lots of odd jobs thrown at us. An interesting and effective one was to find nice juicy targets for the RAF fighter-bombers to tackle. These used to spend hours cruising around and, probably due to their much greater speed and limited visibility from the cockpit, they were reporting nothing seen while we were busy as bees engaging sundry targets.

We therefore found ourselves sitting under a bevy of circling planes, known as a "Cab-rank", ready to pounce like hawks on any prey we might condescend to throw their way. We normally looked after anything within range of our guns but when we found a moving target that was rapidly moving out of range, then we would avail ourselves of the fighter-bombers and watch a first class pasting of the unfortunate Jerries.

Shortly after this scheme was instituted Bob was on a sortie late one evening when he saw something suspicious in a wood deep in enemy territory. A closer look proved that the wood was chock a block with carefully camouflaged vehicles. Jerry had been careless and had commenced preparing for the night move too soon. Bob promptly engaged with a whole battery. As soon as the shells came down the enemy decided to get going although it was still light and the convoy moved out and onto a main road leading north. He immediately passed on the information to the patient boys circling overhead, who had not seen a thing, and he saw them stream off in pursuit. It did not take them long to locate the column and peel off in the approved fashion. They later reported 40 vehicles left blazing and destroyed, transport that would have escaped had it not been for "The Eyes of the Army."

We Camp by Beautiful Lake Trasimeno

With Castiglione del Lago's surrender to Aubrey our troops soon moved on and the Lake was ours. On the 28th June we moved to Panicarola to a site about 300 yards from its shore.

The enemy was retreating fast once more and the following day the 132 Field Regiment was out of range. However that same day while I was on a routine sortie, keeping my eyes skinned, saw some guns, well hidden in a wood firing away. Went back quickly to our ALG and borrowing Scottie's plane, which was netted in to the 75 th Medium Regiment, with 4.5 inch guns and a longer range, I took off quickly and ranged those big guns onto the middle of the wood and let them have it making a mess of anything therein. They did not fire again.

With things eased a bit we could afford to take a breather and for a whole week we flew but once a day and were able to enjoy bathing in the Lake.

Although we were not in a position to fire on the enemy they had not forgotten us. On the night of the 29th June and again on the 2nd July they sent over a party of fighter-bombers loaded up with anti-personnel bombs which they dropped among us with much noise and zooming around, and later they repeatedly machine gunned our camp. They were both clear moonlit nights and they must have found us easily.

While these attacks lasted they were far from pleasant. The first time I even jumped into my slit trench, dutifully dug by Powell, and waited patiently for the party to finish. It usually happened that one heard a plane droning along and took a chance that it was one of ours, as they usually were. When it was overhead and the whistle of a bomb was heard, then it was not one of ours but by then we knew it was too late to duck except under one's blanket. If the bomb should miss, and if the night was cold, then one hoped that it was a lone plane and it was the last bomb; seldom the case.

Despite the frightening noise of hundreds of these kilo bombs bursting, the whine of shrapnel whining all over the place, the thunderous noise of the planes diving down to machine gun the camp and the shudder of the guns, we only suffered a couple of casualties, splinters in fleshy parts, and several planes peppered; nothing that a patch and a lick of paint could not fix.

Made use of the lull to do some exploring and one day took Elsie and went back the way we had come and visited Città della Pieve, a place that had intrigued me. It was a lovely drive along winding hilly roads and the city itself was most interesting, built high up on a sort of plateau overlooking a beautiful valley. Also, out of curiosity, I wished to find out where those guns I had seen firing had been hidden.

I bought some mediocre thick green tumblers for our Mess, the only ones I could find as *"tutti via Tedeschi"* according to the Ities [*Italians call the Germans Tedeschi*].

In which I make a Slight Landing Error

On the 4th of July 1944 we moved on again to a spot near the NW tip of lake Trasimeno where there had been a large Jerry ammo dump. The land thereabouts consisted of a series of long narrow fields, about 25 yards wide separated by the usual line of trees slung with wires supporting vines. We had picked the longest one to land on and the adjacent one to pitch our tents and hide our respective caravans.

The day we moved Aubrey was feeling unwell and I took over his commitments with 138 Field Regiment and flew off in the middle of the afternoon to do some shoots.

According to Bob's story, he was quietly shaving, standing on the tailboard of his caravan, when suddenly a plane swished by, the slipstream whipping the lather off his face. It seemed odd to him so he looked out and there was Holy Smoke III sitting with her nose in the hedge – in the wrong field.

Actually I had been occupied with a lengthy shoot till lateish and the sun was low and dead into wind when I came in to land. I could see the correct long field during my approach but when I turned into wind to come in, the sun shining straight into the scratched perspex windshield blinded me completely. Blissfully unaware that I was heading for the wrong field I flew on, guiding myself by looking out of the side and at the trees that lined the field – the wrong one of course. Luckily, in those days my flying was pretty nifty, and set Holy down very short and by applying the brakes managed to pull up just in time, but only just. The funny part was that I still had not realized that anything was amiss, except that I had made a very long landing.

It wasn't so funny for the poor Erks who had to cut down umpteen trees and make a 36 foot gap in the hedge to move Holy back to the correct strip.

'A' Flight Makes a Cautious Retreat

With the German Army helter-skeltering along we moved the very next day to a new ALG near Ferretto and the following on again to a place by Castiglione Fiorentino, right in the middle of a wide valley, making use of a plum tree lined field. Unfortunately the enemy still commanded all the high ground, or rather the range of hills to our NE. These included several mountains over 1,000 metres high and they undoubtedly still had artillery hidden in the valleys. It seemed to us, thinking it over quietly, that we had left ourselves wide open to their attention.

Having in mind the mess one Self Propelled Gun had made of our Squadron HQ and the stiffening resistance put up by the enemy as we approached the important town of Arezzo, Bill Bolam decided to play safe and ordered us to shift to the shelter of the hills. He found a snug little field tucked into the hills just north of Cortona, a charming little town perched on the shoulder of one of these hills. The field was snug, little, and so tucked into the side of the hill that it was practically impossible to get into it when the wind was coming up from the valley. The slope of the ground was less than our gliding angle and we had to go into a controlled stall, extremely tricky, to sink fast enough. However, we soon got the hang of it. Major Ingram, the Squadron CO, who prided himself on his flying ability, came over to visit us and just could not make it and had to go back. He was most impressed that the four of us were operating normally from this impossible strip.

The field itself was ridiculously short and Bill had evidently just guessed its length without bothering to pace it. Furthermore, at the further end there was a thick hedge and across the narrow road, houses and telegraph wires; nasty things to meet on take off. Once the four of us had landed successfully we began to wonder if we would ever be able to take off again. In these doubtful cases I was the guinea-pig, being the heaviest. If anybody was to hit the wires and pile up in the field beyond it was sure to be Holy and I. It was also logical that if I managed to stagger off the others would do so too. There was no sense in letting a lighter chap try it as he might get away with it but, in the end, I wouldn't. There was nothing for it, therefore, but to have a go; something I did not relish the tiniest bit. To make matters worse I was foolish enough to pace it out and discovered that the entire field was only 128 yards long.

And so, with much foreboding, I climbed into faithful Holy Smoke III. Wilson wound her up and I took great care to warm the motor up properly and check the magnetos. They tucked my tail into the hedge and held her until the engine was roaring at full revs and developing maximum power, all of 125 HP and then they let us go. We seemed to accelerate slowly as we headed for the massive houses and treacherous telegraph wires at the end. They loomed nearer and nearer as the plane ran heavily along the rough field. I was quite certain that we could not make it and could visualize the accident about to happen. When we were three quarters along the field and still not airborne, every instinct and common sense told me to switch off and jam on the brakes; but could not justify this sensible action. Kept my hand on the throttle, to keep it fully on, feeling via the control stick for the slightest sign of her lifting. It is quite an art flying under these circumstances where the slightest error of judgement can add yards to ones take-off run. About here we ran into tall alfalfa and I could feel the plane slow down as her doughnut wheels hit this patch. As can be imagined these details did not add to my peace of mind.

All the lads were congregated at the far end of the field out of morbid curiosity. Our first-aid man was all ready with his box and they had a Jeep started up in lieu of an ambulance. They were not taking any chances; and they evidently did not think much of mine.

The whole episode was over in a few seconds really, but I can remember it vividly to this day. Holy Smoke III, bless her, behaved like a thoroughbred; I felt her buoyant just in time and was able to nurse her up and over the danger spots with inches to spare.

The lookers-on said that it seemed as if we were practically in the far hedge, and all commenced running to the rescue, when they saw us rise, and they held their breath until all was well.

When I returned from the sortie I made the farmer come along and cut down the alfalfa and that helped, but not much.

We operated from that field during six days, taking off and landing innumerable times as the battle was raging fast and furious. Each time we went through considerable mental agonies as the slightest faltering of an engine would be sufficient to cause a nasty crash.

The four of us were keyed up and on our toes and well aware of the danger and for this reason nothing happened. Scottie was flying intensely with the mob he was supporting doing as many as 14 sorties in one day and got away with it every time, only to crash the first time he attempted to land in our next ALG, an easy one. Which just goes to show.

'A' Flight Routs an Enemy Attack

The danger we had foreseen when we moved from the centre of the valley became apparent when the fight moved on towards Arezzo, as the spearhead of the Eighth Army went forward leaving an unguarded flank, easily pierced by a sudden enemy attack launched from any of the valleys leading into their mountain stronghold.

Although we received no instructions on this score, we were all fully alive to the danger and kept a close look out for enemy movement up those valleys. Bob was the first to give the alarm when he noticed and promptly reported, troop movement along two valleys leading into the main one about a couple of miles from where we were. He also noticed that the bridges on the road leading up these valleys were intact, signifying that tanks could speed down them and be on our unsuspecting rear echelon troops in a matter of minutes.

Then Army HQ sat up and took notice in no uncertain manner. Troops and artillery were rushed back to take care of this danger. As we were the only people who could see into the danger spots we virtually ran the whole show, and had a really good picnic. We directed the guns onto the right places, demolished bridges, broke up infantry concentrations and eventually told our Infantry just where to attack and when. They were not taking any chances and the Guards were detailed for this job. Scottie was given the task of taking up the Company Commanders to have a look at the ground before they attacked, a procedure that proved highly successful.

And it so happened that, what might have been a nasty affair, thanks to the vigilant "Eyes of the Army" was nipped in the bud. As soon as the Guards commenced their attack up the hills we directed a heavy artillery fire just ahead of them and onto the bridges forcing the enemy to lie low and preventing them bringing up reinforcements. It was not long before the Enemy realized that the game was up and the sight of bridges being demolished in a large cloud of smoke implied that they had given up all hopes of attacking our flank.

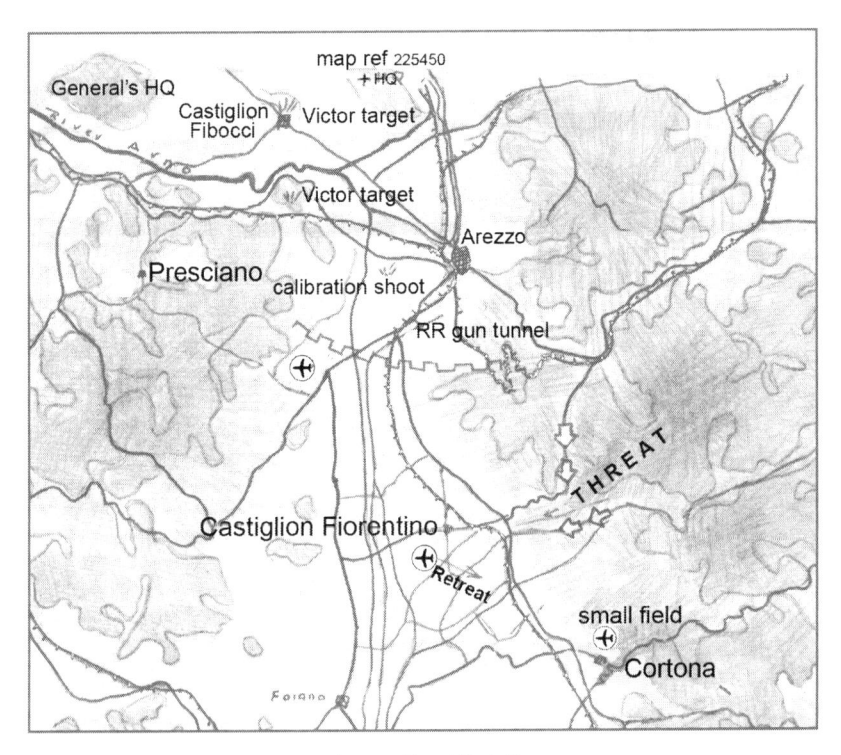

Arezzo Front Detail

THE AREZZO BATTLE AND THE CAPTURE OF FLORENCE

The Arezzo Battle

I already mentioned that, while we were "dicing with death" on the Cortona ALG, the Eighth Army had been chasing the enemy along the main valley leading to Arezzo. However, just before you reach that town the valley narrows to a dangerous bottle-neck, less than a mile wide, commanded by highish hills on either side. A perfect lay-out for defence of which the enemy made full use.

Arezzo did not lie straight ahead of all this but to the right, and was accessible through a deep valley so narrow that it could only carry the road, the parallel railway line having to take to a tunnel to get through.

On the 6th July 1944 the 6th Armoured Division launched a full scale attack on this bottle-neck which they failed to penetrate and had to return to their starting lines. Here again 'A' Flight flew to the rescue and we plastered all the known and suspected gun positions with shells. Considering that at the same time we were also looking after the threatening flank, we had a rather hectic time.

Because I was observing for long range guns I was given the task of shooting up crossroads leading into Arezzo, as well as gun positions. In the evenings, when the gathering dusk made visible the flashes from the guns, we had some wizard picnics. The enemy was firing with all he had, he was pretty desperate, and we were doing as many as three shoots simultaneously at different targets. Bob was the only one who could manage four.

It is difficult to describe all that went on in our small cockpits during a multiple shoot. We had to give initial orders to three lots of guns, receive their acknowledgement and then receive their report of "shot"; timing the time of flight we had to look into the right spot at the moment the shot burst and had to think quickly and give the correct next order, and for this we had to remember what our previous order was for that particular target, then swinging the plane round to be able to look into another target area before the shell, by then whizzing through its trajectory, landed. Besides this, flying the plane, keeping a wary eye on instruments, working the wireless, always terrible towards dusk due to extra static that came up with the setting sun, map reading other guns firing, reporting these in our spare time, etc., etc. It was all quite a strain and I am sure we would all have gone nuts had we kept it up for any length of time.

While this was going on, and they usually kept on firing from all over the landscape, it was getting darker and each minute that passed made landing in the pocket handkerchief field we were using, more difficult and precarious. But it was a point of honour with us that, while the enemy guns kept firing we dealt with them, only making our way home when our petrol was running out.

Lacking such luxuries as landing lights, our Erks would lay out a row of jam tins half filled with petrol which gave us a fair indication of where we could expect to find the runway. Strangely enough the system worked and the morbid crowd, that usually welcomed the last flight in, were always disappointed.

With the advance held up, all our artillery was able to move into range of the enemy again and we used them a great deal during the ten days we were at Cortona ALG.

Thanks to Italian Partisans, accounts of the successes of some of our stonks came through and we received eye-witness accounts of them. Whole gun teams were either killed or wounded, battery positions were disorganised, tanks disabled, trucks knocked out and chaos generally created.

To us who were flying and took on, say, enemy guns firing from a wood with a whole Battery or even a Regiment, we would see the shells bursting nicely amongst the trees and would be satisfied if the guns stopped firing, more so if the flash spotters reported that they never fired again from that position. What we could not see was exactly what damage these shells were doing and they often hit unexpected targets such as HQ's, ammo dumps and the likes without our knowing, unless the partisans told us.

On the 14th July I took on the job of calibrating the guns of the 2nd Troop 2nd Medium Regiment which were then firing badly. I chose a nice flat field in enemy territory as a suitable target and got down to it. A calibration shoot is a long weary process calling for a great deal of patience as it means shooting each individual gun until a verified short bracket is obtained, plus other tedious details unintelligible to a mere civilian. It so happened that there was a farm house in the corner of that field and imagine my surprise when half way through the shoot a gun, a field gun at that, started firing through the window. What cheek! These Jerries are funny guys. They probably had orders to open fire at such and such a time and sure enough they did although they could hardly have been oblivious of my hovering presence.

Needless to say I called a halt to the calibration shoot, gave a couple of corrections to the gun I was then firing and in minutes the house was looking somewhat dilapidated and the gun fired no more.

A Big Gun Hunt

The enemy had been using a huge railway gun that fired huge shells that made an awful mess wherever they landed. A report had come through that this piece was hidden in a railway tunnel through the hills at the end of the valley we were then in, and into Arezzo.

I was ordered to find this monster and fix it. Consequently dutifully climbed into Holy one fine morning, stuck her tail into the hedge for extra take off inches, we were still using the awfully small field, and aged a year or so before we shuddered shakily over the telegraph wires with seemingly nothing to spare. As a matter of fact Holy and I took off no less than 29 times from that field, declared unfit and impossible to land in by our Squadron CO who considered himself a good pilot.

However, flying from this field had its compensations and for the first time since the Cassino Battle commenced, the enemy could not seek us out at night with moaning nasty shells as we were so tucked into the hillside they could not reach us. Besides this, we were making use of a comfortable farm house and had forgone our draughty caravans for bedrooms, a pleasant change.

To get back to the railway gun we were supposed to be hunting, stooged along the line till I was in sight of the tunnel but observed nothing. Of course it would obviously not be lying out in the open in daytime. If inside I would not be able to see it so, to be on the safe side, suggested to control that I should seal up the tunnel; they thought it a good idea and gave me a heavy gun with which to do the trick. Within minutes shells were splashing around and it did not take long to block up the tunnel mouth fairly effectively.

We never learned whether the gun was in that tunnel or not but a couple of days later Intelligence came through with a report that our "friend" was again on the job as could be proved by the wallop it packed and by measuring shell fragments. The Flash Spotters were also able to give us a pretty accurate map reference of its whereabouts. And so it came about that at crack of day the following morning, Holy and I took off again, holding our respective breath till over the wires, and winged our way toward the Front seeking the elusive monster gun. The map reference given showed a profusion of trees and a house, by the side of the railway line, where the gun could easily be camouflaged into the background. We stuck around, floating gently but erratically through the air, with eyes glued to the spot; not caring particularly to fly over the enemy line, we kept at a prudent distance, especially as they had stacks of 88 mm AA guns, our pet aversion, around and also we did not want the gun crew to realize that they were being singled out for a special watch.

This Air OP job was usually mighty exciting but on occasions such as this it could be boring and called for a deal of patience. This time we were amply rewarded, after about half an hour or so of eye strain, a whacking big flash came from that area. I gave it about 90 seconds time of flight and then sure enough, a terrific explosion in our lines confirmed that the gun had actually fired. This check was necessary as they very often employed flash simulators to fool us; and I expect they frequently were successful.

Unfortunately, this target was out of range to my guns and I had no alternative but to pass it on to some other long range guns to deal with it. We were to have another tussle with a railway gun with more success, but that is another story.

A Shocking Story

The weather in "sunny Italy" was good, bad and indifferent, mostly indifferent. In the mountains we got plenty of rain storms of considerable violence and turbulence, which bothered us considerably and our light planes were knocked around unmercifully in such circumstances. However, when the battle was on and a job had to be done we flew regardless, and were proud to say that only lack of visibility ever kept us on the ground.

Many times we were obliged to take off in a shower of rain, splashing our way over waterlogged fields. One particular occasion which I am about the relate, another "line" I know, the clouds that came scuttling low over the mountains were black as the ace of spades and loaded with lightning.

Anyway away we went flying low and we managed to do whatever had been our mission and were returning along the narrow deep valley that led us back to Cortona. The wireless had been terrible, full of static and mush, and I was still trying to send some vital message to Control. The clouds up above were blacker than ever and forked lightning was flashing from one just ahead which we had to go under if we wished to reach home. According to the Flying Manual this sort of situation is supposed to be avoided at all costs, but we had no alternative but to duck and go on in. And then the wicked black cloud got us and filled the plane with high voltage electricity. I was wearing larynga-phones wrapped tightly around my neck and the effect was as if I was wearing a collar of sharp needles – and did it hurt! I need hardly say I snatched them off in a hurry. Then a lengthy and wiggly spark jumped from the wireless set and into my right knee and remained in painful contact arcing nicely. I was rather a close fit in these planes and my knee was jammed up against the dash and I could not get it away so I just had to watch the pretty spark while I wriggled in agony. It really tickled. I was fairly busy at the time trying to keep the plane under control as she was bucking like a bronco while battling with the rain and the high gusty wind; we were also travelling not too distant from the tree-tops. It was quite a to-do.

Eventually I reacted and reaching back wrenched the aerial off the set and the spark subsided; thank goodness.

We Fire and Dodge a Victor Target

On the 18th of July 1944 our Spearheads were passing the important town of Arezzo and some three miles beyond reached the banks of the River Arno, that came tumbling down the mountains from the north. This river then swung west towards Florence.

Jerry was putting up a stiff resistance, the terrain favoured the defenders, and were firing with everything they had, not bothering overmuch about hiding from us. The Arno was wide and they could observe all our movements from OP's in the high mountains. We were therefore called upon to give maximum artillery support to our forward troops and, under these circumstances, we had some super field days hunting enemy guns that kept up a heavy fire from all around the countryside.

And so there we were, zig-zaging along through the air, our customary mode of transport to dissuade people with bad intentions having pot shots at us, though it didn't much and they did, and frequently, when suddenly over the wireless came the urgent call of "Victor Target – Victor Target – Victor Target." Now this meant that every gun in the Corps of Artillery, in other words every gun in that front, had to concentrate on one particular target, and a very special and dangerous target it must be to warrant such attention. As the message came over my wireless net it meant that I too was in the picture and would be called upon to observe. As I have already mentioned, this kind of shoot is an artilleryman's dream shoot and extremely rare, and here I was about to control a second such event in my brief army career.

The map reference of the target came through right away, 195402, and firing time was a brief three minutes from then. I was ordered to observe and correct.

Checked up on the map reference and found that the victim was to be Castiglion Fibocchi, a town some six miles NW of Arezzo. And I soon realized that Holy and I were cruising around right in the line of fire; and it was too late to escape, the target was fairly close, about a mile or so beyond our front troops and at the point where we were flying, the trajectory of the nearer guns would not be higher than a few hundred feet. There was no safe altitude for me. Besides, it was too late by then to do anything so pulled back on the stick and climbed in order to get a better view and be able to correct the fire with increased accuracy. And then gun flashes came from the whole length of the front and the shells were soon whizzing by all around me and the plane was buffeted by their slipstream. A stonk of this kind is truly fantastic and Castiglion disappeared in a fraction of a second and the now familiar boiling smoke and brick dust took its place. No correction was necessary, the guns' firing was dead on.

Not satisfied with all this damage I was ordered to bring down a "Mike" target on a wooded hill. A "Mike" target being a concentrated shoot from all the guns in a Regiment and also a shoot rarely carried out. I knew that particular hill. Inspected it closely the previous afternoon for a reported enemy tank concentration supposedly getting ready to put in a counter attack on our left flank, but I had seen nothing and so reported.

Evidently, further information had been received, probably from partisans, that the tanks were still there and Higher Command were not taking any chances. In that wooded area a chap could pass ten feet away from a tank and not see it if properly camouflaged and, even though I could not see any, yet I could not be absolutely sure. I therefore gave orders for all the guns in the Regiment to be laid on the most likely hiding place for these monsters, establishing a firing time five minutes hence, and to fire scale five, that is five rounds from each gun. The shoot came down beautifully. If there were really tanks in that wood few could have crawled out. It was certainly enemy held and whatever was there had "had it." The fact remains that our Infantry advanced and took that important hill feature without any trouble whereas otherwise, they definitely would have had to fight for it.

We have a Spell of House Hunting

The Italian Partisans, a veritable mine of dubious information, were filtering through with lots of stories of houses being used as HQ's and chock-a-block with VIP's just behind the lines. As a house can be destroyed successfully with one hefty gun, in fact it is the approved method, it did not call for too great an expenditure of ammunition; the powers that be thought it worth a try. Naturally the job was given to the Air OP chaps, we were pretty famous by then – and on the 19th July Holy Smoke III and I went house hunting.

This particular one we were looking for, the address was Map. Ref. 225430, was a pretty little place set beside a road leading into the mountains, it had trees and nice green fields all around. But the tenant, so we believed, was not friendly and our visiting cards were bricks, 4·5 inches in diameter.

Having identified the place, rang through to the 2 Medium boys, and asked them for the loan of one of their pivot guns, and sat back to enjoy myself. Shooting at a nice stationary target on a clear day and with only one gun to worry about, is quite pleasant and relaxing. The wireless was working well, the gun behaved and the ranging shells were easy to see as they made one hell of a splash. With six rounds had reached a verified short bracket and very soon the place looked rather dilapidated with three direct hits and several near misses. The misses only cracked walls, blew in doors, whisked off tiles and the likes, so the place was hardly habitable by the time we had finished. Also Jerry invariably dug trenches nearby and, no doubt the odd shell landing nearby did more damage than we realised.

The following day was given another address to look after. It may sound difficult to the layman finding a map reference, really but a dot on a piece of paper, especially from a moving aircraft, but with the practice we had by then it was a "piece of cake."

This time it was a townish looking house, not pretty and with a flat roof, set in a valley just west of Castiglion. There were other houses nearby and I expect they all contained the enemy in some shape or form.

This shoot was even easier than the one before, it being on a flat piece of ground. Once I was on the target, gave them ten rounds and obtained one direct hit and the rest very much in the neighbourhood. The house was properly messed up. The road alongside leading directly to the front must surely have carried many telephone lines and that too was properly hit

The next job Holy and I tackled in this line was no mere house hunting job as we were told to pay our respects to a leading Nazi General reported to be living in comfort in a castle set in the middle of a dense wood on the northern banks of the Arno.

We found the castle without difficulty, and a pretty place it turned out to be, very old looking and strong and quite a different proposition to our previous soft targets.

At most we gave the General a fright, for our mission was unsuccessful. There was a strong wind blowing, quite a gale in fact, and the ranging shells would burst deep inside the woods and by the time the smoke became visible it had drifted far. I tried guessing, but could not even find out my true line of sight. After putting down a dozen rounds or so inside the woods and near the castle, gave it up as a bad job and returned to base with the mission unaccomplished.

Aubrey Stalks a Bridge Buster

Aubrey was the unlucky chap whose turn it was to get up before dawn and take off at first light. We liked to annoy Jerry from the very minute he was visible until dusk hid him from our watchful and vengeful eyes.

The first chap up had to check on the position of our forward troops. This was easy as the foot-sloggers, with a complete disregard for concealment, went ahead and lit wee petrol fires to brew up their early morning cup-o-char. One had but to draw a line on the map following the flickering pin points of light to obtain an accurate front line. And what a contrast to the Enemy lines where not a light nor any sign of movement could be seen. And all because the Air OP was watching. No wonder they hated our guts, and tried to get us whenever possible.

Another priority job was to check on bridge demolitions. This was rather important as by this we could tell whether the enemy had given up the use of that particular road, which meant they were retreating.

Aubrey was ticking off the bridges demolished on his map starting with a road skirting the north side of Arezzo–Florence valley, which had lots of them, when he saw one go up in smoke. He jotted that one down as demolished and was checking on the extent of the damage when he saw another bridge go up a bit further on. By the time interval between each explosion he deduced that there must be a chap on foot walking along and lighting the fuses, and decided he'd have some fun. He whistled up one gun from the troop he was working with and started ranging on the next bridge, but had only brought a couple of rounds down when that one went up also. He shifted to the next and he had to admire the guts of the chap because that one too went up without any delay, though it must have been pretty unhealthy with shells falling near. His hopes of deterring the demolisher, and maybe saving a few bridges for our own use, failed miserably as the Jerry just kept on doing his job.

I remember, much later, watching a Jerry calmly walking down a paved road which I was shelling with heavy artillery. A big shell burst some twenty yards in front of him but he did not dive for the ditch but kept on walking steadily and went right through the smoke. And he must have known that shells bursting on a hard surface, such as that road, were doubly lethal as they splash more.

'A' Flight has a Well Deserved Rest

Our Flight had been in action since the 17th of March 1944 when we had relieved 651 Squadron on the River Sangro Front and it wasn't until the 28th July that 'B' Flight came along to relieve us and allow our chaps a much needed rest.

Although I had joined the flight just prior to the Cassino Battle, I had yet managed to pile up 171 Operational Sorties and 67 Shoots in less than three months, which was pretty good going, and others had done more. To think that the RAF Bomber Boys were given a rest after 30 sorties, and were taken completely off Operations after a mere 60! Of course our sorties were not quite as lengthy as theirs but, as we pointed out, we were always within range of enemy artillery, from the moment we took off to the moment we landed, whereas they spent hours cruising happily over the North Sea and only an hour or so over enemy territory.

The next morning, after seeing "Marion" and "Elsie" on their way, took off for Lake Trasimeno, where we were to have our rest camp, calling in at the Arezzo drome to visit my old pal Gander of Cambridge days, and had a good chin-wag.

The following day Bill Bolam and myself, he was our CO, set forth in his Jeep for Rome with the excuse of fixing up accommodation for our chaps. It was a lovely drive and interesting to return over the old battle grounds which we only knew from the air. We left rather late, it was after ten, and did not reach Rome until two, in time for a late lunch at an Officers' Club.

Although the Eighth Army was at the outskirts of Rome when it was taken, we allowed the Americans to walk in and capture it for some silly political reason. We were not even allowed to show our noses; in fact, when 'A' Flight had to cross the city to move on with the battle we had strict orders not to stop within the city. My only view of Rome had been from the air and I was suitably impressed by what I had seen.

So Bill and I made the most of the few hours we had there and scuttled around in the Jeep rubber-necking until it was time to head back for our country residence. We left around six and reached Lake Trasimeno about ten, again enjoying the ride.

The following day a brand new Auster Mark IV had to be picked up in Rome, a new type we had heard of but never seen, and I had volunteered for the job. I rather liked flying when conditions were pleasant. Rigby ferried me there and we landed on the Littoira Aerodrome where I was to collect the plane and fly her back. The new plane had an American Lycoming engine and a longer endurance of about 2 hours 40 minutes instead of the 1 hour 20 minutes of the Mark III.

The trip back from Rome took an hour which included a sight seeing tour of the seven hills and a detour to dodge an impressive storm of towering nimbo-cumulus clouds, which are best avoided.

On the 2nd August 1944 set off in Elsie with Aubrey, Scottie and Bill for Rome and we put up on arrival at the posh Hotel Quirinal, on the Via Nazional, then a New Zealand Forces Officers' Club the use of which had been offered to us by these kind colonials. Being the Ugly Ducklings of the Eighth Army, neither Army nor Air Force and too small a unit for anybody to worry about, we did much as we pleased and made the most of our independence. This used to puzzle the poor MP's. If an Army one stopped our Jeep we would say we were an RAF unit but if the chap was RAF then we were very much Army Officers. But we didn't always get away with it.

Poor old Elsie, she had come all the way from Egypt via Algiers under her own steam wasn't as young as she used to be and had worn out a universal joint. I had to take her to the Alfa Romeo works, now taken over by REME [Royal Electrical and Mechanical Engineers] for treatment. Had to leave her there and hitch back to town.

Aubrey, a fast worker, had already made friends with a couple of New Zealand nurses and we took them to dine at the Trocadero, a swanky restaurant, now an Officers' Club, and tucked into a wizard meal not ruined by Army cooks. At these clubs Army rations were used, but cooked by experts they were unrecognizable.

The New Zealanders had things pretty well organised and the following day we joined a sight seeing party in a three ton truck, and did a few of the famous spots and ended up at the Vatican City where we gazed in awe at acres of frescoes. We also could have had an audience with the Pope himself, had we waited a while, but it was too near lunch time for comfort and we voted for lovely grub instead.

We were only in Rome for three days and we made the most of it, going on lots of free trips and doing as many of the free shows as possible. We saw two extremely good plays and did a nightly tour of the Clubs ex "Night", but now very military and under control, but the bubbly was good and cheap.

The days of peace soon passed and on the 5th August 1944 set forth for Trasimeno, a distance of 128 miles, according to my diary. We moved back into harness reluctantly the very next day by moving to Greve ALG to relieve 'C' Flight who were working with the 4th British Division on the siege of Florence which was just ripe to fall. On my very first sortie saw our lads in the streets of Florence but only on our side of the Arno, the Germans had blown all the famous bridges, except the Ponte Vecchio, though that one had been blocked either end causing it considerable harm.

The Taking of Florence

Although Florence had been declared an open city the enemy did their utmost to prevent our troops entering and had, I repeat, blown all the bridges except the most famous one, blocked by destroying ancient buildings, also famous and antique, at either end. This wanton destruction ruined part of the passageway that crossed over the upper part of the bridge, over the little shops that lined it, and which joined the Medici Palace with the Uffizi Palace.

On the 7th August 1944 commenced operations again, working over Florence. This city is built at the foot of mountains rising to its north and facing a valley some five miles wide. The mountain backdrop towered some 3,000 feet; the enemy again had full command of our positions as the Eighth Army gathered for the final attack.

At this time our next ALG was being bull-dozed in that dangerous valley, and the work was under observation from the lofty enemy OP's and attracted plenty of artillery fire. Disregarding this danger the New Zealander at the controls of the completely unprotected Caterpillar tractor kept on with his work until a shell hit near and killed him. Undaunted, another man took his place as the shells continued to rain down until he too was hit and was carried off badly wounded. The work was completed that night. Those chaps were real heroes as they faced the danger in cold blood. We were not amused at having to occupy that particular strip as soon as it was finished, and did not relish the idea at all.

On the 19th there was a great deal of enemy activity east of Florence and they were evidently using Route 70 as far as Pontassieve, as also several lateral roads leading into the mountains. To harass and help them on their way I chose a nice road junction where the main route lay beside the Arno with a steeply rising cliff just across where no detour was possible. I engaged this spot with all the guns of 'A' Troop and then registered it for further treatment during the night when the enemy convoys were surely creeping along. The shells that missed the road would burst against the cliff and shower deadly splinters of rocks on the vehicles and men below.

Our stay on the deadly ALG was brief, thank goodness. We were really extremely lucky and, although they shelled intermittently during the two days we remained there, feeling very bare and vulnerable, no man nor plane was hit. It was unpleasant and one lacked a feeling of security.

We moved on again in a heavy rain storm that did not deter our going, and we occupied a new strip beside a stream, only five miles from the Arno and the enemy. This camp was sheltered by trees but Jerry up in the hills could see our planes taking off and landing and shells would whistle over seeking for us each night; and sometimes by day. We were getting accustomed to the noise of shells bursting close and we badly needed our rest after the nervous strain of several sorties. We slept soundly despite the unpleasantness.

The following day we were all up at the same time hovering around supporting the 4th British Division as they stormed across the Arno. The river was shallow where they crossed and it was funny seeing the little chaps splashing their way across. It wasn't so funny downstairs when the machine guns started up and I saw them being mowed down like flies. We had to bring down artillery close support fire on the houses on the north shore where the machine-guns were situated. As our troops went in the Jerries pulled out the other end of the town, and in that respect they honoured their assurance that they would not fight in Florence. Soon the people of the City, which had seemed to be completely empty, swarmed in their thousands into the streets, certain that their ex-enemies would treat them better than their ex-allies.

Jerry could not quite keep his word and a while later they were shelling the city, and one went through the roof of a famous church killing a number of women and children, who had taken refuge there.

When I observed the shells falling I checked up on the splash they made, it was possible by so doing to obtain a rough bearing on the gun position. By this method I guessed the shells were coming from the NNE and I climbed up to try and locate the silly bastard who was firing on an Open City. After a while I managed to spot his gun flash, he was well hidden, so he thought, in a gully behind the first range of hills, and soon had the guns of the 78th Medium dead on target. He did not fire any more.

The following day the same thing happened and I saw them obtain a direct hit on a hospital. They knew damn well it was a hospital, having just evacuated the place. Although I did my best to locate this other bastard I did not succeed.

The next day, which was to be our last on this front, we were kept busy harassing the enemy, now on the run and disappearing fast up the mountain tracks. To do this I rained hundreds of shells from the 78th Medium Regiment on the high ground to the East. Had one good shoot firing on a bunch of enemy infantry dispersed in a wood. With all the guns in the Regiment stonked an ammo dump and had the satisfaction of setting off a firework display. Finished off a belligerent day by destroying a house reportedly being used as a HQ.

Our lads were over-running Florence by that time and hordes of people were to be seen roaming the streets. The inhabitants had been kept indoors for four days, to nip out meant death, and all were starving. Needless to say they were glad to be rescued.

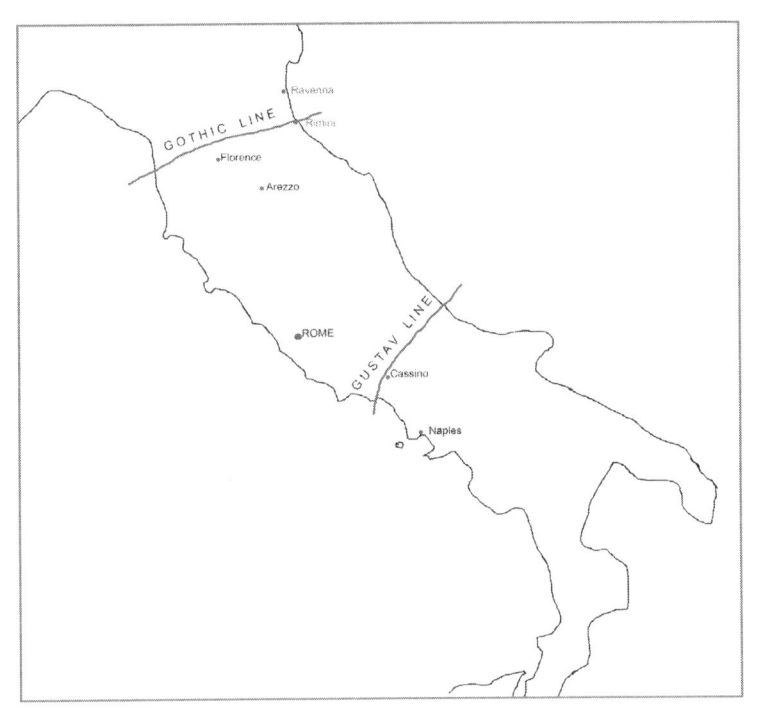

The Gustav and Gothic Lines

THE GOTHIC LINE BATTLE

Secretly and Silently we Creep Away

We had swept the German Army from Cassino, along the valleys, smashed through the redoubtable Hitler Line, the narrow gap at Arezzo, past Rome, the narrow pass by Lake Trasimeno and had taken Florence. Now the foe had been forced to leave the valley and take to the hills, where it could be difficult for an Army to follow.

However there was a tough nut to be cracked on the Adriatic front where Jerry had built what they considered the most impregnable line of defence in Europe [the Gothic Line] consisting of a great quantity of concrete emplacements, many of which mounted Panther tank turrets with high velocity guns, that could easily smash any tank we had then in Italy.

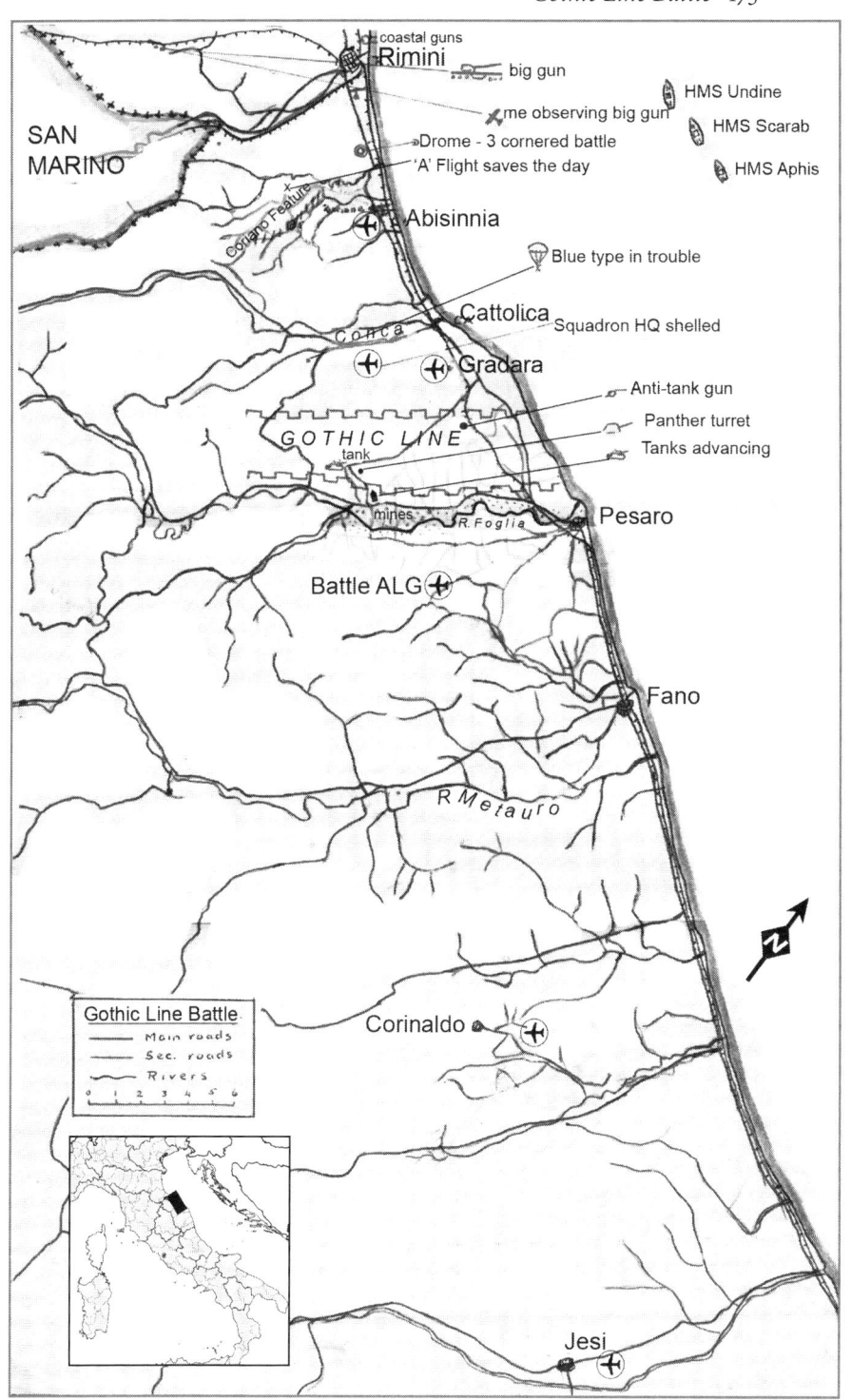

Gothic Line Battle

And so, as could be expected, the Eighth Army and 657 Air OP Squadron with it, was called upon to do the trick. The Army commander, Lieut. General Oliver Leese put it very aptly in a Personal Message to the troops, which read:

> *"You have won great Victories. To advance 220 miles from Cassino to Florence in three months is a notable achievement in the Eighth Army's History. To each of you in the Eighth Army and in the Desert Air Force, my grateful thanks.*
> *Now we begin the last lap. Swiftly and secretly, once again, we have moved right across Italy an Army of immense strength and striking power to break the Gothic Line.*
> *Victory in the coming battle means the beginning of the end for the German Armies in Italy.*
> *Let every man do his utmost and again success will be ours. Good luck to you all."*

On the 15th August 1944 'A' Flight pulled out of the fight and travelled to our favourite camping site by Lake Trasimeno to await movement orders. To move a whole army across the Apennines, along narrow tortuous roads, is some undertaking and calls for superb planning to avoid utter chaos. The tanks had to be carried on huge transporters, so large they could not get round most of the hairpin bends and the tanks had to be off-loaded each time.

Whilst awaiting our turn to move we made the most of our enforced idleness to swim in the beautiful lake and visit nearby towns. Explored Castiglione del Lago, small but quaint, and one day, accompanied by Scottie, went off in Elsie to visit Assisi, a beautiful village set right on top of a pimple hill commanding a view of the colourful valley all around. We had a good lunch at the Hotel Subasio and then strolled down the steep narrow street that led to the Piazza and the famous triple church, built one atop the other, of San Francisco of Assisi. The lowest one of all boasts the oldest *frescos* in the Universe, they certainly looked it and weren't pretty; but we gaped at them with due awe. At the door of this church we met a Mrs. Perkins, a resident of Assisi throughout the German occupation, she said she had been treated reasonably well. She kindly acted as guide and later invited us to her home for tea. There we met her husband, an artist [Frederick M. Perkins, American art critic 1874-1955], who had spent 18 years painting in that area.

We returned to camp in time for the 'A' Flight dinner celebrating the end of an extremely successful campaign, and the fact that "us present" were still alive. We had managed to scrounge some tasty duck and of course there were bags of *vino*. It was a real good show.

On the 18th August 1944 at 8·00 hours our transport moved off in "orderly" fashion to take its proper place in the never-ending convoy crawling into the mountains. Bob, Aubrey, Scottie and self were left behind, feeling somewhat forlorn standing on a bare patch of field which once had been our camp.

As the trucks would take all day, and in all probability longer, to reach journey's end, we decided not to take off until the afternoon, thinking we might enjoy another swim. However, our hopes were squashed as dark cold clouds crept up over the horizon, then the storm broke and kept on for hours. It hailed about eleven with stones so large that Holy became holier in several places and we got wet, the rain creeping into the cockpit of our planes. We ate soggy sandwiches for lunch.

The rain kept on. Though we would have flown of necessity, under these circumstances it isn't good for the blood pressure. We were bored.

Luckily, about what would have been our tea time, the sky brightened and it stopped raining. We helped each other wind up our kites, and soon we were splashing across the runway and into the air. We each had little faith in the other's map reading ability so we soon lost sight of each other as we wended our separate ways across the breadth of Italy.

Playing for safety, I'm a cautious chap by nature, flew on a compass course to Fossato, some 30 miles away, then if the clouds should force me down into the valleys I could Bradshaw my way safely by following the road to Jesi, our destination.

I was flying pretty low for pleasure, well below the surrounding mountains, just beyond Fossato [*Fossato di Vico?*] I came upon a particularly steep sugar-loaf type hill of the type that seem to abound in this country. Having done a spot of mountaineering in my youth, was amusing myself planning a feasible way to the summit and reached the conclusion that it would be quite a job. To have a better look, zoomed up and skimmed over the top. Imagine my surprise to find there a farm house, a tiny cultivated field complete with cows and other domestic beasts. Goodness knows how they ever got up there. Wonder if the farmer knew there was a war on as I could not imagine him popping down with any frequency to the town below.

Although the improved visibility allowed flying on a compass course it was far more amusing and interesting following the road, watching the Eighth Army, crawling along, not very swiftly nor silently for that matter. As far as I could see, over miles and miles of winding dipping road, were lorries, tanks on their carriers, guns, jeeps, ambulances and all the odds and ends that make up a modern Army. Also kept a look out for our own transport; but did not see them.

Our destination was a large Italian aerodrome on the outskirts of Jesi and about 10 miles from the Adriatic Sea. Didn't dare land on those huge runways so did so instead in a friendly field lined with fruit trees and dotted with haystacks, these proved to be Aubrey's undoing. He came in nicely but his judgement was slipping and a wing tip touched a tree and this changed his course sufficiently to head him straight into a haystack, and the resultant gentle crash did not improve his plane. Aubrey was famous for this sort of thing and he is still remembered in Cambridge for having taxied hurriedly into an Airspeed Oxford and a Mosquito, chewing large bits off each with his prop, and severely damaging the Tiger Moth with which he did the deed.

The chaps from the other Flights drifted in and we stood around and waited for the convoy to arrive. Tired of waiting and peckish we managed to scrounge food somewhere, then I found a barn and went to sleep on a soft pile of hay. Just as well I did so because the trucks did not arrive until 4 am the next morning.

The Lull Before the Battle

Having sneaked into Jesi airfield [18 Aug 1944] we hid the planes among the vines and covered them with camouflage netting. They were to remain there un-flown until the 28th August when we moved to our battle ALG

The blue Adriatic was within Jeeping distance and we made many trips to the nearest beach or to Ancona, for some good bathing. We thoroughly enjoyed swimming and fooling around in the bracing sea water, and the peaceful atmosphere.

Harry Simms of 'C' Flight was awarded an immediate DFC [Distinguished Flying Cross]. and that, added to the splendid news of the fall of Paris, made an excellent excuse for a Squadron party; and a good time was had by all.

Trucks and Jeeps were thoroughly overhauled and "406'd." Stores were checked, batteries repaired and recharged, wireless sets seen to and things were put into first class order in preparation for the tough assignment ahead of us. The Gothic Line had taken months to prepare. In that hilly terrain there were thousands of ideal defence spots where a well sited anti-tank gun emplacement, topped by a Panther turret with a high velocity 88 mm gun, could knock out any of our tanks at long range. These tough defences were built to a depth of nearly twenty miles and, besides, we were to attack against the enemy's crack regiments that once again were facing us.

So we made the most of these last few days of peace and quiet.

The Attack Commences

The Eighth Army had successfully crossed the Apennines and everything was now set for the Assault on the Gothic Line. At the Jesi drome there were hundreds of Spitfire and Kitty Hawk Fighter Bombers, each a vast improvement compared to German Stuka. They could load up with 1,000 lbs. of bombs – one of 500 under the fuselage and two of 250 under each wing. It was fascinating watching them trying to take off under that enormous weight. They staggered off eventually after using up most of the long runway. Besides the bombs they carried multiple machine-guns to add to their destructive force.

To make the most of our powers of observation we had ceased to be attached to the famous XIII Corps and were transferred to the 1st Canadian Corps. 'A' Flight was to work with their AGRA [*Army Group Royal Artillery*] and this gave us a terrific fire power making it possible for us to inflict serious damage on the enemy whenever we saw something worth damaging, and we were to see plenty.

At first light on the 25th August 1944 'A' Flight was to move forward and occupy our battle ALG, and go into the fray without delay. By that time the Canadians would be pushing over the Metauro River on their way to take up positions for the Gothic Line attack. To cover this advance all our artillery was firing and to reach our new ALG we had to fly through all this hardware. We all managed to dodge the shells.

Altogether I did three sorties that day but saw no enemy movement, they were taken completely by surprise and evidently beat a hasty retreat to the shelter of their prepared line.

The next day our advance continued meeting little opposition and I did a couple of shoots; one a "Y Target" on a road junction and another one a ford where enemy infantry was wading across. I saw the rounds splashing in the river and the movement of troops ceased at that point.

We were becoming increasingly obnoxious to the enemy and that evening they sent another lot of bombers to plaster our camp with hundreds of one kilo anti-personnel bombs that crackled wickedly all over the area. The following couple of nights they repeatedly shelled us; which was worse. One can hear the bombers fooling around and the bombs on their way down, and it is soon over, but the shelling is a deliberate business that can go on for hours; it interferes more with one's sleep.

We spent these days harassing the Gothic Line, softening it up for the impending attempt by the Eighth Army to smash through. This was likely to prove a really stiff job. The enemy had spared no effort to make that, their last fortified line before reaching the Northern Plain, as impregnable as possible. We knew that the Todt

Organisation had spent many months pouring cement into numerous gun-emplacements and strong points.

'A' Flight also moved forward and we were now over the Metauro and within 12 miles of the Gothic Line itself and in a good position to offer effective support during the attack scheduled to commence on the 30th August. This nearness was all very well from the efficiency point of view, but not from that of our nervous system, we were now well within range of their artillery, and they did not like us one little bit. However, they only shelled us at night, having a healthy respect for our powers of observation during the day.

A Ripley Line

Long before dawn on the 30th August 1944 the Canadian boys were storming across the Foglia River under desperate circumstances. They had commenced their advance across a half mile of flat valley, with no cover whatsoever, obstructed by a wide, if shallow, river, and a deep mine field the other side.

As can be imagined, Jerry was fighting savagely with everything he had, and casualties were high. The troops that did manage to get across that lethal bit of no-mans-land were confronted by a line of hills, swarming with enemy sitting snug and safe in concrete pill-boxes and pouring deadly fire upon them.

By the end of the first day the infantry was across the river and the sappers had managed to clear lanes through the mine-fields. By dawn on the following day some of our tanks were across.

I did a couple of sorties on the 30th but no shoots. Our guns were fully occupied with predicted targets and barrages. Besides, there was not much to be seen through the smoke of battle. The tanks were, as yet, not involved.

It was my turn to do the Dawn Patrol on the 31st August 1944 and was thrilled to spot Shermans across the Foglia, close in against the hills where they could not be reached by shells. Others were then wading across. Mist and smoke prevented me seeing much but returned to camp with the good news which I promptly sent over the telephone to Brigade. For obvious reasons reports on our troops were not sent by wireless.

Bob Barrass was next man up and by then the enemy evidently knew that our tanks were creeping across and he spotted three large enemy ones, either Panthers or Tigers, both equally formidable, moving forward into position where they would be ready to stage a counter attack on our armour. He promptly engaged with a troop of 4·5's and they scuttled for cover. Two of them disappeared into a vineyard but the other settled itself comfortably in a shallow dip behind the crest of a hill, just short of a lateral road. In this position he could obviously watch the line of advance of our tanks and whistle up the others when necessary.

All this took some time and by then Bob was running out of petrol. He got on the "blower", reported the score, and in minutes Holy Smoke III and self were buzzing along the runway and on our way to carry on with the good work and do our darndest to prevent those tanks coming into action.

We were so near to the front line that I was soon up front and spotted Bob's plane weaving his flak evasive way around the sky. As soon as I had climbed sufficiently to see the terrain, he indicated the position of the three tanks by the simple expedient of putting a round near each and telling me when to watch for the explosions.

Bob's well directed shells were dropping spasmodically near the lone tank and it was difficult to tell if it had been damaged. I was having a good look at it through my binoculars, when I noticed, out of the corner of my eye, a vague circular shape in a field nearby that did not look natural. I was still climbing but quickly levelled out to gain speed, and flew towards this object to have a better view. My suspicions were confirmed when I discerned, through the clever camouflage covering, the long lethal barrel of a high velocity gun. Recognised it as a Panther turret and it was sited just over the crest of a hill and covering a road leading up from the river and over which our tanks were obliged to travel. And I knew our Shermans were then assembling preparatory to advancing right into this danger spot.

There was not time to be lost if I was to try to save the lives of many of those chaps in the tanks about to creep up that dangerous road. I knew only too well that they did not have a chance of

Gothic Line Battle 183

Our tanks were creeping up that dangerous road towards the Panther turret - and they did not have a chance of survival.

surviving when fired upon by this powerful anti-tank gun which could fire solid shells through their armour with ease, and from a great distance. Added to this, I knew that three Panther's were in the area, ready to pounce.

On the other hand there was little I could do to help. Even the whopping 4.5 inch shells I had at my disposal could do naught against that gun emplacement. At best, I could hope to hit the turret and, maybe, if I was lucky, damage the traversing gear or, by placing plenty of shells in front of their line of fire, blind them to a small extent and maybe spoil their aim.

But something had to be done, and fast. Had already reported the gun to Brigade, who would warn the tanks. With one quick correction I switched the single gun I was using on the stationary tank onto the new target, and engaged for a destructive shoot. What

My Panther turret bag. "Elsie" on the right.

Bob Barrass

a hope! This calls for extreme accuracy and that means going to a verified short bracket. That is, two plusses and two minuses fifty yards apart. Carried on doing this with the Pivot Gun but, at the same time, gave the Jerries the benefit of several rounds from the troop, to shake them up a bit and get them jittery

I had by then explained the problem to the guns and they were on their toes and keen as mustard to save the tank boys if possible. In a matter of minutes we were down to the verified short bracket and ready to go to fire for effect. The tanks at the bottom of the hill had begun to roll and were already moving up the road. Another 400 yards or so would bring the leader into the trap. The drama deepened! Orders were going back and forth as fast as my wireless could carry them and, without pause, called for "Three rounds gunfire." They came down dead-on for line, the first bursting about 25 yards beyond the target. The next came down, just minus splashing mud and dirt over the gun. The third I did not see at all and presumed it had been a dud.

The rounds had come down nicely and it was not necessary to change the lay and I ordered a further "Five rounds Gun Fire." The Troop had barely acknowledged my order when I was thrilled to see a tall sheet of flame jet from the Panther gun turret. This could only mean that the cordite charges inside were going up in flames. Gleefully ordered "Stop" and gave the boys at the guns the good news. The third shell had hot been a dud after all but had accomplished the impossible feat of passing cleanly through the man-hole on top of the turret, a chance in a million, and truly a Ripley line if ever there was one. The round had burst deep inside the gun emplacement where it made rather a mess of blokes and things inside. It was for this reason that I had not observed the flash.[1]

After we were safely through the Gothic line Bob and I took time off to Jeep it back and have a look at my bag to find out what really happened. Sure enough, my supposition turned out to be correct. There was no sign of damage outside the emplacement but inside gun fittings, instruments and cartridge cases were to be seen twisted

---

1   This "Ripley Line" is confirmed in *The Story of 657 Air O P Squadron* by Captains Barrass and Owens on page 41.

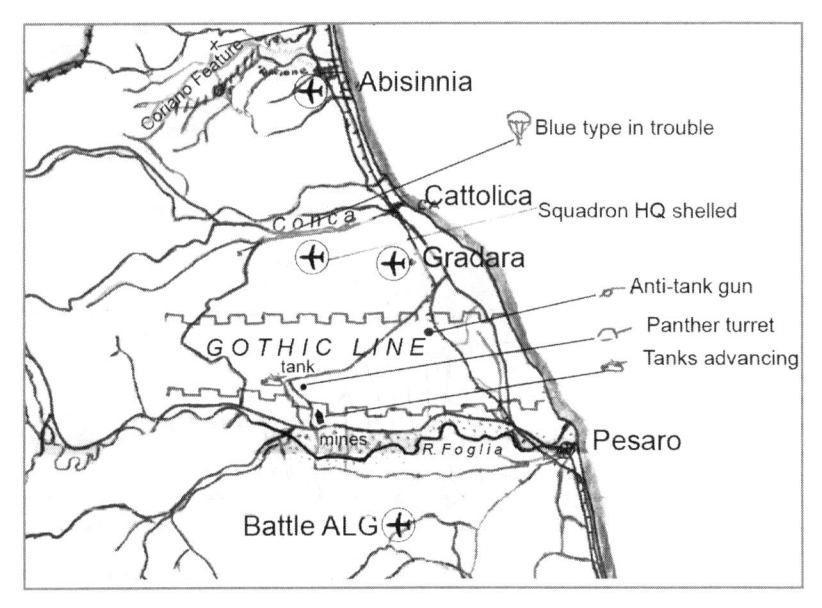

Gothic Line Battle - Detail

and bent by the explosion and heat. The gun itself was a high velocity long muzzle 88 mm mounted on a Panther Turret and there is no doubt about it that the lucky shell had saved the lives of the crew of several of our tanks which would have been picked off at leisure, by this powerful rifle, as they advanced up the road.

By early afternoon the Eighth Army was well over the river and swarming up the hills the other side. Bob's affair with the three tanks and my little effort at gun busting had weakened a link in the enemy's first line of defence and our tanks were soon over the first line of hills and out of the dangerous flat lands. Furthermore, our infantry had driven them away from the high ground commanding the river and its approaches. I felt that, whatever happened now, I had justified my existence in the British Army and had put in my penny's worth towards final victory.

Aubrey Young with one of the 88 mm dual purpose gun knocked out by the 2nd Canadian Medium Artillery directed by him. 1 September 1944

The Gothic Line Battle Continues

On the 1st. of September 1944 it was my turn to do the Dawn Patrol. At an unearthly hour of the night Powell climbed into my caravan and shook me awake with a steaming mug of "char".

I could hear Holy Smoke coughing and spluttering as her engine was wound up by Wilson and Green. Then she awoke with a roar. I dragged on my battle dress trews over my pyjamas, struggled into fur lined flying boots and jacket, made sure my map board was in order with code signs for the day written on, then stumbled sleepily towards the strip.

Holy was ticking over gently by then, purring like a contented kitten, and also mewing as Wilson fiddled with the wireless set.

By then the sky was commencing to glow and when I could make out the surrounding trees silhouetted against the dawn, clambered in and taxied along the narrow runway. I turned at the very end as, per usual, there wasn't too much room for an easy take-off.

Holy flew beautifully in the calm pre-dawn air. Despite the fag of getting up so early, it was the pleasantest sortie of the lot, usually quiet and peaceful. We climbed, circling gently to meet the sun.

That morning there was little peace. The God of War does not wait upon the sun; his deadly children, the mighty tanks, were already stirring and creeping, belly to the ground, smelling out the enemy.

The position of our forward troops was easy to trace by the petrol fires lit for their, inevitable, morning cup of tea, and I was kept busy marking their positions on my map.

Spotted a Squadron of Shermans creeping along. By the cautious way they were travelling it was obvious they were sounding out the enemy and expecting trouble at any minute. They were deep in hilly country by then, surrounded by well camouflaged defensive positions.

To offer what assistance I could, I lost height and hovered over them keeping a wary eye out for trouble, warning my guns to be on their toes. The tanks came within sight of a farm and started pouring tracers and bouncing shells off the buildings. Soon there was smoke and fire all over the place. The enemy were retaliating by lobbing over mortar bombs; some of them smoke. Then I saw that a concealed anti-tank gun was active as one of our Shermans suddenly burst into flames from a direct hit. I went hunting for the bastard and spotted a gun firing from the corner of a village. But by that time my petrol was running low and I would not have time to engage. I therefore rang up Control and reported the gun position to Scottie, who was next up, and he was able to "stonk" the gun good and proper.

It wasn't long before I was whistled up on a tank hunt. Some of these monsters had been reported massing near a cross-road in no-mans-land. Went up and had a good look at the area and saw their tail ends scuttling into a vineyard. I had already sent the map reference of this target down to the guns and was all set to engage. All this time I had been steadily approaching the target and, before giving the final order to shoot, I had a closer look at them through my binoculars. It was just as well I did so because I was now able to recognise them as Shermans. Cancelled the shoot by saying they were out of sight, a whopping fib, but I had given the map reference of this friendly target in clear and I did not want Jerry to realize my mistake and profit by it.

I was up again for the Dusk Patrol, and concluded a nice party started by Bob who had engaged a HQ and a gun pit. I spotted another of the latter nearby and had nasty HE shells falling all around. Did not see much else, because of the smoke, dust and gathering darkness, so returned to a tricky landing.

Blue Types in Trouble

The battle for the Gothic Line had been raging for three days and we had the enemy on the run. Bob, who was first up, saw them scurrying across the dry bed of a river and engaged with HE and planted a shell right in the middle of one group of foot-sloggers, knocking them about like nine pins.

Holy and I were next up and we kept a good look out for movement across the fords, and roads leading to them. However the

190   Warlike Sketches

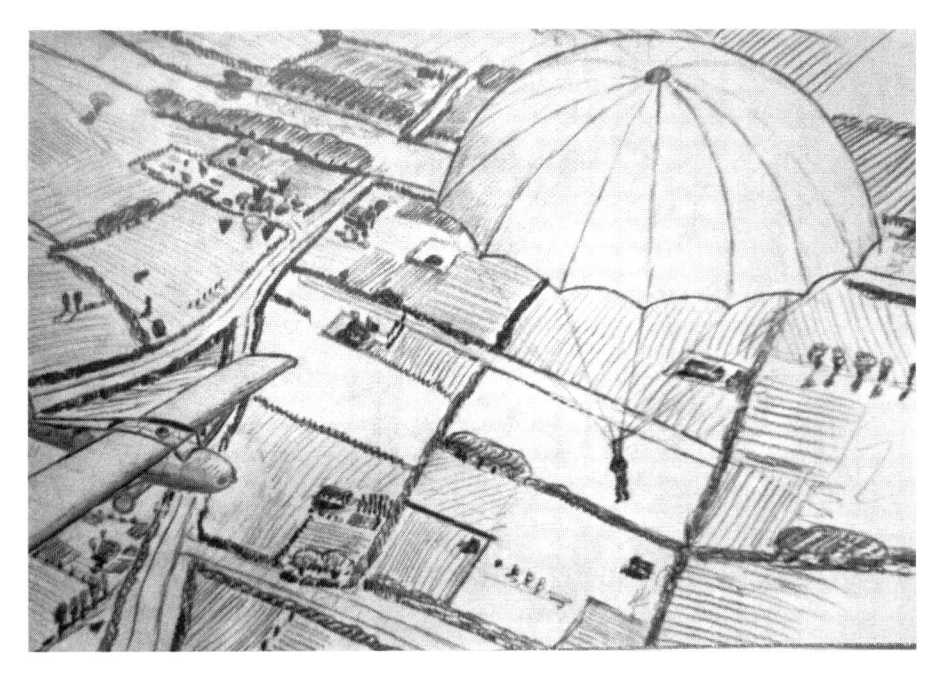

Heading straight for a great white parachute — and another white parachute drifting down — nearing my target area

enemy had learnt a lesson and were now wary and not to be seen. A while later we spotted a lorry speeding along one of these roads, obviously in a hurry to escape our advancing troops. I got onto my gunner boys and ordered a troop of 4·5's laid on the ford the lorry was heading for in anticipation of a nice picnic, then sat back and watched the victim heading steadily towards the trap. But he didn't quite walk into it. When he was only some 100 yards short of the ford, and I was just about to give the order to fire, he nipped into a farm yard and halted beside a house. This suited me fine, a stationary target, is far easier to hit. Quickly ordered a fresh map reference and commenced ranging on the lorry. I was engrossed in this task when I found myself heading straight for a great white parachute with a chap dangling underneath and it was only by taking immediate and violent action, that we missed hitting this, chap. I'll bet he was scared stiff.

As we whizzed by I was able to see that he was one of our Blue

Types. He did not look very happy but did not seem the worse for wear. Had a quick look round for any other odd things floating around and saw the burning wreckage of a plane that told its own story, and another white parachute much further down, rather near the enemy.

Carried on with the ranging and soon I had the shells landing just where I wanted them and called for fire for effect with a troop of guns.

All along I had been keeping an eye on the Blue Type. The wind was in the wrong direction and was carrying him rapidly towards the enemy lines and, what was worse, towards my victim and into the line of fire of my Troop. When I thought he was within range of the splinters of the shells bursting I stopped the shoot to give the poor fellow a chance. The parachute drifted on and when within some 100 yards of my lorry, it went limp as it touched the ground. Gave the chap thirty seconds to get free and away from the danger area then resumed my shoot making a mess of the farm house which must also have been a HQ

I hoped I did not hurt the new "Caterpillar" who presumably was caught "off side."

We Order the Navy Around

While we were battling along following the Adriatic coastline, the Royal Navy had crept along with us. Now they demanded a look-in on the fight in order that the BBC could tell the World how they were helping to win the battle.

The *Undine*, *Scarab* and *Aphis*, sundry destroyers, were stationed at Ancona and would steam out but, not too early, and fire umpteen broadsides haphazardly at the Italian coastline, and then steam back and send the score to the BBC. It became too obvious that they were chucking precious ammo away so the ubiquitous Air OP were called upon to help the Navy boys plant their bricks where they could do some good. Naturally they wanted the very best guidance so 'A' Flight was detailed to lend a hand.

The task was fraught with difficulties. The wireless sets we used were not in harmony with the ship-borne ones and it was a devil of a job tuning in to them. Although we were politely warned that any plane approaching one of their ships would be fired on, quite a few of us risked this uncalled for attention and beat them up after we got fed up with twiddling knobs and not hearing a glimmer of the pre-arranged tuning call. Quite often the beat-up brought results the which made one think.

Personally, I never did manage to break their reserve. I was detailed to contact the *Undine* on the morning of the 4th September and took off with the code sign, tuning call and time all set. Although I could see the destroyer sailing prettily along, a prudent distance from the enemy held coast, I never heard a peep out of her. Another attempt in the afternoon, when the shoot was supposed to take place, also proved futile and I went home in disgust.

Aubrey was more successful. He had been detailed to look after the *Scarab* and did three shoots with her. He managed to tune in and suggested they shoot up the port installations of Rimini, then out of range of our land guns. They agreed and he gave them a map reference and ordered "fire." He saw them shoot, not with one gun as he had expected but with all the guns they possessed in their sharp end. He never managed to spot just where they landed. He then politely asked them to "drop 800 yards." Again he did not see anything splash near Rimini. However, he did observe some splashes away to the north, somewhere near Venice. Suspicious, he ordered "repeat" and, sure enough, the splashes appeared away up there again. He afterwards reported that, instead of correcting their line by degrees, he ordered them to traverse five miles south. This order brought them within easy distance of their original map reference and, by the time he had finished the shoot they had altered their line by 16 degrees. So much for their map reading.

As soon as Aubrey was sure the guns were firing in the correct direction he ordered "four rounds gun fire" as the target did not warrant greater number of shells. But, the Navy types had their score to think of and they just carried on pumping broadside after broadside into the same buildings, quite needlessly. Although they were steaming away out to sea, some enemy gun or other was having a go at them and they appeared in a mighty hurry to return to their base.

That evening we purposely listened in to the BBC and, sure enough, it was reported that units of the Royal Navy had engaged shore installations and enemy troops in the Rimini area, firing a large tonnage of shells, no mention was made of the many troops of artillery that had done far more useful damage with but a fraction of that weight of shells. Expect it impressed the public – but not us.

The next day I was up early working with my old crowd, the Heavy Artillery boys. As usual I was flying over the sea, where it was somewhat healthier, when I observed two of our destroyers steaming along at a goodly distance from the coast, obviously bent on popping off another day's ration of ammo. I forget what I was doing, but when next I had time to look their way I discovered they were being fired on, by the large splashes that appeared near them. After a bit of searching with my binoculars, spotted flashes coming from what appeared to be a row of four coastal guns, nicely emplaced, and protected about half a mile north of Rimini; I rang up my boys, gave them the news, and came to the rescue of the Navy with a troop of 4·5's.

Meanwhile, the navy boys did not seem to be enjoying the party one little bit. After hiding behind a thick smoke screen they turned and sailed for home. BBC or no BBC, I kicked up plenty of dust from around the Coastal guns which I later inspected and found bits off the outside emplacement. But the pieces themselves, of 1890 vintage, were untouched.

'A' Flight Again Saves the Day

The battle was going well and every pilot in the Squadron was working flat out, hitting the Enemy wherever and whenever they stuck out their necks too far. We were up against their crack troops, well experienced, well armed, employing thoroughly thought out and prepared positions and with a pretty good knowledge of our tactics.

By the 6th September 1944 we had pushed the enemy beyond the

Conca river, and they were making a determined stand on what was known as the Coriano Feature that dominated the narrow battlefield, some ten miles wide, between the Adriatic and the wishfully neutral country of San Marino.

At first light that morning the flight moved forward to Cattolica, as always too near the front line for comfort.

It was my turn to fly second that morning and no sooner was I in position to look around than I saw a gun firing rapidly from the boundary line of San Marino. This was easy to see as they had placed huge white crosses all around their small country in the hope that their neutrality would be respected. I placed a troop of guns onto this target and it shut up pronto. The bricks came down nicely right on the wood in which the gun was concealed and presumably did some damage. It was unfortunate that some of my shells burst on the wrong side of the line of crosses; as there weren't any houses nearby I am sure they would not take umbrage at a few shell holes lying around.

Scottie was up next. After scouting around for a while he spotted some movement beyond Coriano village, built on the top of the line of hills of that name that was our next objective. Our tanks and infantry were then attacking. He dove down to obtain a better view and received a shock when he saw a number of enemy tanks moving steadily towards the front. So far they had used their tanks rather stupidly, in penny packets. It soon became obvious to Scottie, once he had counted seven of these monsters that they were about to make full use of their armour. This was extremely serious considering that our Shermans and Churchills were no match for their Panthers and Tigers armed, as they were, with high velocity 88 mm guns. A surprise attack by this number of tanks would, undoubtedly, play havoc with our forces and possibly turn the tide of battle that day. Our positon was precarious. The contending forces were about equal in weapons and supplies and there was not much to choose between them. A sudden lunge by the enemy, at this moment, could easily suffice to upset the fine balance, disrupt our plans and cause the Eighth Army to fall back.

Scottie's report to Brigade HQ caused quite a panic and every gun in the Corps was placed at his disposal to smash the impending counter attack. He afterwards reported that the shoot he called down was terrific. In an engagement of this nature ranging is unnecessary and the first the Jerries knew about it was when a "Yoke Target" came whizzing and whining down amongst them. They kept on for a short while and then lost their pattern and commenced dispersing in an effort to escape the punishment. Scottie kept ordering more rounds, to be put down. Although it is impossible to see if a tank is damaged unless it brews up, and they rarely do from long range fire, damage was being done to their tracks, traversing gear, etc. and several remained where they were.

We later worked it out that over 4,000 rounds of heavy stuff had been put down among that crowd. The fact is that not a single armoured unit reached the starting line, and none went into the attack.

Aubrey took off before Scottie had finished to carry on with the good work, and he engaged two Panthers that were still creeping around and refusing to lie still. This he did with one gun as they were far behind the battle, evidently endeavouring to get out of range of our artillery. He also spotted and engaged a Nebel firing.

Bob, up next, spotted and destroyed two enemy trucks that were speeding along a road beyond Coriano, and knocked them out. It was my turn to do the Dusk Sortie, which could be relied upon to be interesting to say the least. Keeping my eyes skinned and weaving, as presumably some dirt was coming up at us, soon spotted guns firing from the NW edge of Rimini airfield, and engaged with a battery of Mediums, plastering the area with shells.

The sun sank below the horizon and then, rather late to be sure, realized that it had been a beautiful day. Wished I had taken time off to admire the wonderful scenery over which we were flying. With the dusk I commenced to see far more of the battle than was evident in daylight, as tracer ammunition became increasingly visible, darting wickedly across the landscape and bouncing off objects.

Several of our tanks were engaged in a pitched battle with the enemy and it was thrilling to see streams of machine gun bullets leaving their dark hulls and darting towards the source of other streams of tracers coming in the reverse direction. Their heavy guns were also in action and bright flashes showed where their shells were bursting against some pill-box or emplacement.

Tracers were criss-crossing over the whole battlefield and shell and mortar bomb bursts added Dantesque brilliance to the scene, all very pretty but it was high time I headed for home. As per usual we were using a pocket-handkerchief sized field, difficult enough to find, let alone land in without appropriate landing lights. Luckily, there weren't any trees around but the ALG was small and neat, tucked away rather too close to a hill, which called for some tricky flying to get in. We managed fine and it was not long before Holy was picketed down, after three hectic trips that day.

A Duel with a Big Gun

Whilst 'A' Flight ALG was safe and snug in the shadow of Gradara Castle, or rather of the pimple hill on which it was built, Squadron HQ, for a wonder, was ahead of us. They were using a large field south of the Conca River, actually about five miles ahead of us, but in a rather exposed position, the surrounding country being fairly flat. It wasn't long before the enemy saw lots of the hated "lame ducks" sitting in a nice straight line and one morn a dull moan heralded the first of many whopping shells that were to land in the very near neighbourhood, causing much alarm and despondency among the Erks. By the shell fragments picked up it became evident that they were being favoured by a large railway gun, firing from a long range. That the enemy thought it worth their while to dedicate such a gun to us was deemed rather an honour and showed that our nuisance value was rated high.

Naturally, all the Squadron pilots kept their eyes skinned to locate this gun and Squadron HQ sent out a loud cry whenever the big shells came moaning over.

One morning, it was the 9th of September 1944, Holy and I were up on the Dawn Patrol minding our own business and nearing the end of our endurance with nothing much observed, when HQ piped up with the usual imperative order to "stonk that bloody gun firing at us."

I knew it must be fairly far away and trained my binocs up the coast and kept looking through them for what seemed ages. The plane flew itself, I knew not where, but I kept on staring, very rude, and at long last was rewarded by seeing a little flash away in the distance. Marked it well in my mind and then whizzed round to look in the direction of Squadron HQ. After a long time, it must have taken nearly two minutes, a hefty fountain of mud heaving from the middle of the strip confirmed that the gun had fired. I did not have enough petrol to remain up much longer and passed word to Flight to saddle up a new steed for me. By the time I landed another plane was being warmed up. Took a couple of minutes off for a quick cup of tea and a leg stretch and was soon chasing tail up along the runway and off a-hunting again. Meanwhile I had managed to borrow a super gun, a fat 6·2 incher the only gun in AGRA capable of reaching out sufficiently to give the railway gun a wallop, and it had to reach nearly 12 miles, it was soon tuned in on my frequency.

In the interest of efficiency, and with great reluctance, flew high-ish and out to sea as I headed up the coast and miles inside enemy territory. This was just begging for attention from their 88mm AA guns, not to mention the odd fighter plane that could be in the area. I had seen the flash coming from a gap between two white houses built just off the railway line running east from Rimini, about 10 miles away from that town. As soon as I was sure I had re-identified the precise spot where I had seen the flash, ordered "Fire." The gun had already been laid on a rough map reference I had given them.

It was a lengthy leisurely shoot. It takes quite a while to load the huge shell and stuff sufficient charges up the spout in a long distance duel of this nature, and the time of flight of the shell was in the neighbourhood of 120 seconds. It was a bright sunny day. The Adriatic was a beautiful blue and the mountainous domain of San Marino with its little town perched on top made a pretty picture. The enemy gun was skulking behind part of this small country and my shells, therefore, invaded the neutral air above to reach their destination.

It was the first time I had fired, or rather, ranged one of these big guns, and it was a pleasure to see how accurately they shot. And

198 Warlike Sketches

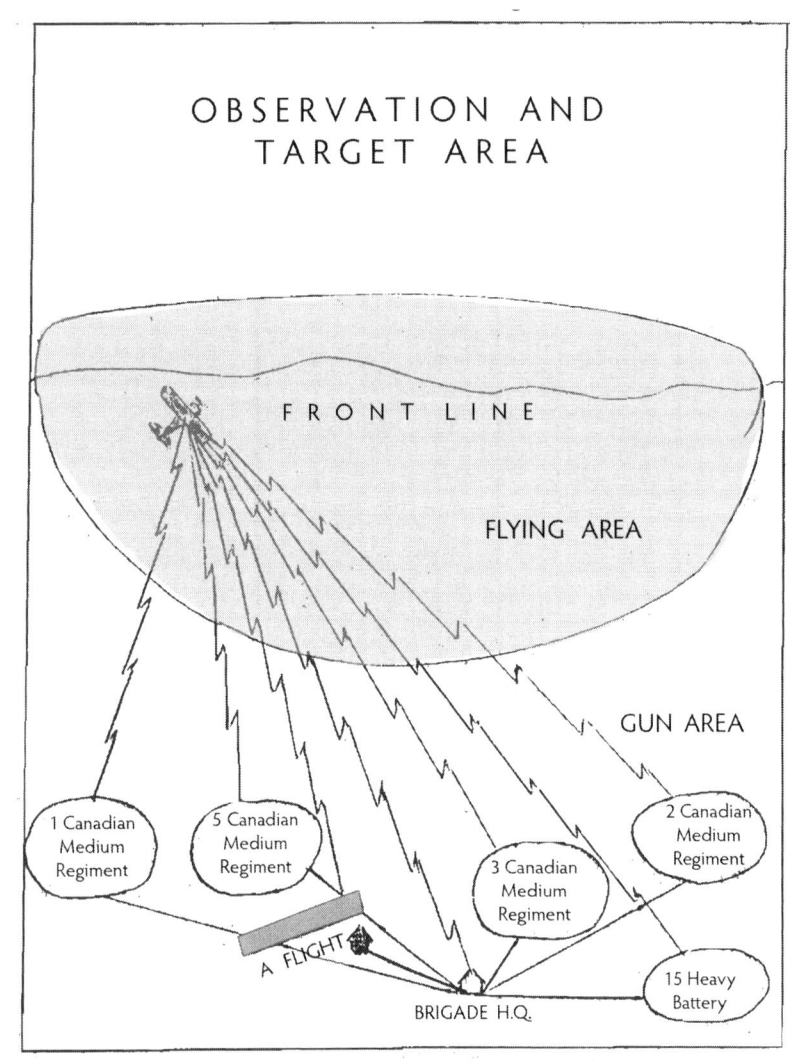

OBSERVATION AND TARGET AREA

FRONT LINE

FLYING AREA

GUN AREA

1 Canadian Medium Regiment
5 Canadian Medium Regiment
3 Canadian Medium Regiment
2 Canadian Medium Regiment
15 Heavy Battery
A FLIGHT
BRIGADE H.Q.

Lines of Communication:-
Wireless
Telephone

Battle Communications Diagram
Canadian AGRA and 'A' Flight

what a nice visible splash they made. Consequently the shoot was a piece-of-cake and simply could not go wrong. The shells were soon falling on and around the two houses and, it was hoped, damaging the big gun which could not have been far away, tied as it was to the railway lines. The fact remained that it never fired again from that position nor, to our knowledge, from any other.

Peace reigned once again at Squadron HQ.

I Break in Holy Smoke IV

The Holy Smoke Dynasty commenced years ago in the peaceful Parana Delta, in the shape of a nifty vessel pushed around noisily by an outboard motor. This object was owned jointly by J.E. Walding now a lowly "blue type" [RAF] and myself. In honour of my first love I had named my first war plane, to wit, a noble cannon-firing Auster III.

Holy Smoke II had met a "brilliant" death as will be recalled, during a dive bombing raid on our air-strip just after the battle of Cassino, when she had been hit by a bomb and went up in flames.

I took over Holy Smoke III a brand new plane on the 26th May and by the 14th September 1944 had flown her 240 hours and she was due for a major overhaul. This meant sending her back to base. I flew her into Squadron HQ and bade her a fond farewell. Then I took over a real swanky job, an Auster Mark IV with an American Lycoming 128 HP engine; it even had central heating consisting of a tube off the exhaust aimed at my left foot, which roasted slowly. Instead of the one hour twenty minute endurance, these planes flew well over two hours – a ruddy nuisance this, as it meant we could not nip back smartly for a cuppa every hour or so, but had to keep right on doing what we were doing for more than double the time.

We took off from the Squadron strip and feeling pleased with my new steed, climbed up a bit and started to chuck her around checking her for stalls, spins, that wings were well stuck on, and generally enjoying myself while I was getting the feel of her. It was a lovely sunny day and I flew towards San Marino, which had fascinated me for a long time and had a good look at the pretty little town balanced on the top of the mountain ridge. Flew close enough to see the people walking around the streets, but not too near as this was a neutral country and they had threatened to take pot shots at any intruder. Then I flew back and landed in the shadow of Gradara Castle where we had a cosy little strip where nobody could find us.

Hilton quickly had the new wireless checked and tuned into our working frequency. After tea away we went on our first sortie. Holy IV received her baptism of fire as a nasty machine gun kept pumping wicked tracers up at us, while we were busy engaging two lots of guns firing. However, they missed. A careful inspection once we were back home proved she was still un-holey.

Although the enemy was doing his best to stop our advance, we were slowly pushing our way up the coast towards the bottle-neck formed by neutral San Marino and the Adriatic. All this side was flat country and excellent for tank actions.

The next day I was up again on a couple of sorties and took on a vehicle hurrying along a road, after having stalked it for miles. Stayed up over two hours. The following flip took on a gun firing, and the shells came down nicely in the target area, and the firing promptly stopped.

On the 17th September our chaps were launching an attack on a strategic airfield, built beside the main road leading up the coast. I went up to keep an eye open for trouble. We hovered over a troop of Armoured Cars belonging to the New Zealand types, as they crept cautiously towards their objective. The leading vehicle did not quite make the airfield boundary before she was hit by an anti-tank shell and brewed up. Although I could not see where the gun was, I plastered the most likely places with a troop of 4·5's. The armoured cars took advantage of this stonk to make a goodly advance without meeting further trouble.

Later I received orders to silence a Self Propelled Gun that was causing trouble. We soon fixed that.

A few days later we went along and had a party with the New Zealand boys and they told us about the attack. It seemed that whilst they were attacking the airfield from the SW corner, the Greeks were doing likewise from the SE and the Jerries were defending themselves in no uncertain manner from the north. The Greeks had had a pretty rough time of it during this War and hated all and sundry. When they saw armoured cars and infantry approaching to their left, they promptly shot them up, just in case. The tough New Zealanders took a dim view of this unfriendly attitude and they sent back an equal amount of bricks. A pretty hectic three cornered party developed. Luckily, the Jerries were the main recipients of all this hate and backed away. After that the Greeks decided to behave and were friendly.

They later apologised to the NZ types saying that they thought they were "friendly" Ities. The Italians had stabbed them in the back not long before and they simply hated their guts. To get their own back they destroyed everything Italian they could lay their hands on. It got so bad that after they had smashed everything they could find in Rimini they were sent back someplace. We never came across them again. Just as well too or we would never have been able to replace our very expendable Flight glassware and crockery.

On the 18th we left our cosy Gradara airfield, where we had been for all of twelve days without being shelled. A record. We then flew off to occupy an ALG by the seashore near a place called Abissinia [now Riccione?], a bathing resort, where we managed to get some bathing hours in.

Another Field Day for 'A' Flight

The Eighth Army was hammering at the Rimini Defence Line and finding it mighty tough. The Fortunato Feature, slightly to our left, a long lowish hill and Jerry's best defence feature, had been receiving a terrible pasting both from our artillery and from the Desert Air Force. All this did not seem to deter them much and they kept fighting back with everything they had. The fighting, once again, was becoming both grim and nasty.

As can be imagined, 'A' Flight was right in the middle of all this noisy activity, eternally hovering just over the worst spots, intent on putting in our penny's worth and giving the lads on the ground our moral support, if nothing else. The PBI types told us repeatedly that their morale would soar way up whenever they found themselves in a hot spot and one of our box kites put-putted into view. The Jerries had a healthy respect for our powers of observation and quite often would cease firing on them.

By the 20th September 1944, the battle was going fast and furious. With the success of our arms the enemy increased his endeavour to ward off our attacks and brought up all the guns he possessed for this purpose. Our principal role those days was counter battery work. This meant we had plenty to do. That day 'A' Flight took on no less than 18 shoots, all directed at the enemy guns then firing.

The Dawn Patrol chap returned with the news that things were humming. By the time Holy IV and I took off, after partaking of our morning cup of tea, there were wicked eruptions, bumps and plenty of smoke to be seen and heard all over the landscape. We were hardly over the front when we saw flashes coming from a small wood, probably from a troop, and promptly engaged with a Battery of 4.5's. In a moment our shells were dropping nicely into this wood and no doubt did plenty of damage. They shut up for a while.

Later, having finished with this target saw more enemy guns firing fast from a group of houses just beside Route 9, that runs west from Rimini. Normally, the enemy was chary about firing off while we were about, but they must have received a frantic SOS call from their infantry and had no option. Rang up the same Battery of 4·5's, ranged accurately on the houses, an easy thing to do if you are practically sitting over the target, and splashed them thoroughly with five rounds G.F. [gun fire] putting them out of action.

By that time I had been up 1:30 hours and was wondering what there would be for lunch, when I saw the unmistakable dust whirlpool that is blasted up by a Nebel firing. Automatically pin-pointed the spot for immediate destruction, which I proceeded to do with a troop of Mediums, hoping some of the crew would still be near. They usually made themselves scarce before pulling the trigger by remote control. These rockets are somewhat unpredictable in their habits and were wont to blow up in the firing tubes.

By the time this last target was disposed of, it was pretty late and I had flown for more than two hours, so slid down for a quick landing beside the sea at Abissinia for a late lunch.

The other chaps were reporting shoots on vehicles scooting along the roads, no doubt bringing up much needed ammo, tanks nosing around, Nebels and odd guns firing, and we evidently were pulling our weight that day.

It wasn't my turn to fly again until after tea, and we climbed up into the sky knowing that we were headed for plenty of excitement.

The enemy was using Nebels wholesale, causing serious casualties to our forward troops. The situation was becoming serious. The Nebels fire nine six-inch rockets, and devastate a huge area wherever they fall. They are thin skinned and their whole weight is made up of high explosive and the blast effect is tremendous. That day they were definitely our Public Enemy No. 1.

I had been flying around for but a short while when spotted and stonked another Nebel firing from behind a small wood.

Things were far from quiet, but failed to spot any sign of enemy misdemeanours. When it was getting dusk, when conditions become favourable for observing gun flashes, but, on the other hand become steadily worse from the communication point of view and static rears its noisome head , I received a shock. No less than four sets of Nebels and at least the same number of gun groups fired simultaneously from distant points on the landscape. The damage done to our boys on the ground can well be imagined. I quickly ordered a whole Battery of 4·5's to fire "Predicted" that is, without my ranging them, onto a map reference I gave them. With this I hoped to make them hold their fire for a while at least. Meanwhile I called up Control and requested permission to punish the enemy with a greater quantity of guns. Brigade did not take long to reach a decision and, within ten minutes, they authorized me to make use of a "Yoke Target", which means firing every gun in the Corps. At the moment that consisted of five Regiments of AGRA and all Mediums or Heavies.

The infantry must have been yelling for the Artillery to do something about the heavy fire being pumped across by the enemy for HQ to resort to such a desperate measure.

Within seconds of placing the order I had passed down a

corrected map reference, based on the Battery fire I had observed. When so many guns are involved it is impracticable to control the fire from the air. Instead Control takes over, checks on the "Readys" coming through and establishes a time for the guns to fire. A few minutes later I was told to observe at a given time and the belligerent area was soon blanketed by dirty black clouds, heaving and belching as shell burst caused bloody havoc among the gun areas.

All this had taken time and the sun had long sunk behind the mountains of San Marino. It was rapidly becoming dark, a decided and disliked hazard that invariably had to be faced after a hectic evening.

Luckily, our ALG was near the coast and easy to find. As soon as I was satisfied that the target area had been effectively dealt with, I headed for home in a long dive with motor revving near her maximum rpm. As I came over the field saw that they were lighting up the odd tin can half filled with petrol that we used as a flare path and which helped quite a bit. Came in cannily and glided over the trees without touching, but landed rather far up the strip and had to jam on my brakes, pulling up too near the boundary hedge for comfort.

Bob, Aubrey, Scottie, plus most of the Flight, had come to watch me fly in. The last Dusk Sortie was always the anxious one because it usually meant returning to land way past the safe visibility time. The chaps on the ground would gather around the Control set and listen in and speculate on how much longer the chap up in the air would have to remain before he could head for home with a clear conscience.

I can remember many anxious waits, on worse fields than this one, wondering if the chap up could possibly land safely in the dwindling light. Then we would hear the splutter of the idling engine, and the peculiar whistle Austers made as they swept by overhead to appear a while later skimming over the far trees, seeming about to hit them. A split second burst of throttle and she would stagger onto the field and swish down the runway. The chap would climb out of the cockpit, line shoot a bit, then we would all wander over to the mess, if we possessed such a luxury, and drink a much needed drop of *vino*.

THE RAVENNA FRONT, THE BATTLE FOR THE PLAINS OF LOMBARDY

Eclipse for Santarcangelo

The rains came on the 21st September 1944 and low, moisture laden clouds, plus exceedingly sticky runways, not to mention the driving rain, made observation sorties impossible. Although I did try early that morning and managed to stagger off after being pushed by the Erks, ran into thick clouds at 600 feet and, over these, another layer at 2,000 feet. Turned back as things were hopeless.

That day our forward troops entered Rimini and the following day Rigby and I Jeeped it into this town, also a famous bathing resort. We roamed around for a while gazing at all the damage. Rimini was in a frightful mess, it having received a pasting from all angles and, what little remained, had been smashed by the Greeks, first troops to enter this town.

However, by dint of some hunting, we managed to discover and liberate some glassware that had been hidden in the cellar of a house that had since collapsed. This acquisition proved a welcome addition to our Mess where we had been reduced to drinking "*vino*" from cut down beer bottles. We also visited the large and imposing Rimini Hotel, it must have been a beautiful edifice a short while back, with a huge dining room and even larger elegant ball rooms, all very much the worse for wear and draughty. Every single pane of glass was shattered and strewn around the polished floors.

We returned to our ALG for lunch, the weather was clearing slightly and our boys were fighting fiercely, just beyond Rimini. Therefore, as soon as possible, sailed away in Holy to lend a hand. We went up to check the cloud base and found it much too low at 700 feet. Nevertheless, went zig-zagging up the line to see what we could see; which wasn't much as rain was coming down here and there making observation difficult. However, our mere presence was always welcome to the chaps crawling around the ground and the enemy invariably eased off their firing, the cause being credited to us, most flatteringly, with our uncanny eyesight. After stooging

206 *Warlike Sketches*

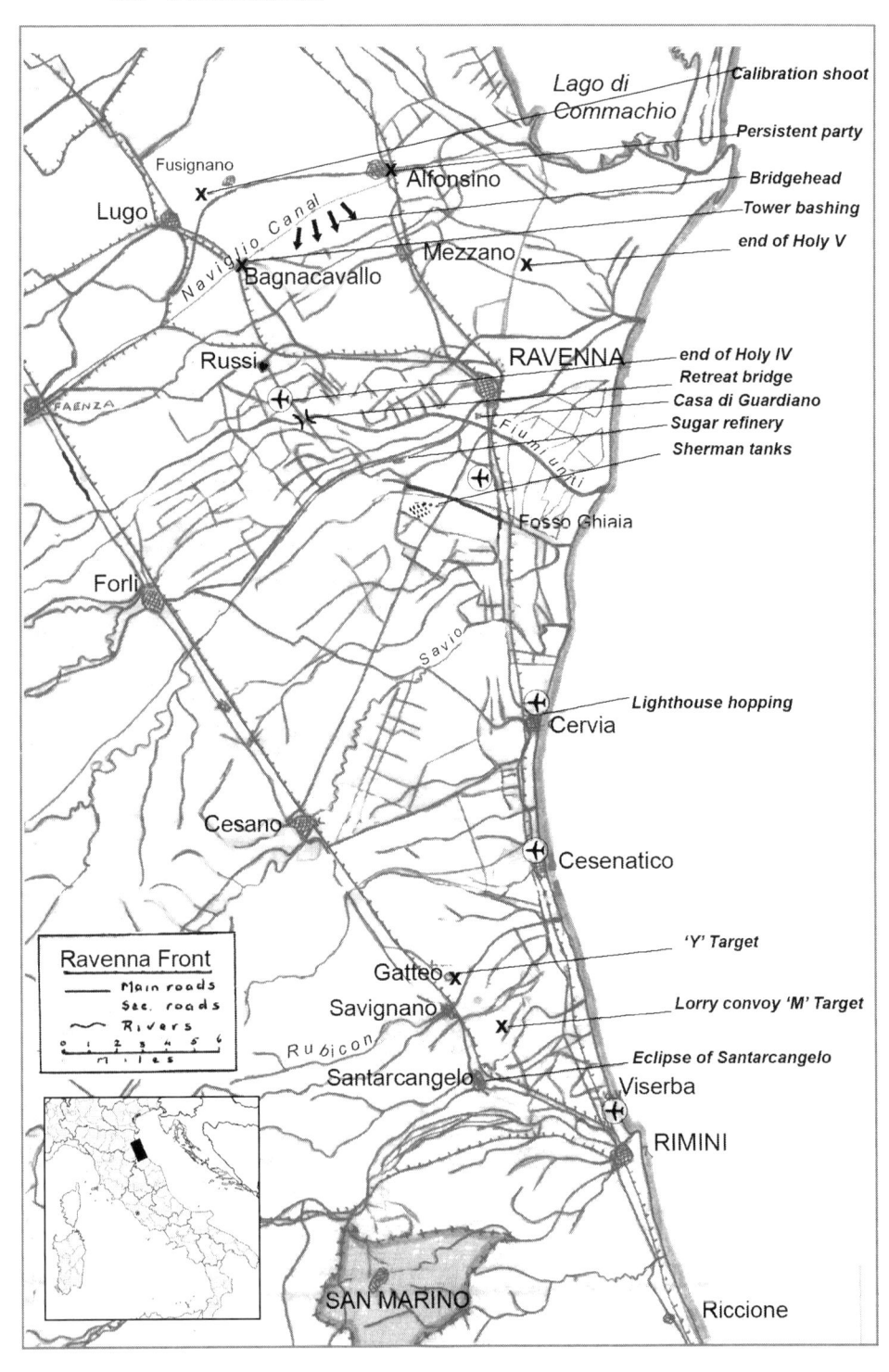

The Ravenna Front

around for 1.40 hours, and seeing nothing, nipped back home for tea.

Later on, the rain stopped and the sky cleared, the weather was improving at last and decided to take off to see if we could put a stop to some of the firing that was causing serious casualties to our forward infantry.

Flew around for a while without discovering any hostile act, although there was plenty of smoke and the flash of bursting shells on the ground. As the sun was going down I began to see gun flashes coming from the outskirts of a small village, at least from three guns firing rapidly; I silenced them with a Battery of Mediums. As this general area had been giving trouble for some time, and the village was a suspected HQ, registered this target accurately for further stonking during the night.

Had been up for over two hours before I could head for home, and of course it was pretty dark by then. As I have already explained these Dusk Sorties finished up far too late. On this occasion, to make things more interesting, there was a gusty stormy wind blowing at right angles to the strip and said strip was ankle deep in mud. Was obliged to approach crabwise to make up for a considerable drift and if one did not kick the rudder-bar hard at the precise instant of touch down, so swinging the plane into the ruts on the muddy runway, the doughnut wheels would dig sideways into the mud and ups-a-daisy, over she'd go. The darkness made it difficult to judge one's distance up, for the fraction of an inch tolerance required for this sort of flying, and chances were pretty slim. However, good old Holy never let me down and would respond instantly to my violent corrections, necessary when flying at such low speeds.

The following day Bob was first up and saw a Don R [despach rider] chasing down a road, obviously with a high priority message, and he amused himself chasing him with one gun, with such skill that he managed to get a burst so near that he knocked the man off the motorbike and laid him out.

Holy Smoke and I only did one sortie, a nice pleasant mid-day one, and had plenty of fun spotting and firing at a SP [Self Propelled] gun hiding behind a hedge, a Nebel firing, and again at the SP gun as it scuttled away to another position. All these in rapid succession, and we were down in just over 1.30 hours.

With the battle again going fast and furious the 24th was a particularly hectic day and the chaps who were up first were taking on targets wholesale and reporting lots of enemy activity. Holy Smoke and I were up fourth. This meant a late lunch and usually doing the Dusk Sortie.

The weather had cleared and visibility was good as we soared into the air before noon. Our troops had recently captured Santarcangelo and were pushing on towards Savignano, an important town on the main railway line and Route 9, both leading on to Forli, Bologna, and all points north

No sooner were we high enough to see into the enemy lines than we commenced observing things and engaging interesting targets, such as Nebels firing, guns doing likewise and towards the end of our sortie a Panther tank that kept roaming around rather aimlessly in quest of a haven as my shells kept peppering his tail. Although I managed to obtain several bursts fairly close none quite managed to hit him.

Returned for a late lunch, then lay down in my caravan for a siesta until tea time. After this, strolled around to the Control Wireless Set to listen in to Scottie's comments as he was then up and it was my turn next. He was doing a shoot at the time. Checked the map reference of the hostile battery he was engaging and marked it on my map as also those taken on by the other pilots. By so doing, if any of these guns opened up while I was up, I could direct the guns right on the target without wasting time ranging by simply giving the Code Number under which these targets were registered.

My "Erks" Wilson and Green did not have to be told when to get my plane ready. By then we had fallen into a simple routine so when Scottie reported he was packing up, Holy Smoke was being wound up. Unless the previous pilot called for help, or Brigade asked for continuous air cover, we normally waited for the previous man to land in case he should have some important information regarding our own troops which could not be given over the wireless. Although each pilot kept the front line on the Flight War Map up to date after every sortie, we could easily jeopardize the lives of our own troops during these fluid front days if we did not know exactly where they were at all times.

As soon as Scottie had landed and had given me the latest gen, I climbed into my plane, an uncomfortable procedure. I really did not fit properly even though I had removed the armour plating which was supposed to protect my sit-upon and back from ground fire. The field we were flying off had dried considerably and take off was normal.

I soon spotted some guns firing, they probably had not seen me coming into the sky, and engaged with a troop, splashing shells all over the target area.

Remembering that I still had to settle accounts with that Panther tank, kept a wary eye out for him. After some searching discovered the bastard trying to hide in the back yard of a house near Savignano and, no doubt, he had orders to counter-attack our boys as they advanced on their present objective. A tank hunt is jolly good fun and is normally carried out with one gun, but after ranging onto him I engaged with a troop presuming that that particular area must be chock-a-block with Jerries, and the added weight of shells increased the probability of obtaining a direct hit.

I was still intent on bagging that tank, when the whole immediate countryside flickered with guns and Nebels firing simultaneously. Promptly let go of everything. Grabbing my map I was able to pin-point the positions of four Nebels and about the same number of groups of four guns. There were many more but my eyes and memory could not cope with them, but I estimated that at least 30 guns and 16 Nebels were involved on this terrific shoot, the heaviest I'd ever seen during this campaign. It probably was the heaviest concentration of fire ever put down by the enemy against the Eighth Army.

As already mentioned, we had recently taken the large village of Santarcangelo. When I looked around to find out what the target had been, saw this place boiling and billowing smoke, red brick dust and dirt as buildings disintegrated. The whole village was still scintillating wickedly with bursting shells and Nebel rockets. Luckily, the majority of our troops were encamped behind the town but our losses must have been terrible inside. The Ities who had come out of their holes, thinking themselves safe, must have suffered too.

I immediately contacted Brigade HQ and gave them a report on the active gun areas and they offered me every gun they had with which to deal with this menace. The Jerries had made the mistake of bunching their artillery rather close together. I expect they had been retreating and just drove a short distance off the main road and went into action for this shoot.

This made it possible for me to group them into two general areas, not too large, and engage one lot with the concentrated fire from three Regiments and the other with two Regiments, all these Heavies and Mediums. This being a Dusk Sortie, it was impossible to engage each enemy position individually and, in any case, speed was essential; it could be presumed that they would move off as soon as possible to avoid our retaliatory action. This sort of shoot takes a few minutes to organise. In order not to waste time, switched the Troop of Mediums I had been firing on the Tank onto two lots of guns that were rather outside the general gun areas I had visualized, and put down plenty of rounds where they surely did the most damage.

With the dusk I commenced to see, all too clearly, the machine gun fire that was directed at Holy Smoke with me inside. How I missed that nice armoured seat! Then some sod opened up with bigger stuff, probably 20 mm and the tracers arched up beautifully towards us and seemed to pass too darn close. As can be imagined, old Holy was jumping about the sky like a cat on hot bricks, mighty necessary to keep one jump ahead of those particular bricks.

Had told Brigade to fire when ready, not to waste time, and "Shot" came over the blower while I was still engaging the second target with the Troop of Mediums. Saw the whole lot fall with a nice spread that covered most of the areas. After firing two rounds from each gun, corrected "East 400" to cover a bit that had been missed out and gave them two or three more rounds. Simultaneously with this "Shot" also came from the other three Regiments and the "stonk" landed so beautifully in the area and must have covered all the remaining guns and Nebel positions, that I gave them a good pasting Scale 5.

By the time I had dealt with that bit of trouble the sun had been down for ages and, once again we had to face the danger of bad visibility. Luckily it was a calm night and we landed nicely.

These Dusk Sorties were pretty grim affairs, what with the excitement of the shoot, seeing shots coming up at you. Then we had to face the nervous strain that came from executing an extremely difficult landing under most adverse conditions. All this played havoc with our nervous system, which was none too good considering that we had averaged something like 250 operational sorties virtually without a break.

Lagoons and Pink Flamingoes

It is amazing how one particular space in time should persist in ones memory for many years, and for no apparent reason.

Bill and I had been trudging through orange groves all day, as was our wont at that time, seeking out a different enemy, the lowly orange scale. We were pleasantly tired and it had been hot.

It was late afternoon and very quiet as we rode back to Bella Vista, Corrientes [*Argentina*], and the doubtful comforts of Saravia's Hotel, in the good old "Surubi."

Past Yataiticalle, running smoothly along the sandy tracks, the swish of the tyres and an occasional splash as we went through shallow lagoons each splash adding its quota to the gray film that covered the once sea green car.

Orange groves either side, for miles and miles. Dark green foliage, golden fruit and a sprinkling of late orange blossoms. In the stillness of the evening their aroma seemed to thicken the air around us.

The sun itself a gigantic orange as it neared the shimmering horizon.

We do not talk, nothing unusual for me but Bill sometimes likes to express himself. Easy to guess of whom he is thinking.

The closely packed orange groves give way to open grass land, with tall feathery palm trees scattered about and a large, sand encircled, lagoon. Maybe it is about a mile across.

Still and mirror like with rushes growing near the shallow shores.

The shady track leads us right to the water's edge and we follow it around.

White storks and pink flamingoes, doubled by reflection, stand about in the shallow water. Some on one leg others headless, asleep, nearby ones take fright, flap their great wings and fly off in lazy circles. But they do not stay up long and land before we are forced to break away from the lake, ruffling the still waters as they do so.

Even the storks glint pink in the rays of the setting sun.

Alligators are also present. Maybe that log floating, half hidden by the reeds, isn't what it seems. Maybe those two dots, level with the water, are crafty eyes watching us.

The tall feathery palm trees, darkly silhouetted against the sunset, lend enchantment to the scene.

We leave the lagoon and are winding through orange groves again.

The sand gets deeper. We are nearing the outskirts of Bella Vista and have to go canny or we will get stuck. Soon we are in the town and grate to a halt outside our hotel.

Fat Saravia is sitting in the patio his fat belly stretching a near white vest. He is sitting on a creaking chair playing cards with some *viajantes* [*traveling salesmen*]. He was in that precise position when we departed that morning.

A quick sluice down and we stroll over to the *cafe* at the corner, sit down at a table set out in the sandy street, and order two large iced beers.

It is cool in the twilight and pleasant.

This scene persists in my memory. Maybe because its quiet peacefulness is such a contrast to the scenes to be seen around here.

It is September 1944 and the guns are rattling the windows of this room in a small Italian farm that is our Flight HQ. The Battle for the Plains of Lombardy is raging. There is no peace here but only War, and it has been like this for a long time.

More Routine Belligerancy

On the 25th September was woken by Powell at an unearthly hour of the morning with a mug of tea. It was my turn to do the Dawn Patrol. It was still quite dark. Not bothering to dress, pulled on my battle-dress trousers over my pyjamas and wriggled into my fleece lined flying jacket and ditto boots. Then staggered off the tail board of my caravan into the mud, and slushed along in the dark towards the landing strip, where Wilson and Greene were swinging Holy's prop to the tune of "contact" splutter-splutter "off", "contact" splutter-splutter, etc., etc.

After a while, and with a modicum of patience, the Lycoming engine, a hard starter as it lacks the impulse starter magnetos of the more trusty Gypsy engine, sprang into life with a roar.

While I waited for the engine to warm up and be given a final check, as also for a glimmer of natural light, mooched over to the dim glow in the wilderness that emanated from the cook-house, to enjoy another cup of tea.

Dawn Patrol was always a delight, once we were safely clear of the trees surrounding the field, we could look forward to a peaceful and pleasant flip, borne on the smooth new air of a day just born. Cast a fatherly eye upon the line of twinkling fires where our lads were brewing their morning cup of tea and went further forward to check that no trouble was coming their way.

After the hectic Dusk Patrol of the day before cruised over and had a good look at the many gun areas I had stonked and one cheeky type had the nerve to fire his gun just as I was hovering over him. Had no alternative but to shatter the morning quiet with a troop of Mediums as one could not allow them to get away with that sort of thing. Visibility was superb and just sat up there enjoying the scenery while I directed a perfect shoot. Everything went like clockwork. The wireless was strength five and clear and the rounds splashed just where they were supposed to fall.

Cruised around for a while after that. The remaining enemy lay exceedingly low and nothing stirred; quite a difference from our side of the lines where fires flared, dust could be seen rising from all over the landscape and bods and vehicles roamed around openly.

After 1.30 hours of gentle flying headed back to base. Then rang up G.3 Brigade [officer responsible for operations] and gave him the latest Gen., marked up our Battle Map and told Bob that nothing stirred. After another quick mug of tea crawled back into my fleabag, it was still early, and snoozed until Powell brought me my shaving water at a reasonable hour.

Was up again after lunch and had quite a party. I managed to spot two Panther tanks moving together down a road leading to the front; obviously up to no good. Engaged immediately with Troop fire and when they saw the nasty crumps from medium shells falling all around them they ran for cover and attempted to hide among some farm buildings. That did not do them much good as I was sitting right on top of them and could see their every move. However the houses offered them some protection and they had to be destroyed before I could get at the Panthers. After several rounds on the houses, and some splashes near the tanks themselves that must have shaken them, tried the nasty trick of stopping the firing for an uneven number of minutes, then sending over a bevy of shells all together, just when one could expect the chaps inside to be out and looking at the treads for possible damage. As the Jerries were invariably methodical types, they could not understand anybody not sticking to the traditional 5 or 10 minutes intervals; and this trick worked quite often.

While this stonk was going on I suddenly noticed something move in a wood close by and spotted the unmistakable form of a large lorry moving. Had it remained quiet I would never have noticed it, so well was it camouflaged, but our sense of sight was so developed that we instinctively noticed the slightest movement within our range of vision.

This was unusual and I became suspicious and went over to have a better look at this wood. Was thrilled to spot a score or so of vague bulky objects spaced along the fringe, as also many black shadows, by no means natural, inside the wood. Immediately reported to Brigade that I had discovered a convoy consisting of, at least, a score of lorries. As I have already mentioned, thanks to our vigilant eyes the enemy was forced to run all their convoys at night and we rarely managed to spot and engage a vehicle. Therefore, made the most of this opportunity.

Brigade told me to make it a "Mike Target", which meant engaging with a complete Regiment of Medium guns. This sort of target is ideal. After a few ranging rounds, which came down well in the wood, ordered scale 5 and in no time at all smoke from the bursting shells was billowing above the trees. Continuous black smoke showed where some vehicles were burning and, undoubtedly, quite a few were unable to move back that night to fetch much needed ammo.

That night the rains came again.

Next morning Bob and I went into the nearby village of Riccione and enjoyed a civilized breakfast at the Officers' Hotel there. Afterwards enjoyed a swim in the Adriatic.

Did only one sortie that day and, strange to relate, did not see a thing worth engaging. Bob, who was on the Dusk Patrol, ran into the usual packet of trouble, the Jerries evidently did not believe we could remain up after the sun went down and would open up with plenty of guns thinking they were safe.

Next day we moved to another ALG near a place called Viserba, north of Rimini. This was far too near the front for our liking and Jerry, hating us intensely, took advantage to shell us good and properly throughout the nights we were there. Luckily no damage was done, except to our nerves. To add to the excitement, a 3.7 inch gun firing over the top of us from a nearby field (we certainly were far up) had a premature, the shell burst in the barrel, which kicked up a hell of a noise. Nobody was hurt.

Actually we had our landing ground right in the centre of the AGRA gun area, and they were busy all night replying to the enemy shelling. This also caused an awful din and was hardly conductive to a peaceful nights sleep. When it wasn't our turn to fly on the Dawn Patrol or on the second sortie we could afford to take things easy, get up late, and shave after breakfast if one felt so inclined. In fact, we were most un-army like.

The following day it was my turn to fly third so took things very easy and did not take off until after partaking of elevenses, knowing that we would be back in nice time for lunch.

Although I looked carefully into all the known gun areas, and kept an eye open for tanks that had been reported on our front, did not see anything of particular interest and returned hungry without having fired a shot.

After lunch crawled into my caravan for a short *siesta* and then helped Hilton check the ignition system of the 3 tonner. Then went across to Control to find out what was happening up front to ascertain what I could expect when I flew off on the Dusk Sortie that evening.

Was on the strip when Bob sailed over the trees to a gentle landing and he said he had engaged some guns firing, but had dealt with them successfully. I took note of their map references, just in case. Climbed into Holy Smoke, squeezed into the seat, taxied to the far end of the small strip, pushed on full throttle and away we went rearing along the muddy ground, unsticking in time to soar over the trees.

We were lucky. Shortly after we were in position to observe, I spotted a large tank heading fast towards a village called Gatteo and promptly engaged with a "Mike Target" at Brigade's request.

They were certainly keen on bagging this chap. The shells fell well in the area and, incidentally, taking chunks out of Gatteo, and the tank changed its line of advance and turned into a farm where it tried to hide behind a haystack. This served him little with me sitting right on top, and I proceeded to hit its immediate surroundings with shells from one gun. With the dusk I spotted some guns firing from about five miles north of Gatteo and ordered another Regiment to engage whilst I finished the tank shoot. I had ordered "fire" on the second target when more guns commenced firing some miles to the east and I placed another lot of guns on this third target. To add to the fun, having then moved rather too far over the front lines for comfort I observed tracers arcing their gentle way towards us, and quickly edged away in the right direction. Holy was weaving most erratically around the sky, I was flying with feet only, my hands being too busy coping with the screechy wireless, message pad, marking maps, etc. and the 20 mm tracers slid harmlessly by.

Gave up the tank hunt and concentrated on the two gun areas that were causing trouble. Once I had ranged, gave them a good pasting with a Battery each, which must have caused considerable damage in their general area. They stopped firing.

Of course it was too dark for safety when I felt we could head for home with a clear conscience. It was a calm evening, the boys had lit the tin-can flares and we got down fine.

During most of that night the enemy kept sending shells over that crumped most unpleasantly in the near neighbourhood. The AGRA guns, all around us, replied and a counter-battery duel went on all night long. The silence of the night was most definitely – NOT. Too lazy to crawl out of my warm flea bag and into the dank uncomfortable slit-trench I cowered under the wishful protection of an army blanket and waited for the one that wouldn' t whistle.

Stormy Weather

Jerry definitely did not like us and thought up many schemes to do us mischief. Although I had sampled many of their hate efforts, I still received a shock when next up, whilst flying low about 100 ft with dirty black clouds whizzing by just above, Holy was blasted upwards by several powerful explosions on the ground just below as Nebel rockets burst. During the same sortie, and flying at tree-top level, found myself going through a quantity of streaks of smoke spiralling down to the ground. Looked up and, sure enough, saw the corresponding black puffs of smoke where shrapnel shells had burst sending nasty bits of metal hurtling down. We certainly led a charmed life and nothing hit Holy. This sort of thing had happened too often for it to be a mere coincidence, and it seemed that Jerry was aiming deliberately at a spot beneath our planes, whenever we were forced to fly low, as in this case.

On the second sortie that day spotted a Panther tank moving along Route 9. Of course engaged promptly, first with a Battery to stop him moving, then at leisure with a troop. It moved off the road and tried to hide behind a tall hedge. They never did seem to realise that this was a useless procedure with us Air OP types hovering overhead but expect this was the correct manoeuvre according to the book, and they stuck to it. Several rounds fell in the immediate area and it was still there when I packed up for lack of fuel.

My third Sortie that day was flown in a regular storm, with rain squalls and bad visibility, which called for tricky flying.

Several tents were blown down that night, causing much wailing and dampness. My caravan was draughty and leaky but it remained all in one piece. Next day we commandeered a nearby, nearly intact house and moved in.

It was too stormy to fly so went off for a long walk along the sea shore towards Viserba. The stormy seas were grand to watch, but I hastened my stride when I saw a big mine just off the shore and about to bump. Whilst I was still too near it did bump, but nothing happened. Must have been one of ours.

Passed by and had a look at the naval guns and concrete emplacements I had fired on some days ago while they were engaging units of the Royal Navy. Found they were 6 inchers and built in 1885.

The end of the month came and it was still raining and taking off from the usual small strip in the mud was decidedly dicey. We never knew if we would pick up sufficient flying speed to rise above the trees.

It was my turn to do the Dusk Sortie. Spotted plenty of guns firing and kept two Regiments fully occupied. Then had to face the nervous job of landing in the dark into a slithery mud in a too small strip.

More Routine Stuff

All this is becoming monotonous and I will just quote direct from my diary:

October 1944.

1st Nothing much doing. Only saw 1 gun and Nebel firing and had three shoots. Lt McCorquadale arrived to be IO (Intelligence Officer) Had a long chat. He was in SAS [Special Air Service] and had done 8 jumps, 2 in Sicily pre-invasion leaving by submarine (McCorquodale was with me in the 95th LAA Regiment in Scotland).

2nd Another rain storm. Sparrows walking. CO disappeared to see MO and found he had jaundice.

3rd George Riley of 'C' Flight now CO. Bob Barrass went to Flight Commanders Conference. Major Purvis G.3 Air visiting us. Things should happen now. On sortie saw car entering house – stonked as enemy HQ.

4th Did Dawn Patrol. Nothing seen, Wells arrived to take over from Bob, who is acting CO.

5th Raining again. Did one shoot and chased a Jerry tank.

6th Hectic Dusk patrol. Guns firing all over. Had 4 shoots. Shelling at night. (They were, and at us)

7th We are not yet over the Rubicon (this river was actually in that area). Did Y Target on Gatteo. SP gun shelling our camp that night. Bricks fell too darn close.

8th Raining again. No flying. Pat Henderson, ex 655 Squadron, arrived as new CO. Major Ingram out at last.

9th THE SIGN OF THE BEAST. It was still raining – no flying – and we were sitting around in our requisitioned farmhouse, when a terrific explosion and debris falling just outside had us scampering. At first we thought it was our old pal the railway gun back on the job. It did not take us long to learn the truth.

Friend Jerry, with his usual nasty mind, had planted a devilish delayed action booby trap in the house next door, and several Teller mines had gone off as the farm folk were having a meal. The blast killed three men and a child outright, wounded four other children taking the leg off one of them. Our Medical Orderly did some good work, and we did the best we could until an ambulance arrived to carry off the wounded. These Ities were paying dearly.

10th Nothing much doing. Jerry again moved an SP gun close up after dark and started firing, searching for us, their pet aversion. Two New Zealand tank boys for dinner. Oysters and roast duck.

11th Jerry has pulled out and is across the Picatello River.

12th Nothing exciting happened, New Zealand boys came along to dinner and we had quite a party till midnght.

13 th All quiet. Only one shoot.

A Spot of Leave At Last

Desert Air Force Brass woke up to the fact that, whereas RAF lads were getting leave after 30 operations, us Air OP chaps just kept on and on, with never a rest and, furthermore, whereas the blue types faced enemy fire during a relatively brief period each sortie and returned to safe bases far from the front line, we were constantly within range of enemy guns, whether in the air or on the ground, and this sort of existence was decidedly detrimental to our nervous systems.

'A' Flight had been at it practically continuously ever since the Cassino Battle six months ago. When Regiments and Divisions pulled out for a rest we had been handed over to the incoming unit and told to keep on with the fighting. Apart from the break we had when we moved from the Florence Front to attack the Gothic Line, we had been flying without a pause except for a few days when visibility was too bad.

It was decided that Air OP pilots would get 15 days rest every 250 hours of operational flying. Scottie was the first to go, having done nearly 300 hours; he was already acting strangely and was a bag of nerves. Aubrey Young also was jumpy under the strain and was pranging kites too frequently. I had done 270 Operational Hours, with about the same amount of sorties, so we were all pleased when news arrived that Bob, Aubrey and self could go on leave.

We decided to head for Florence and on the 14th October 1944 around 14,00 hours, we started off in an ancient utility.

It was a beautiful spring-like day. We sped south along the road to Jesi where we looked up old friends and were invited to partake of *vino* and *salami*. Carried on through a fantastic pass which we had flown through on our move west; it appeared even more impressive from road level. We were still winding our way through it at dusk and it was dark by the time we reached Forli where we were told there was no accommodation. We therefore decided to carry on to Assisi, a weird little village perched atop a hill, made famous by St. Francis. There we obtained rooms at a pretty, minute hotel where a dance was in progress. Our holiday had started.

We left early the next morning and it was grand driving through that beautiful countryside. We found it interesting as we were revisiting old battle-grounds. We reached Arezzo in time for lunch. Then we carried on and arrived in Florence around 17.00 hours in time to check in at the Majestic Hotel, taken over by the Desert Air Force, and enjoy a wizard hot bath before dinner. We promptly went out to see a flick, *Pin Up Girl* it was, and then to a dance at another hotel where we met old pals Piper and Gander.

The following day we roamed around that beautiful city, had lunch at a Club, tea at the Savoy, went to see another show and back to our hotel where a dance was in progress.

On the 17th October, with a couple of New Zealanders and ditto nurses, we squeezed into the utility and headed for Pisa where we climbed to the top of the leaning tower, explored the Field of Miracles, churches, etc. and had a picnic lunch in the open. That place was swarming with Brazilian Army types.

Thereafter we did Florence pretty thoroughly, besides seeing every show we could find time for including *By Pass to Berlin*, a Yank show and pretty good, *Barretts of Wimpole Street* with Brian Aherne and Katharine Cornell, *Jealousy* with Barbara James, and also some good films.

A highlight of our holiday was a really super-civilized dinner party at the Hotel Excelsior, which had a wonderful dining room and a ten piece orchestra gently playing. We had just been to a good show, the *vino* was excellent and army rations unrecognisable. Our party of ten included several New Zealand nurses, all good scouts, and the atmosphere was just right.

After four days Bob and Aubrey decided to carry on to Rome. There was still much to be seen in Florence and travelling to Rome meant losing two days on the move so decided to remain on by myself.

Thereafter roamed around to my heart's content exploring the Ponte Veccio, Santa Croce Church, the famous mosaic works next door, the Duomo, Palacio Veccio, and generally going on long walks through the city and surrounding suburbs.

Met several old friends, one ex the Mountain Regiment, and attended the first concert given by the Florence Choral Philharmonic Orchestra. It was truly impressive, with an 100 piece orchestra and sixty in the choir and it took place in the beautiful Verdi Theatre. Florence had only recently been liberated and the choir was dressed in the weirdest assortment of clothes imaginable; but that did not prevent them putting all they had into their music.

There were a number of Air OP types about, conspicuous with their "wings", and whenever we met we got together and swapped yarns. There were some good and some sub-good night clubs, all patrolled by the MP's. The lowest was undoubtedly "Smoky Joe's," buried in an underground grotto affair, ages old. The "Music Box" had a good floor show and as champagne was cheap we could manage without too frequent visits to the Field Cashier.

Bob and Aubrey arrived back on the following Thursday, the day before we had to head back home.

I took them on a quick conducted tour of the places they should see, according to me, and the next day we departed after lunch. It was raining and we made Perugia by dark, staying at a swell hotel which happened to have a dance organised for that evening.

Left the following morning, not too early, it was around 9.30, and drove through the rain to Jesi, again traveling through the wizard pass, stopping at friend Dario's for a while and made Savignano by dusk. We dined at Squadron HQ and then were guided to 'A' Flight's new ALG and so ended a wizard leave.

We meet Popski and his Private Army

The Eighth Army was moving up Italy fairly fast and when we returned from leave 'A' Flight was at Cesenatico, living in style in a large white building beside the sea that had been a Fascist infant colony, and were using a strip of road in front to land on. On the 16th November we moved on to Cervia, also a coastal town, and there we met Major Popski and his merry men.

Vladimir Peniakoff, alias Popski, was a remarkable person. He had carried out some amazing feats of daring in North Africa where

A page from 'A' Flight 657 Squadron RAF Operational Record Book now held by the Museum of Army Flying in Middle Wallop, UK. This page was chosen because it shows a lot of Arrol's activities and describes a dinner hosted by Popski and staff.

he had set up a HQ in the Jebel area [Jebel Akhdar] south of Derna and organised the Arabs against the enemy, carrying out demolition raids on dumps and aerodromes, practically single handed. The Powers that Be, recognising his worth, eventually agreed to allow him to run his own Private Army which, despite its grand name, never numbered more than some 80 odd men.

Amongst the lesser feats performed by PPA was the reconnaissance of a detour south of the Mareth Line through which part of the Eighth Army managed to outflank Rommel. They were also the first to link up with the American Fourth Army in Algiers. By carrying out sundry raids behind the enemy lines in Italy they managed to create a lot of alarm and despondency, with but a handful of men, creating the impression that a much larger force was operating in the district. This caused Jerry to panic retreating prematurely.

Popski had been born in Belgium of Russian parents, after an English education he had spent most of his life in Egypt where the war caught him working in a sugar refinery. His hobby of wandering deep into the desert in an old model A Ford fondly nicknamed the "Pisspot" fostered a natural flair for navigation which stood him in good stead later on.

I met Popski for the first time on the 11th November when he came along to our ALG with the object of getting an aerial view of the approaches to Ravenna and the state of the roads over which he intended leading his men on the morrow. I was flying an Auster Mark IV with a small seat set sideways in the back of the plane which I had recently used to take up the G3 Partisan forces on a like errand. And so Popski climbed into Holy Smoke III and off we went to tour the front lines. He himself was soft spoken and mild looking of medium height but sturdy. At the time he must have been about 50 years old.

His small force operated with nothing but Jeeps, but these were highly lethal, armed with a 303 machine gun swivel mounted in front, another half inch one at the rear, all around in racks were rows of hand grenades and, for good measure, under the floor they carried slabs of demolition charges. Their pet scheme was to infiltrate through the enemy lines, travelling over the most impossible country in their highly mobile vehicles, then surprising the enemy in no uncertain manner by careering hell-for-leather through a village shooting off their two machine guns and lobbing hand grenades right and left.

His lads were all hand picked and Popski had been granted the privilege of recruiting men from any unit of the Eighth Army. They had a fine disregard for danger. Powell, my batman, made the mistake of expressing curiosity regarding an Italian hand-grenade lying in the rack of Popski's Jeep. The driver obligingly demonstrated its use by pulling out the pin and lobbing it into the middle of the street where it burst with a nasty crack, scaring the odd passer by.

PPA happily raided several farms converted into strong points, but they could not approach one called Casa del Guardiano as it was surrounded by flooded land and glutinous mud. This annoyed Popski no end and he resolved to do something about it. He therefore came along to us, we were known to be able to solve problems by unorthodox means, and he thought up a scheme. It was highly irregular and to my mind most impractical, not to mention unhealthy, but Bob and Aubrey were keen to try it out. The plan was to convert our Austers to bombers by the simple expedient of carrying the bombs on the floor of the cockpit and lugging them out of the window.

Next day Popski and his second in command, Captain Yunnie, came along with a load of old 25 lb. bombs. They flew off with Bob and Aubrey to practice dropping them on the beach.

They were not satisfied with the 25 lb. as too many failed to explode so they decided to load up, for the real attack, with such things as 4.5 inch mortar bombs, PIAT projectiles and ordinary hand grenades as well as a couple of healthier looking 25 lb. bombs. Popski and Bob took off first and flew into cloud at 300 feet. Under these circumstances there was no question of having a look around first before going into the attack. They found the Casa del Guardiano; the farm consisted of a house and a couple of haystacks in the yard each with a shelter dug underneath. Haystacks offer perfect protection against shells and bombs and these shelters were common.

They did their first run in at 60 feet. Popski dropped one 25 pounder which fell short, but exploded nicely. They then turned fast and came in to drop a couple of 4.5 inch bombs. They then observed

Jerries running around below and chased them with more bombs, but by then Spandau's were chattering and holes appeared in the wing fabric. This decided them to run for home.

Aubrey had the unpleasant task of commencing his attack at the height of these harmful activities and he and Yunnie chucked over as much as possible on two quick runs over the farm house at tree top height until they too decided that playing at being a target to irate soldiery with diverse weapons firing from close range was no way to pass an afternoon.

This was really a foolhardy adventure, more so if one considers that the impromptu bombs had their various safety devices removed. This meant that they were set to go off at the slightest jar and a bit of carelessness in pushing them out of the window or even a rough manoeuver would have sent these types sky high.

I met Popski again at the farewell party given when Porter Force broke up. We both belonged to this small Force for special duties. Later I was to support his crowd and Partisan forces on the approaches to Lake Commacchio.

Some days later, Popski set off in his Jeep heading up the road leading north from Ravenna to visit an outpost of the 27th Lancers and Partisan Forces. He unfortunately ran right into the middle of a Jerry attack and was caught on top of this raised road devoid of any cover and had no option but to sit in his Jeep with his driver, Burrows, and fire his machine guns into the enemy as they swarmed across a bridge. A Jerry stopped in full view and calmly proceeded to aim with a rifle grenade. Popski tried to pick him off with his machine gun but the grenade came sailing over towards him. Next he knew his left wrist was shattered into a pulp; despite which he kept on firing until the attack petered out. He then discovered his right hand had also been shot through by a bullet.

Popski was sent to Rome to recover but a short while later he was back on the job, sans a left hand.

We learnt that, after we left Italy for the Belgian and Dutch fronts, whilst PPA was attacking a village near Lake Comacchio, Lt. Ian W. McCallum of Buenos Aires late of the 27th Lancers, was killed when a panzerfaust landed right on his Jeep.

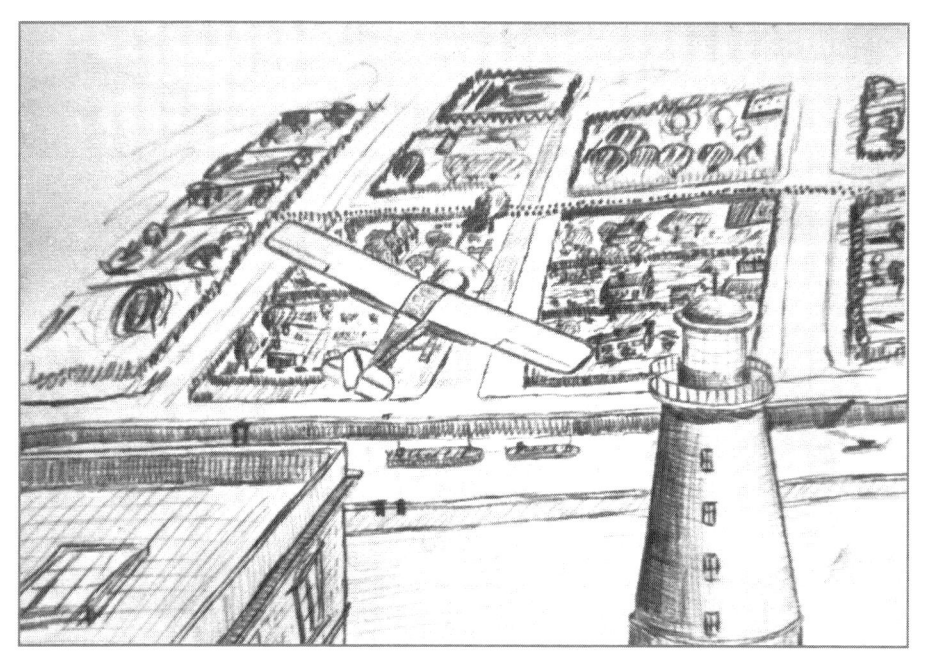

Lighthouse hopping in Cervia - We had to crawl over a four story building, miss a tall lighthouse and then plummet down fast.

Lighthouse Hopping

We had been landing in weird and far from wonderful ALG's in Italy but the one Bill chose for us in Cervia [16 Nov 1944] about beat the band. He had picked a narrow, nine foot wide, strip of road that ran parallel to the sea, through a row of small bungalows. This offered no problems to us ace airmen but it so happened that, to get at this nice level roadway, we had to crawl over a four storey building and miss a high lighthouse, then plummet down fast and at very low speed, always highly dangerous, so as to hit the road urgently because 200 yards along it there was a row of armoured cement anti-tank teeth. Once over the building came the width of a road, a watery cannal and then the beginning of our landing road. From the building to the strip there may have been fifty yards, probably less. To make things more interesting the wind was invariably in or out from the sea, in other words, we landed cross wind. The drill we worked out was to come over the high building with the right wing scraping the lighthouse, the engine roaring at full throttle with the nose away up, literally hanging from one's prop just above stalling speed. Once clear of the roof we would snap off the revs to fall sickeningly fast towards the canal, making sure to catch the plane before she hit the water with a spurt of throttle. Just too bad should the engine fail to respond promptly. We were all really trick pilots by then by dint of saving our necks. It is satisfying to report that none of us ever strained an under-cart at this ALG.

The RAF were running a Communication Flight which was supposed to take over our strips as soon as we went forward but, to date, they had never dared take over any of ours. However, this time when we were about to move on, one of their Austers flew over and we had great fun watching it attempting to land. The pilot, an ex-Fighter Command type, was determined to get in – or else – and attempted all sorts of ways going round three times but he just did not have the knack of losing speed and height at the same time. In the end he staggered over the high building at the point of stall and side slipped down towards the road. But this was still not good enough and he landed too far along it. He sat down nevertheless and applied full brakes but even so we watched him go tearing towards the tank trap. Rather than hit those hard concrete teeth he swerved off the road and deliberately crashed into a tree with one wing, which brought him to an abrupt stop.

Next day the sappers came along and started blowing up the tank obstacle, tooth by tooth, with "beehive" charges. They hadn't bothered to do that for us!

A Mystery Voice Comes Over the Ether

We were friendly with the New Zealand Division boys. They were kind enough to allow us to use their leave hotel in Rome and we had had several pretty good parties, especially with the tank chaps. In the part of Italy we were then working they often found it difficult to make headway through the rough terrain of gullies, hills, rivers and innumerable irrigation canals and ditches, especially when they were being pinned down by anti-tank fire or even by machine guns which prevented them sticking their heads out to have a good look around. At one of these parties we worked out an ingenious scheme which, we hoped, would enable us to help our pals when in difficulty.

A while later Brigade and Control were most intrigued, and somewhat worried, when a mysterious new station came up on our wave length with a call sign of "Cobber" and was answered by another equally mysterious station giving a like call sign, with a voice remarkably like that of the Air OP pilot then flying. The highly irregular arrangement we had worked out infringed umpteen security regulations. It worked like this. When the tank boys found themselves in difficulty they would switch their wireless set onto our wave length, first looking up to see if any of us were flying overhead. We usually were. Politely waiting for a lull in our messages to Control they would come in with "Cobber" as a call sign and ask for help in a most discreet way.

I recall that once, while I was flying covering an attack across a river, three New Zealand tanks were pinned down and unable carry out a reconnoitre commitment to locate a fordable river crossing.

Under the circumstances they either had to turn back or make a suicide dash across the stream, vainly hoping that they would pick a suitable spot for the crossing and not drown. Then it was that "Cobber" piped up and the following mysterious chat was heard over the ether:

"Hullo. Cobber – We are slightly NW of your balcony. Can you get us across the street."

Looking out of the plane towards the NW I saw two lots of tanks not far from the river so asked:

"Hullo Cobber" – "Do you dance in threes or fours?"

"We prefer threesomes" gave me the needed clue. Giving them "Wait" dove down to have a closer look at the river and discovered that about 150 yards west of their present position there was an obvious ford of sorts and could see tracks crossing slantwise to avoid a deep part.

Within a minute of their original query was able to reply:

"Hullo Cobber – Carry on 150 west to dip in Curb and cross street slantwise NE. Should have no trouble with other curb."

To give them a better chance put a troop of 4·5's firing into a nearby wood where an anti-tank gun would obviously be placed if it had to cover that particular ford. As a result of our clandestine chat the three tanks started up, ambled along to the ford, and crossed the river as directed without any difficulty; a job they could not possibly have done by themselves as easily and without harm.

It was a very happy arrangement. Listening in to the guarded back-chat was often most amusing. It must be remembered that Jerry was also listening in. The wizard parties we held afterwards, to talk over the various incidents more than compensated for any trouble taken. We never found out if Brigade discovered the origin of these weird calls, but we wondered.

More Cooperation with the Tank Boys

It came to pass that the tank boys were not finding sufficient targets worthy of their big 75 mm guns and their ammunition was accumulating faster than it could be expended. It was decided, therefore, to use their useful fire-power in an ordinary artillery role. Naturally the Air OP could not be left out of anything as unorthodox as this and, in consequence, I found myself briefed to proceed up into the air and direct the fire of no less than 21 Sherman tanks owned by the 27th Lancers.

The problem I had to face was quite different to that of any normal shoot and no standard procedure existed governing an aeroplane shooting a herd of tanks.

Intrigued by the novelty I dutifully took off from our lighthouse strip and soon sighted the tanks all lined up neatly in three rows of seven, a lovely target for any enemy dive-bomber that might come that way. They were all pointing roughly in the direction of the chosen target, a large sugar-refinery on the outskirts of Fosso Ghiaia which was also scheduled for an attack by the Lancers on foot, the RAF Regiment and Popski's Private Army.

Managed to contact their Control without any difficulty and

asked them to range with a pivot gun. To make their task easier I sat over them and could see what they were up to. However, although they fired on a given map reference I never saw the fall of shot until I asked for "smoke" which I found to be landing miles beyond the target. These guns have a very high muzzle velocity and, for this reason, with their flat trajectory the slightest error in elevation added miles to the range. Ordered the pivot gun to decrease elevation until it was hitting the wall of the factory, then called for a good old blaze away from the whole shooting match. They were all supposed to be pointing exactly the same way as the pivot gun but the visual results belied this as splashes were to be seen in several counties and hardly any on the target.

A little juggling was called for and a while later high velocity shells were perforating the walls of the sugar factory and bursting inside. There were plenty of rounds to be spent and we had a satisfactory party. The tank boys enjoyed themselves and I pleased them by giving a running commentary of the shoot.

It was somewhat unfortunate that a bare 100 yards to the north of this factory stood the famous and ancient church of Sant'Apolinare in Classe, then declared non-military and the refuge of many women and children. I am glad to say that not a single one of our shells hit this sanctuary but, when I inspected it some time later I found hits from shells coming from the other direction, as Jerry deliberately and unethically fired on the tower as soon as they pulled out of the area, and managed to kill several Ities.

I was detailed to fire tanks on six other occasions, our targets usually being rows of houses swarming with Jerries, ideal for this sort of shoot, it was a case of aiming low thus making sure of popping shells through the front door or, should they fall short and ricochet, go nicely into the upper story.

As I fired the 75 mm tank gun as well as the 105 mm gun carried by some Shermans I think I can fairly state that I had, by then, fired practically every type of gun used by the Eighth Army in Italy.

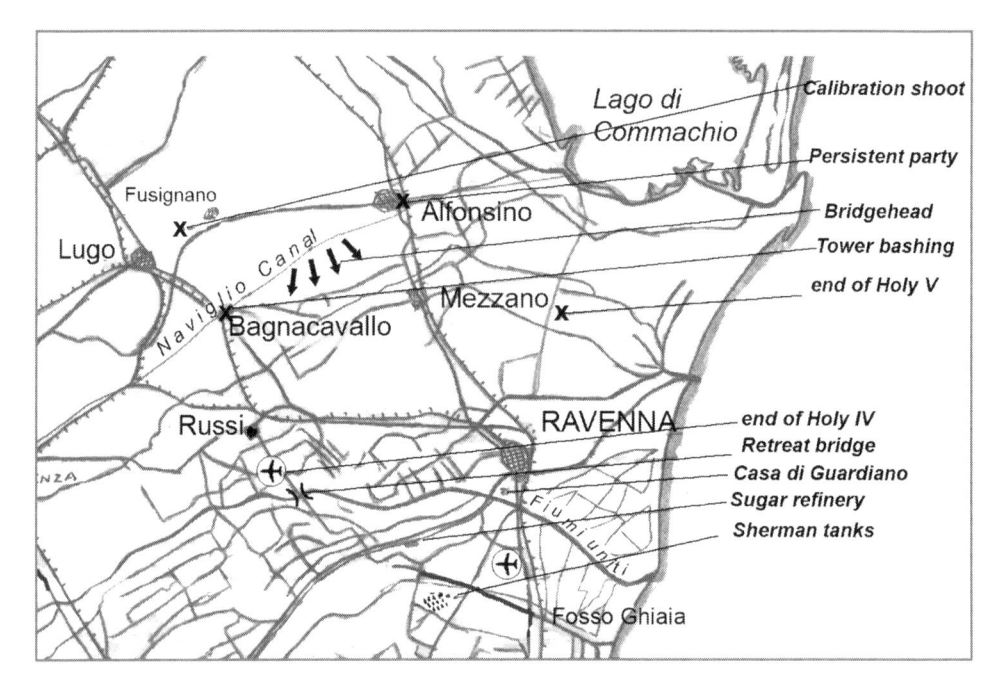

The Ravenna Front – detail

The Fall of Ravenna

We had been within firing distance of Ravenna for some time but mud, swollen rivers, and canals bogged down our advance. Jerry was becoming desperate and hated us more than ever. They invariably opened fire on any Air OP plane flying over the front with their versatile 88 mm dual purpose guns. It seemed we had plenty of luck on our side and despite this usually pretty effective hate no real damage was done, barring the odd hole in the planes' fabric. This is rather surprising considering that these guns are extremely accurate and their bursts are lethal over an area of 100 yards or so.

We were kept busy, at that time, controlling the enemy traffic entering and leaving Ravenna; also dealing with guns caught firing on our forward troops.

On a dusk sortie I left it too late and lost my way returning to the ALG. Discovered in the nick of time that I had gone way past

Cervia and by the time I eventually found the place it was quite dark and had to face a dicey job evading the lighthouse and getting down fast onto the narrow strip. I slid down successfully on my last drop of petrol.

The final assault on Ravenna was supposed to go in at 5 am on the 2nd December 1944 but it was cancelled due to fog cutting down visibility to but a few yards. The attack was launched the following day and this called for another hectic spell of flying for 'A' Flight. We could spot little opposition and our main job was to fire on bridges and to prevent reinforcements coming along.

By the 4th our tanks were entering Ravenna now meeting stiff opposition and I was up in time to see the first one brew up. It was impossible to detect the anti-tank gun that was doing the mischief as it could be hidden in any of the many buildings facing us across the river. The DAF [*Desert Air Force*] bombers were in active support and another of our jobs was to protect them against ack-ack fire by firing with our artillery on the AA areas. The enemy had a large concentration of 88 mm guns on this narrow front and, whereas they did not have much success with us, we saw them bag quite a few fighter-bombers. A Mitchell came down not far from our ALG the crew managing to bail out before she crashed. To add variety to the bellicose scene, one evening we saw one of our Spitfires come at our ALG in a graceful dive and, as we watched, a bomb was released that burst with a most unfriendly crump but 50 yards away from us.

When we spotted and reported Jerry blowing up bridges in their methodical way we knew that the battle for Ravenna was nearly over.

A couple of days later Scottie and I spent an afternoon exploring that ancient town and visiting Dante's tomb. It was not much to look at from outside but exquisitely beautiful within, made so mainly by the windows of translucent alabaster. We also visited the Basilica of Sant' Apollinare Nuovo this being the "new" church of that name, it only dated back to 500 AD.

A posh Officers' Club was opened in Ravenna and we were able to organise as well as join some pretty good parties held there.

A Spot of Panic

For the first time, as far as I can recall, actual steps were taken to cater for a possible retreat and a "retreat bridge" was built over the Fiumi Uniti south of Russi where we then had our ALG.
Visualising a long stay now that the rainy winter season had arrived, the CO had decided to concentrate the whole of 657 Squadron on this strip which boasted a luxurious coconut matting laid over its length, a pleasant change from our normal variety of mud ones.

The Eighth Army had succeeded in putting a bridge-head across the Naviglio Canal but on the 16th December 1944 the best of the German Army put in a vigorous counter attack. By best I mean our old friends the Panzer Grenadiers, Herman Göering Regiment, Paratroop Regiment, etc. and they most certainly knew how to fight.

For some time now it had been painfully apparent that the more we advanced and lengthened our lines of communication, the balance of belligerent power of the two opposing forces, pretty nearly equal numerically, tended to favour the enemy. This attack, therefore, caused everyone much anxiety and a spot of panic ensued.

The enemy had chosen an excellent moment for their strong counter-attack, when visibility was extremely poor and the low ceiling could be depended upon to keep the dreaded "Eyes of the Army" grounded.

As soon as we received the bad news, despite the bad weather and low ceiling, Scottie took off to lend a hand. He was forced to fly at tree top height but managed to reach the salient there to discover a regular mix-up with a full scale tank battle being fought. The battle was so involved that he dared not bring fire down and therefore, had no alternative but to sit over the battle and await a favourable opportunity to get in his penny's worth. He was not at all happy with the situation. The Jerry tanks would insist on firing their machine guns at him, generally acting unfriendly. Aubrey Young was up next and he experienced much the same difficulties and returned with both wing struts hit and damaged. He was lucky in that they did not collapse. Next on the job, I found the scene most interesting as the bad visibility and ensuing darkness accentuated the battle scene, making more visible the gun flashes and tracer bullets that darted wickedly about. Every now and again some would curve gracefully towards me as some sod had a go at Holy Smoke wriggling around at a mere eighty yards or so over the battlefield, this being the highest I could go without putting my head into the scudding clouds overhead.

Throughout that day the battle raged and we dared not fire a shot with our AGRA guns, but the infantry gave the tanks what support they could with their 25 pounder guns and anti-tank rifles. Ted Wells, a newcomer to 'A' Flight was the last and, as usual, everyone was listening to the Control set this being the dusk and critical sortie. He was on the air around 16·20 giving a routine report and then nothing more was heard from him. Just after 17·00 hours a report came through that a plane had fallen in flames. Just in case we hopefully set off flares and Very lights to guide him in. Time passed with no sign of his plane and when his maximum endurance limit had lapsed we had no alternative but to presume that the plane reported crashed was his. A rather despondent bunch of pilots wended their way to the farm-house that was our mess at the time. A short while later the glad news came through that Ted had forced landed not far away. Bob went to his rescue in his Jeep, it was his kite he had been flying, and found the chap comfortably ensconced in a farmhouse digging into fried eggs and *vino* which the farmer had produced. He said he had been hopelessly lost following the battle and, unable to get his bearings, headed south and landed in the first large field he could find. Those two came back via AGRA where a humid stop was made at their Mess. The next day the plane was flown off the field by Bob without any damage.

Luckily our tank boys and infantry were able to cope with the fierce counter-attack and we were not called upon to beat a hasty retreat as could well have been the case under the circumstances.

The End of 1944

Some rather unwise person, hearing there was strong resistance from a largeish town called Bagnacavallo, gave orders that our artillery should proceed to destroy all probable OP's and I was given the job. This town, like many around these parts, had several ancient towers rising above the houses which were obvious targets. It was a pleasant day, cold but sunny, when I took off after breakfast. My assignment was silly, any experienced gunner should know how impossible it was to knock down massive brick-work with shells, but as far as it went it was a "piece of cake" especially as I had chosen a huge 7.2 inch gun of the 61st Heavy Regiment with which to do the job; this gun sends over a hefty shell with a terrific splash. As I said, the job was easy but the results meagre. Even those huge shells hardly made an impression on those ancient but thick walls of the medieval towers. Many a time I was obliged to delay the fall of a shot until the cloud of blasted brick-dust cleared. This job kept me busy all day and, in the end, although the towers were much the worse for wear, they were still usable for OP work if somewhat draughty.

The weather broke and sleet and snow became commonplace. Despite this, from the 18th until the end of the month I did eleven sorties and took on 21 shoots, four of them with whole Regiments, at guns firing. Bridges were a favourite target. They were much in use and destroying them annoyed the enemy.

We had several parties as the festive season approached and on Christmas Day started off with a Visit to 'C' Flight" then back in time to look after our boys, feeding them and wining them as per time honoured custom. The officers were in honour bound to accept the numerous toasts offered us by the lads and by the time the plum-pudding came round several of us were more than jovial. In the end Bill and I were the only ones able to tuck in and enjoy a wizard feast of turkey, pork, etc. with all the trimmings, the others having lost consciousness long before. These types revived around tea time and started off again and kept it up till midnight.

Luckily, Boxing Day turned out to be real duff with "sparrows walking" so we were able to sleep in and recover.

Whenever I could I would go for a long walk around this pretty countryside, even though it meant trudging through snow and slush. On one of these I saw a Spitfire come spinning down out of control. At about 800 ft it straightened out then did a half-roll, the usual drill for baling out. Something went wrong, maybe the hatch stuck or the pilot was too badly wounded and he did not make it. The Spitfire went into a steep inverted dive hit the ground quite near to where I was with a sickening crunch and burst into flames. There was nothing I could do about it so proceeded with my walk.

We kept flying whenever the weather permitted and kept up a fair average as regards parties.

'A' Flight was invited to Squadron HQ for a party on New Year's Eve but we returned to our Flight in time to see the New Year in with our boys.

The Beginning of 1945

After the party, which finished in the early hours, I was unfortunate in being the first pilot to fly in the New Year and was up before the sun doing a quiet uneventful sortie and it was not surprising that I did not see a thing. I was also stuck with the Dusk Sortie this time spotting a group of guns firing which I promptly engaged with all the guns of the 2nd Canadian Medium Regiment.

For some time now we had remained stable, in fact, we had moved to our present ALG on the 13th December and the pattern of our operations was vastly different to that which we had become accustomed to when we were forever on the move.

It was then mid-winter. The weather was usually foul and heavy rainfall had filled the hundreds of rivers, canals and deep drainage ditches that criss-cross this area making it extremely difficult for our forces to advance, hence it seemed likely that we would remain stable on this front until the spring.

For the first time since Cassino we were able to make use of air photos marked up with gun areas which had been spotted by the Survey Corps by means of their flash spotters. If we took on these gun areas early in the morning after they had been spotted, it was likely that some damage was done.

Apart from these photo shoots, which kept us busy in the early morning, we found plenty of other things to do. Vehicles were seen to move with greater frequency in the enemy rear areas, bridges were always available for stonking as the enemy persisted in rebuilding them during the night and, as usual, the last sortie could be depended on to produce an exciting duffy with guns firing from several spots and the odd pretty tracer arcing towards the chap then up. And of course the usual hazard of having to land after dusk had to be faced.

Because of the weather we were unable to fly every day and advantage was taken of these non-flying days to go into Ravenna, which now boasted a couple of good cinemas, to do a flick. The Officers' Club there was much frequented and many a shindy was had. On one occasion the gaggle of Air OP types then present were slung out by the MP's with much lack of ceremony.

The End of Holy Smoke IV

As I have already related, it was a point of honour with us of 'A' Flight to fly whenever it was humanly possible and we would take off into any weather provided the ceiling was higher than the trees and visibility fair enough for us to do some good at the front.

On this particular day, the 19th January, it was my turn to fly and I had been waiting all morning for a chance to take off. Nobody had been up since the 12th when I had done a weather test without success, not having been able to see a thing. Since then fog had descended and stopped all air activities. Consequently we were receiving reports from the PBI that the Jerries were obnoxiously active, taking advantage of our hovering absence, to put in numerous attacks, some on quite a large scale. It was imperative that something should be done as soon as possible. When I saw that visibility was improving around noon I told my lads to get my plane ready.

The sun had not been seen for days and it was freezing cold even at midday. Decided to take off at 13·00 and was all ready with the plane warmed up when a sudden cross wind hit the ALG. This was nothing unusual and proceeded to take off regardless. The strip we were then using, the one with coconut matting, was about 30 yards wide and protected on either side by tall elm trees. Consequently the cross wind did not affect the plane really until we were barely airborne, when we received the full benefit of its force as it came tumbling in a turbulent mass over the trees, just when we were struggling to gain height and speed, at the same time hovering just over the stall. However, we made it.

First of all I checked the ceiling and found it a surprising 1,000 feet up, good enough for observing. Then headed for the front where some trouble had been reported. Was flying over Russi when we ran into rain and such was the cold it immediately froze on my windscreen, blacking out all forward view. This made things awkward. To make matters worse I noticed ice forming fast on the struts. Without a doubt it was also forming fast on the leading edges of the wings of like airfoil section. There was nothing to do but to turn back as I could not be of much use under the circumstances. However, whilst normally one can get out of a rain storm by turning through 180 degrees, it was evident that this rain storm had broken over me. The trick did not work in this case as it was already raining all over the landscape.

By then the sluggish controls warned of a dangerous increase in the weight of ice. The altimeter was showing an alarming rate of descent. By increasing the throttle setting to FULL managed to cancel out this sinking feeling. It seemed we were in trouble and getting Holy back down on the ground this trip was going to be rather awkward.

The stalling speed by then was obviously several times higher than normal. I dared not check it by cutting the engine, scared that the plane would go into an uncontrollable spin; which was more than likely. I guessed that Holy would fall out of the sky at anything under 60 mph. Considering that we had to land at less than 30 MPH to avoid hitting the trees at the end of the strip, there was no doubt about it that poor Holy Smoke IV was doomed to end her days in the very near future.

To add to our difficulties the windscreen was completely iced over and I was obliged to steer by looking out of the side window and into the raging rain storm.

At last I saw the ALG and gingerly manoeuvred until the strip was slightly ahead and to port, where a gentle turn and a controlled glide would get us in.

Holy was handling like a waterlogged boat, sluggish, slow and likely to sink at any minute. By then I was convinced that we were going to crash. How badly remained to be seen and depended on what feverish skill I could impart my piloting over the next few minutes.

The wind was now blowing at gale force and right across the landing ground thus creating a dangerous cross wind and turbulences at the critical height where we had to do our final approach. The plane, at full throttle, roared along slowly and crabwise as I endeavoured to line up on the strip. To see better I had stuck my head out of the side window and the freezing rain was hitting my face hard and painfully. It was difficult to see what lay ahead. The report that we were returning had been sent and I took off my earphones as I had found that I could fly with greater skill if my hearing was unimpaired.

And so we crept slowly towards the strip, battling all the way with the elements. While still quite a way up the tumbling air knocked the plane around affecting her aerodynamic efficiency and this set her sinking faster than intended even though our airspeed was around 70 mph and the engine was at full throttle. As we descended flying got worse, despite frantic juggling with the controls and the use of flaps. Holy would simply not respond and kept going down like a lift. I felt pretty hopeless at that moment.

The road that edged the strip loomed ahead and I pulled in my head smartly to avoid it being chopped off. Had a vision of trees swishing by, then the horrible rending sound of a crash as the under-cart hit the ditch and was left behind and the rest of the plane hurtled itself against the thick hedge. With bits and pieces flying around and the sound of rending metal Holy smashed through and went careering along on its belly in the slithery mud heading fast for the line of picketed planes. Luckily the line of slither was curved. A wing tip hit a tree and we swung round to stop jarringly with her nose against another, where she came to rest.

There was no sign of fire, hardly surprising with the rain coming down in buckets. Had switched off somewhere along the line, couldn't remember when, and that helped of course. I could not get out as the door was stuck so connected the wireless and reported, should Jerry be listening in, that Holy wasn't feeling so well and would be resting a while.

The lads had come to the rescue and were swarming around by then and they helped me out. Poor Holy Smoke IV was in a sorry mess, all twisted and torn and a complete write-off. I was OK except for sore knees and bruised shins. The ice was still thick on the wings, what was left of them, and that told the story.

Inspected the tracks we had made and it shook me to discover exactly where we had hit. It was only by a miracle that the engine had missed burying itself in the ditch in fact, had we hit but a few inches lower we would have dug into the ground there and then with most regrettable consequences.

And that was the end of the third of my War Planes and the second real prang since taking up this flying business.

From then until the end of January, despite the rough and frigid weather, flew on 11 sorties and carried our a total of 21 shoots using a spare plane borrowed from Squadron HQ.

Not so Sunny Italy

Sunny Italy did not live up to its name and, in fact, the long persistent winter was really miserably cold and wet with scarcely a glimmer from the sun.

We were living mostly in our caravans as we crept up the length of Italy. These were really Chevrolet 3 ton trucks with steel floor and sides with canvas atop. They had very roughly been converted by our own efforts into rudimentary habitats. The final results were a most refreshing combination. With the prevalent humidity, it rained most of the time, everything inside was cold, clammy and damp, this included all our clothes. Getting up in the early morning was an unpleasant operation.

My Section possessed a kitchen stove. A small highly inefficient, smelly, two burner pressure job. This I commandeered to ease the frigidity off an evening and so that I could enjoy a spot of reading after going to bed. Had rigged up a couple of bright lights off a wireless battery. Snug in my flea-bag lying on three folded blankets and several layers of *Mundo Argentino* sent from home, this would absorb the frost coming up from the steel floor, and with two blankets on top plus wearing thick woollen stockings, my fur lined flying jacket worn back to front, and head stuck into a balaclava helmet I could enjoy a read in relative comfort while listening to the patter of rain on the canvas roof and, of course, the ever present sound of battle.

Once I had put out the stove the cold would invade in seconds and the temperature would be about the same inside as out. It was understandable, therefore, that people would prefer the dubious and wishful safety of their flea-pits to that of a soggy slit-trench whenever the enemy would decide to send nasty shells wailing and moaning into our area.

For months on end the temperature was freezing, and under. Beer kept in a cupboard alongside my bed, despite its alcoholic content, would freeze solid.

While we were encamped for around a fortnight in the same place, a family of ducks became friendly. They would appear each morning whenever I commenced shaving standing on the tailboard of the caravan. They had noticed that after shaving I would empty the canvas basin onto the ground, and they would promptly dig in and gobble up the soapy but warm water. The reason was that this was the only wet water available all the rest being frozen. In fact the ice in the ditches was several inches thick, and every puddle was frozen solid. This friendly ritual lasted throughout our stay at that place.

Whereas we complained bitterly about the cold it must be remembered that the PBI were a darn sight worse off, especially those who were caught up in the mountains.

The Ravenna Front 243

LAC's Wilson and Green with Holy Smoke V

Aubrey Young, LAC Worral with Rover, LAC's Davies and Penney, and Sammie II.
Arrol standing on the right, in the mud of an Italian winter, San Pancrazio January 1945.
Photo courtesy of the Estate of A. C. Young via VF.

We Christen Holy Smoke V

Having finished off my third War Plane, the kind RAF sent along another to take its place. This was a Mark V Auster, more or less the same as the previous one but with a third seat at the back. A chap from Squadron HQ flew her along to our ALG at Russi on the 21st January and I took off after lunch to try her out doing an observation sortie at the same time. Chucked her around the sky a bit and she behaved fine.

The front line by then was decidedly static and we made ourselves comfortable at Russi patiently awaiting winter's end.

Ted Wells, a new type, went up one windy day and not having our experience he did not dare attempt to land with the violent crosswind that was blowing. I was around at the time, realized he was in difficulties and came to the rescue on the blower advising him to try out HQ landing strip, a larger affair than ours. After a while he returned and reported that he could not find the HQ strip and had only some ten minutes petrol left. Advised him to head due west where he might be able to find the Ravenna aerodrome which covered a huge expanse of land. He made it.

Scottie turned up from Naples where he had been to attend Gunner T's Court Martial. This man had been his batman but had deserted just after Cassino when our camping ground was being used as a target for the first time by Jerry. Evidently his nerve broke and he fled to a safer spot. A rather grave misdemeanour which, in the past, would have called for action by a firing squad. His was the only case of desertion we ever had.

One fine day, having invited a Sergeant from the 5th Canadian Medium Regiment to come along for a flip, ran into rain and a real scare as my windshield promptly froze over and ice started to form on the struts. Mindful of our recent accident I became uneasy. We had, however, a bit more ceiling than last time and was able to do a peel off for warmer climes down below. Was relieved to see the ice disappear.

Right then spotted a gun area and rang down to the boys of the 15th Heavy Regiment to do their stuff and commenced putting down 7·2 inch shells in that area. Had forgotten all about my passenger until strange static, seemingly coming over the wireless, had me puzzled. Then I realized it was the Sergeant being sick; the horrible noises that accompanied such doings being transmitted via his laringa-phones, strength five and warbled. Should have warned him that on these trips of ours we never flew straight and level.

A Persistent Jerry Working Party

Took off on a sortie after lunch on the 30th January 1945 with the intention of engaging a gun area marked on a photo flash-spotted the previous night.

While I was gaining height to get into position to look into the area was surprised to see quite a crowd of men, about 50 strong, marching down a road leading to Alfonsine. Could not let them get away with that sort of thing so promptly engaged with 4·5 inch guns of the 2nd Medium without bothering to range. This meant that a fair number of shells would drop out of the sky without any warning. These guns had been firing from their present positions for some time and their coordinates were accurate and the stonk came down about 50 yards plus of the party. Watched them scatter fast, taking shelter in shell holes and nearby buildings. Changed to the 15th [Canadian] Heavy Regiment and asked them to put two of their 7·2 inch guns on the job and whiled away the time before tea demolishing the houses these chaps had entered. The near misses splashed amidst the others cowering in their shell holes.

When I went up the next morning had a look for my party and, would you believe it, there they were busy as bees reconstructing a bridge over the Senio not far from Alfonsine that Kitty bombers destroyed. Naturally, could not allow them to work peacefully in full view of an Air OP plane and had a 4.5 Troop plaster them for a while, breaking up the party. Told the guns to send over a couple of shells on that bearing at odd intervals for the rest of the day to ginger them up. On that flight engaged two hostile batteries causing trouble.

The following day went up after lunch, this time taking aloft as passenger Major Wright of the 2nd Canadian Medium Regiment with the idea of showing him how his guns were firing. In that flat country he had not seen a round fall in ages and his guns were not firing too well. Naturally, my first look was to see how my old friends were getting along and darned if they hadn't nearly finished that wooden bridge they were building, despite the shelling they had received for their pains. Now a decent bridge is a dangerous thing as it means the enemy can switch their tanks around with ease and, as I have already mentioned, the balance of the opposing armies was pretty even. So the Major had to wait until I settled my little quarrel. For this particular job chose the good old heavy guns because of their accuracy and whopping shell. They were firing well and in no time the single gun I was using was properly lined up and went to fire for effect with five rounds. At that moment, the now familiar sound of gurgling static came over the wireless and, sure enough, poor old Major Wright was being violently sick; not at all pleasant whilst tied up with divers straps and lacking the needful to do it into. By that time was receiving the report of "shot" from the guns and was pleased to see three rounds fall on the embankment on the far side of the bridge, presumably damaging the supports. We both cheered when the remaining two fell plumb in the middle and the bridge disappeared. The Major was most impressed. Bridges are notoriously difficult to destroy with artillery.

After that ranged his 4·5 guns on a railway bridge over the Senio that had been damaged but was being used as a temporary foot bridge. Although we used a whole Battery of guns on this job we did not manage to damage the bridge at all. However, the shoot served its purpose as the Major had taken careful note of every fall of shot and could now correct the lay of his guns.

The next two days were non-flying with the ceiling down to the ground and raining. Took the opportunity of visiting the 19th Heavy Battery and watch their 7·2 inch guns firing. Went along in Elsie taking Hilton and Green with me. Found the Battery billeted in a farm with their guns in action nearby. One was sited in the farm yard itself and was about to fire on Aubrey Young's orders. He had ventured up despite the weather. We stopped to watch it do its stuff. These guns are so huge and powerful that instead of having the usual spade trail that would dig into the earth and a hydraulic recoil system, as is usual with normal guns, it had no spade at all depending on a weird and wonderful method to take up the tremendous shock of discharge. This consisted of a sort of wooden ramp shaped somewhat like a half moon that was placed behind the two huge pneumatic tyred wheels and the gun was supposed to career up these until the recoil force was expended, then slide back again to its original position. However, whilst behaving fairly well with low charges on firm ground in this case Aubrey had called for "supercharge" and the farm yard was knee deep in mud. We stood at a safe distance to watch.

With the first two rounds the heavy gun tottered dutifully up the ramps which wobbled and threatened to slip sideways, but didn't quite. When the gun eventually came to rest after its little journey, it invariably finished up a few feet away from its original position and had to be re-laid again. The ramps, heavy things, would be manhandled until they lay correctly behind the wheels.

The third round went off and this time the gun skidded at the start, ran up the ramps askew, jumped off when half way up and went slithering across the farmyard, knocking a large chunk off the corner of the house and eventually stopped some 30 yards from its firing position. The poor gunners had to manhandle the beast back again through the mud, an awful job, rig up the ramps and only then were they ready to carry on with Aubrey's shoot. This lengthy pause in the firing had happened to me several times in the past, while I had fussed and fumed at the delay. Now, knowing the cause, I would be more patient with the "Heavy" boys in the future.

The End of Holy Smoke V

The Canadian AGRA had recently received a batch of a different type shell with a lighter fuse ring to be used specially for airbursts, that is bursting in the air thus splashing a nasty lot of steel onto the ground below.

A change of weight alters the ballistics of a shell and it was necessary to re-calibrate the guns. This job is normally carried out at a firing range but we were at war and what better place to do this sort of thing than the enemy lines, where two birds could be killed with one brick. And so it was decided that the versatile Air OP would be given the job and I was chosen to carry it out. There being room for a passenger in our new planes Major Young, CO of the Battery we were to calibrate, decided to come along and have a look at the first shoot. Sunny Italy had been anything but, the ALG was a quagmire and it was necessary for four Erks to man-handle Holy onto the strip.

The coconut matting was so soggy that though the engine was pulling at full throttle we failed to get going and once again the Erks had to push us. All this no doubt used up an appreciable lot of petrol.

It was a pleasant day for a wonder, with excellent visibility. We chose a flat bit of country SW of Lugo, with a white farm house in the middle as our target area. It did not take long to get the shoot under way but the tedious job of ranging each gun of the Battery, one at a time into a verified short bracket, lasted a long time. Actually took 1 hour and 45 minutes. Major Young was satisfied with the visual results which, incidentally, made rather a mess of the farm house and a rail junction nearby. We still had around 45 minutes flying time, or so I reckoned, and decided to fly NW along the front line. The petrol gauge marked a quarter tank and thought we could safely see if all was well.

Naturally we waltzed around, our kites were always in season to Jerry. We were approaching Lake Comacchio when all of a sudden the engine spluttered. A rapid glance at the petrol gauge showed we still had some left, sufficient to get us safely back, but the engine nevertheless stopped.

So there we were, sitting in a flimsy silent little plane right over the front line; feeling rather silly. There was no option but to head as far into our own lines as possible hoping to find a decent place to land. This was not at all an easy matter as the ground underneath had been fought over for months and was pitted with deep shell holes all filled to the brim with rain water. The Ities do not believe in wasting land and all the fields thereabouts had the usual rows of vines strung between rows of tall trees. Once again we were in trouble and sure to come to a sticky end with all that mud around.

We had been flying rather high, about 2,000 feet and were therefore able to glide a fair distance before I became acutely aware of trees passing close underneath. There was no object in worrying about picking the best landing ground, they were all equally bad. The wind had been behind us and this helped us glide away from the enemy who could be depended upon to shell us the minute we touched down. And so we were flying downwind, along the length of the narrow fields. Soon I could estimate more or less where we were likely to hit and picked out three possible strips, side by side, each bordered by trees of uneven heights. I had, of course, to turn through 180 to land into wind. When abreast the far corner of these fields, I jerked the aircraft sharply left. There was no room for gentle flying, now I was at right angles to these fields and one more left turn would get me in, but had to really judge mighty carefully. If we turned in too soon we would be too high and would not be able to touch down before we hit the trees at the end of the short field. If we left it too late the necessary sharp left turn with one wing dipping far down would, like as not, hit a boundary tree with regrettable consequences. And doing it just so, would land us in the mud.

With a passenger up we were coming down like a lift. Although it was evident the far field would suit us best, it was unploughed and our height would be just right, a high elm loomed ahead and prevented us reaching it. There was no option but to make another violent turn and land in the middle field that was ploughed half way along its short length.

Never came out of the turn as deliberately kept the plane askew with one wing away down in a violent sideslip desperately trying to lose height and speed. Things happened fast. We were but 30 yards from the far trees when we touched down hard. Of course we had reached the ploughed land by then. The small doughnut wheels squelched deep and hadn't a chance to roll and we tripped up. The engine hit the mud, dug in and we slammed to a violent stop, with a loud noise of snapping and bending tubes and rending fabric. My poor knees, it was quite a jolt. Am sure we broke all existing records for short landings having slid a bare yard from touch down, and the poor young plane was bent beyond repair.

My passenger received a nasty dig in the ribs as he was sitting sideways in the back seat. Tried the wireless to advise Control of our predicament but it was useless. Then we nipped out of the plane in a hurry and did not linger near, but hurried away just in time as shells commenced crumping around.

Another amazing coincidence occurred here. Although we had glided haphazardly our only aim being to put as much distance between the enemy and ourselves with little regard to our whereabouts, we had, nevertheless landed but a couple of hundred yards from Major Young's caravan, where we repaired to settle our nerves with a couple of the real stuff. There Powell found me in due course and drove me back home.

This little episode brought me a "Red" endorsement in my Logbook, my first and last. Highly uncalled for I thought under the circumstances, my flying time and petrol gauge justifying the extra trip to the front, but did not bother to complain as these "Red" endorsements were considered honourable; no Log Book was considered complete without at least one.

We Help the Backroom Boys

The Backroom boys had invented another new type of shell for the heavy guns. The corresponding Range Tables had not yet been completed and it was necessary to carry out a calibration shoot if these shells were to be used in action.

As vast experience and great accuracy was called for naturally the Powers that Be insisted that the job be given to the Air OP and, for obvious reasons Aubrey Young and I were chosen for the job.

And so it was that on the 13th February 1945 commenced the shoot with 5.5 inch guns belonging to the 3rd Canadian Medium Regiment, using Major Hickson's Battery.

I took off first and started the series of shoots using a gun with a new lining and firing Charge IV. From a gunner's point of view such a shoot was ideal, the OP could not be better, high up and comfortable with the target area in plain view. The target, naturally, was well inside enemy territory. The weather was clear and the whopping size of the shells guaranteed a big and visible splash. A "piece of cake" in fact.

By this time we had become *blasé* and found the job tedious and lengthy. The pivot gun had to be taken to a v.s.b. (verified short bracket) which meant an average of seven rounds, followed by ten rounds more from each of the other guns in the Battery laid on the same range, bearing and angle of sight. Then each "splash" had to be marked carefully on a photo of the target area. After this, the same sequence was repeated with the normal shell that weighed 100 lbs. All this again repeated with different charges, of which there were five ranging from Charge I to Supercharge.

It took me two hours to complete the Charge IV series, not bad going really, then Aubrey carried on with the Supercharge ones.

It went on all next day, I completed Charge III and Aubrey Charge II and the lower the charge the longer it took the shells to lob over onto the target. Major Hickson came along and congratulated us on the way the experimental shoot was going and was pleased with the results so far.

We had been lucky but next day our luck changed and fog clamped down. Thinking it was clearing around eleven took off for a try. Although I managed to find the target area and look into it properly was obliged to fly low and near and soon found this decidedly unhealthy. Besides the fog threatened to clamp down again so beat a hasty retreat.

Despite the duff weather, knowing that this shoot was important, tried again in the afternoon but I could not see the shell splashes as they merged with the fog and had to give up.

How important these shoots were we only discovered much later. It seemed that these new shells were the very first ones with a radar fuse and they were urgently needed for use in the Second Front, where the Canadian AGRA were soon to be fighting.

The following day we were able to complete the calibration shoot and Aubrey and I went along to the 2nd Canadian Mediums for a party which was also a farewell party as they were leaving this front and heading into the blue. Actually they were going post haste to Belgium to help extricate the Yanks from the mess they were in due to the Battle of the Bulge.

The following evening all of 'A' Flight repaired to AGRA HQ for the official farewell party. We had worked for them for a long time and many kind words of praise about our work were heard. In fact the big-shot himself promised to fix it so we could follow them and help them fight in the grim battle that lay ahead. We accepted that statement with a pinch of salt, knowing the ways of the army, but he did keep his word and we were to join this bunch of jolly good types a while later in 21st Army Group.

And so the Canadians disappeared and for the first time in many moons 'A' Flight found itself jobless. We moved into a huge airfield south of Ravenna and occupied a farmhouse. There an Itie family adopted us and produced some dream grub from our Army rations and we spent some pleasant, peaceful restful days.

Here it was we commenced training rear observers who, for 2/6 [2 shillings and 6 pence] extra pay were willing to sit in the rear seat and look out for enemy fighters, sharing with the pilot all the danger but little of the fun.

In which I Invent a Radar Homing System

The mist and foggy weather was causing us a great deal of trouble in finding our way back to our ALG. Often enough it was necessary to carry out a shoot in the late evening, or in worsening weather, when every minute that passed meant that our chances of returning safely to our landing-ground became slimmer. Although so far the more experienced types had reached their base under these unfavourable conditions, others had to force land or head for large aerodromes.

Being ex Heavy AA and knowing something of the workings of the GL sets (now known as Radar) it occurred to me that a system could be evolved whereby we could make use of the two sets in our area to home by.

Presented the scheme to Brigade and they thought it a good

idea and authorised me to go ahead and carry out any necessary experiments.

The scheme was simple. When a pilot felt he was lost he'd come up on the blower "XYZ 6 calling for cabbage patch." Cabbage patch was our code name for ALG. The GL set would come onto our net and order "XYZ 6 circle to port." The lost pilot would then circle left which would allow the men on the GL set to identify the plane which would be the only one to be moving around in a circle. They would then work out the compass bearing from the plane to the landing ground and report it, say: "XYZ 6 head 286."

The pilot would then set this bearing on his compass grid and head in that direction. If necessary a correction would be given. When, the plane was seen on the Radar screen to be approaching the ALG they would transmit, "XYZ 6 look now" and by that time the pilot should be able to recognise landmarks.

Tried out this procedure a couple of times and it worked perfectly, it being so simple and fool-proof. This invention was adopted officially by Brigade for that particular front. However, as we were due to move in the very near future we were never able to try it out in earnest. I never did find out if any pilot used this system after we had left but it may have helped somebody some time.

A Wizard Leave in Rome

Things were quiet. The front had been stable for months. The mud and plentiful rain precluding any likelihood of a recurrence of bellicose activities and, besides, I had clocked over 400 hours of Ops. with 372 operational sorties and it was high time I had another spot of leave.

And so it was that with F/Lt. Harding, our Adjutant, on the 25th February 1945 caught the 13.00 hour train at Rimini for Rome. I was made OC train and, making use of my exalted rank took over the best compartment, allowing a lowly Colonel to share it with us. A good move that as this chap proved well stocked with the very best Scotch.

It was a lengthy trip and arrived in Rome in the very early

morning the next day. Walked through the dawn to the Albergo Reale on Via 20 Setiembre where managed to wheedle a good room on the 4th floor with private bathroom. Such an unaccustomed luxury was most pleasant and, for the first time in months, felt really warm and clean, besides the bed had real white sheets.

And so commenced a fortnight of first class rubber necking in one of the most beautiful and interesting cities in the World. Did all the more famous churches and museums and explored the Vatican on several days, even unto the copper ball that supports the cross at the very tip of St. Peter's.

At that time, what must surely have been the greatest accumulation of art ever seen in the World, was on exhibit at the Vatican. All the art treasures from the principal European countries that had been sent to the Vatican for safe-keeping were on show. It was really too much for anybody to absorb. Each single picture or statue should have warranted a lengthy study, but there were literally hundreds of superb masterpieces around and in one afternoon hastened through the many rooms that comprise this museum gaining a hazy idea of such magnificence.

There were plenty of shows on. Seeing *Carmen* at the Rome Opera House was unforgettable. The magnificent interior is breathtaking, especially enhanced by cunning lighting effects and the interior of the boxes are lit up gently while the rest is dimmed slowly. We did not last out through the fourth act as we were feeling hungry and did not want to miss our lovely grub, difficult to come by after nine.

There were also lovely spots to visit and our favourite place for lunch was the Trocadero in the Pincio Gardens. There we could tuck into wizard food whilst sitting out on the terrace taking in the spring sunshine and looking down upon Rome shining in all its glory.

Usually dined at our Hotel, which was first class and sported a five piece girl orchestra playing softly in the lounge. The bar was not bad there either. As regards company, apart from Lofty the Adj. bumped into lots of old pals and Air OP wallahs. Buchanan and Walker who happened to be in town as also chaps from the different Artillery Regiments we had been supporting for so long. My Air OP wings and Argentina shoulder flash made me an odd type.

Rome, Pincio Gardens — tucking in with elegance

Me and Lofty - (F/Lt A.C.G. Harding RAF)

Of an evening we were wont to hit the bright spots, not entirely authentic as they were MP controlled, but some were pretty good. The lowest dive of the lot was undoubtedly Buffalo Bill's, way down in a cellar-cum-catacomb, eerie, dusty and noisy. Here one could have grub and good *vino*. Later on in the evening one could cut the atmosphere with a knife. It was my showpiece whenever I had to look after any newcomer. We made up parties usually with New Zealand nurses, who also made our hotel their headquarters whilst in Rome, and a jolly good mob they were too.

The Nirvanetta had a good classy floor show but where we enjoyed ourselves the most was at the Colibri. After I had been there a couple of times found that the group of Spanish dancers that did the floor show, in fact they ran the place, were real and from Barcelona. It did not take long before we were great pals, they being tickled to find somebody who could speak to them in *cristiano*. They used to come and join us and, in consequence, we got the very best service and excellent champagnes, not the mediocre stuff they gave the *ingleses* and what is more important, at reduced rates. This made me popular with the other Air OP types and they were most impressed to hear me jabber away in "dago" to the dancers.

I had been looking around for a 35 mm camera to replace my old one that used unprocurable 120mm films. Found a natty Agfa Karat with a 6.3 lens which suited me fine even though the lens was a bit slow and price high, 12,000 lire in fact. I had no alternative if I wanted to document the War, so went to the Field Cashier and took out the needful. 35 mm film was easy to "acquire" via the RAF film units.

Again We Meet the Sign of the Beast

One Sunday, Lofty, Hern and myself set off in our Jeep to visit the Catacombs. Arrived at the church of San Sebastiano, built on top of this old burial system. There a real live monk in gown and hood, carrying a lighted wax taper, stacks of atmosphere, led us down into the eerie catacombs; in fact several layers of them where we crept silently by stacks of old tombs built into the solid rock with odd bits of skeletons still lying in them.

After that we thought we might try and have a look at the quarry where the SS bastards had liquidated over 300 Italian hostages in brutal reprisal for the killing of some 30 Germans in Rome. We never thought we would be allowed to enter but a spot of bluffing worked and we were let in. We walked down an incline and into a lengthy tunnel cut into the rock face for about 200 yards.

I have never seen, nor wish to see, anything like that again. There in the dark dampness of this man-made cave were to be seen myriad clusters of flickering candles, each cluster surrounding a coffin lying on the ground around which drably dressed figures knelt or sat, and over all, polluting the atmosphere, the sickly stink of rotting human flesh. On each coffin was a photo of the deceased. What made matters worse was the fact that the Jerries had shown a fiendish callous disregard for any decency in picking their victims. Many of the photos were of young girls and boys in their teens. One was of a priest and another an Italian General. All to be sure were completely innocent. These poor people had been forcibly dragged there, shot down by machine gun fire, a messy way of doing the job, and then an attempt was made to hide their crime by blowing up the tunnel entrance. They were not successful and only part of the mound of bodies was buried under the rubble.

We left with a nasty taste in our mouths and a fervent hope that many of the shells we had been instrumental in sending across into the enemy's midst had liquidated as many as possible of these inhuman beasts. Not a very Christian wish for a Sunday morning.

A Spot of Diplomatic Touring

Thought it would be correct, and a good idea, to locate the Argentine representative, then a chargé d'affaires by name Oscar Oneto Astengo and rather a decent type.

Looked him up around midday, he did not arrive at the Embassy till around then, and introduced myself. This promptly produced an invitation to his house for lunch. So there I went a couple of days later where I met his wife, a genuine Italian *marquesa*, and had a wizard lunch, including *ravioles* and *dulce de leche*, a rare treat. Later they took me out for a drive in their car plus chauffeur and we did most of the Seven Hills of Rome. This gave me an excellent chance to commence using my new Agfa Karat; in the afternoon we visited a famous collector of canaries and saw stacks of these birds in an amazing variety of colours.

Back to the Embassy for tea. Afterwards we were joined by their blonde daughter, not bad at all, and went to the select Quirinal Cinema.

On Sunday morning, it was the 11th March, Astengo sent his car to fetch me at my hotel and we all, plus a Miss de Bon, attended a benefit concert given by leading artists at the Eliseo Theatre. It was pretty good.

After that back to their residence for a drink and a swell lunch this time with *bifes* finishing up with *milhojas con dulce de leche*. This was followed by us younger types setting forth in a Jeep driven by a Major plus a couple. They all spoke Spanish so we could converse. We headed for the seaside to have a picnic tea. The other chap was a once-famous Italian pilot and had flown one of the Schneider Cup planes; not a mean achievement. On the return journey inspected Astengo's summer house and found it stripped and pretty well smashed up by the occupying Tedeschi [the Italian word for Germans].

Astengo himself very decently sent a letter to Mother telling her he had seen me and that I was looking well. Mrs Astengo was worried about her brother, last heard of heading for Malta on a bombing mission. Not a very friendly gesture especially considering he was a Knight of the Order of Malta. She endeavoured to obtain my help to find out his thereabouts but, of course, I was hardly in a position to help.

On the 12th March 1945 took a last look at Rome and then caught the 1 o'clock train for Rimini, so ending a wizard leave.

In which I Help Cremona Gruppe do Battle

When I arrived back from Rome discovered that 'A' Flight had moved once again and was occupying buildings on the outskirts of

Ravenna. Powell, my Batman cum Jeep driver, was on 21 days detention for neglecting his vehicle. Hilton, my wireless operator and caravan driver had been lucky in the draw and had sailed for home. Spedding, another decent Army type, took over instead.

The very first morning I was on the job and flew off in Holy Smoke V to check up on the front line, taking Green my A/C [aircraftman] fitter as observer. When I returned found that I was expected to cooperate with the Cremona Gruppe, the first Italian Army unit to be formed and to fight against the Germans.

Their Commander, General Bertucci, turned up soon after lunch with a request that we should show him the front. He could not speak English but understood Spanish and, in consequence, I was detailed to look after him. It was really funny. The General was all of 5 feet tall and came all resplendent in a comic opera uniform. I am 6 ft. 5 odd. As we walked across to the plane broad grins were much in evidence.

Settled him in, well strapped up and with his parachute on in the little rear seat, then we set sail for the front that was then just south of Lake Comacchio. Flying erratically along the length of the front I pointed out where our forward troops were. Since we were speaking in Spanish and we got on fine.

I took him up a couple of times. Then he requested that I should be assigned to act as Air OP to his artillery. This I did on several occasions again making use of Spanish. Thus for the first time in history an Air OP type fired the Italian Army guns. It was all rather amusing and called for the use of most unorthodox orders being sent down the blower but I had them firing pretty accurately in the end.

As will be recalled, Popski and his merry men were active around the lake Comacchio where Italian Partisanos, gliding around in their small boats, were risking their lives to harass the enemy.

The remainder of the front was very much at a standstill and was likely to remain so at least until the end of the rainy season. But elsewhere in Europe the Second Front was gathering momentum.

Ravenna, March 1945 — Wells, Bob Barrass, Self, Aubrey Young, Rigby and an Italian Family: Mama, Papa, Viola, Sultina and the boy next door

MOVE TO NORTHWEST EUROPE

We Bid the Eighth Army Farewell

It soon became apparent that we could not possibly be allowed to remain idle on a cushy front. A rumour had spread that the Canadian's promise was likely to be kept and we were to follow them into battle somewhere in Belgium or Holland, where the Battle of the Bulge was then raging.

This was sufficient for the holding of a series of parties, not only with other Eighth Army units but also with the local inhabitants. Here I was to appreciate the notorious ease by which the lowly Tommy could conquer the sympathy of the people of occupied countries.

Without knowing a word of the lingo, nor bothering to learn it except for a few functional words, they lost no time in establishing friendly relations witvinoh the natives where they were accepted without question and treated as one of the family.

Went along to a farm for one of these parties. It was the usual affair with stables, housing cows, horses and the odd pig downstairs which also had a large livingroom-cum-kitchen, then on top on a second floor, the bedrooms.

There was plenty of *vino* to be sure and the Ities had camouflaged army rations into appetising local dishes. An old fashioned gramophone scraped out music and sturdy farm girls were dancing with the lads. Enjoyed chatting with the folk there. They all had cousins in the Argentine and were interested in learning all about that country.

The rumours became a certainty and we received orders to hand over our planes to a new, recently formed, Polish Air OP Squadron. In the end Rigby and I were the last ones to possess trusty steeds and we kept working right up to the last. On the 22nd March 1945, on my second sortie, I did my last shoot on the Italian front for the Desert Air Force.

That evening we had a terrific farewell squadron party at the Ravenna Officers' Club, a most uninhibited affair, nobody worrying about the morrow.

And on the 23rd March 1945 I flew faithful Holy Smoke to Forli, landing in a street and handed her over to the Poles of 663 Squadron. Returned by Jeep to attend another wizard party given in our honour by the owners of the farm house which had been our abode during our last stop on this front.

In Convoy over the Apennines

At an unearthly hour of the morning 'A' Flight vehicles joined the Squadron and commenced the long trek that was to take us to Belgium, there to join Montgomery and his 21st Army Group.
The hour was 3.30 am, the day the 24th of March 1945, when we manoeuvred our vehicles into place on the large Ravenna aerodrome.

Apennine Pass en route to Florence, March 24 1945.
Photo courtesy of the Estate of A. C Young via VF.

At 6 we moved. I was driving "Marion" my Chevy three tonner with Gunner Spedding as co-driver. She had just had a new engine put in by REME and we were expected to tow a heavy four wheeled trailer. However, found the clutch was slipping, and were obliged to hand this vehicle over to Aubrey to tow behind his lorry.

Our immediate destination was Leghorn. This meant we had to traverse the Apennine range of mountains, with all the climbing on narrow twisting and turning roads that that entailed. Driving one of the better lorries I was placed near the tail end of the convoy so that I could come to the aid of any that fell by the wayside. Shortly after we had started the long climb we came across the cookhouse three tonner in trouble. They were hauling the water trailer and, as Marion's clutch had ceased to slip, we relieved them of its weight thus allowing that most important vehicle to keep on crawling up the trail.

The day had turned beautiful and spring was in the air. The route was really magnificent and driving a truck is an ideal way of seeing the countryside as one rides high and slow. Driving the heavy lorry plus trailer called for quite an effort, not to mention knack, but it must be remembered that I had been an MT Instructor during part of my Army career.

The Squadron was out of training as regards moving in convoy and the lot was stretched over many miles of winding roads. Luckily traffic control had placed this mountain route entirely at our disposal. Stopped at Pontassieve for lunch and there we caught up with most of the Squadron.

Really enjoyed that ride. Marion was behaving fine even though the engine was not developing full power and was consuming petrol at an alarming rate.

Eventually we wound our way into the flat lands where we were able to make better speed. By 17·30 we were near Leghorn. Sign posts appeared which led us to Harrod's Camp, a transit camp set in the middle of a large wood. This was made up of large US Army tents with plenty of comforts such as a well stocked Naffi, cinema and plenty of US grub in our rations.

We spent five peaceful days resting in that camp and preparing our equipment for what lay ahead. On the fourth day part of the Squadron left and on the 30th March 1945, in the afternoon, I drove Marion into Leghorn and boarded LST 177 of the U.S. Navy. We sure were made mighty comfortable, we shared a four bunk cabin and tucked into lovely grub. We remained in port all that night but by the time I appeared on deck next morning we were well away. Eight of the Squadron's pilots were on board, including Bill Bolam and Ted Wells of 'A' Flight.

We formed part of a small convoy of four LST's with a sloop in attendance and met with no trouble at all as we sped smoothly over a tranquil Mediterranean. We passed quite close to Corsica, looking pretty in the bright sunlight and a large force of Liberators rumbled overhead on their way back from some mischief.

And so we spent another night as guests of the US Navy. By morning we were in the roads outside Marseilles where we dawdled

Harrod's Camp near Leghorn, March 24-30 1945.

awaiting permission to land. There we had our Easter Sunday lunch with toasted buns and mince pies. A signal came at last and the LST shoved its nose up against what seemed to be one of the main streets of that city, opened up her enormous mouth and disgorged us and respective vehicles, and so we landed on French soil, it was April Fool's day.

We Follow the Gold Flake Route

After landing we were told to follow "Gold Flake" signs till our journey's end. Doing so we soon found ourselves in another large transit camp on the outskirts of the city. Like Harrod's Camp, all comforts were laid on and it was well organised. There the Squadron took

The Gold Flake Route April 1–6 1945

stock of itself and, amazingly enough, naught was missing.

Much secrecy was attached to our move. The Powers that Be evidently did not want Hitler to learn of his fast approaching doom, and all our Air OP identification marks had been painted over and shoulder flashes removed. When we landed at the port a barbed-wire fence had kept the populace at bay, a great pity that, from all accounts, and no fratting was the order of the day.

The Gold Flake Route, established by the Canadian Army, was well organised. "Gold Flake" sign posts were placed at every road junction and transit camps were sited at the end of an easy day's run. They all boasted good cookhouses with their respective cooks. Well pitched tents, a plentifully stocked NAAFI and a cinema showing new films. Apart from that the gentle drive through the beautiful countryside of the South of France was delightful. Riding high in the cab of our trucks we could see over the hedgerows and away into the distance; and it was early spring.

Our route took us up the Rhone Valley through Aix-en-Provence, Orgon, Valence and we finished up that evening on an old aerodrome outside St Rambert [*Saint-Rambert-d'Albon*] having travelled 152 miles.

Next day we started up lateish, around 8·30 and formed part of a convoy of 50 trucks. It was another beautiful day and pleasant driving. Marion, now towing our original trailer, was pulling well and it was no trouble keeping our place in the convoy travelling, as per usual, at an average 30 mph. We went right through the centre of Lyon, everybody waving at us and stopped a few miles beyond Mâcon. Distance run was not great and we were at our overnight camp by 15.00 hours, there we had a late lunch. From there we could see the broad Rhone and that afternoon went for a walk to its banks and watched the boats passing by.

Next morning we were away by 7·30 as we had to tackle a longer stretch. Always heading north towards the battle ground, went through Chalon-sur-Saône, Chagny, Dijon, Vitteaux and Les Laumes, climbing steadily after that place for around 14 miles until we pulled up just before 16·00 on what was a wide plateau. Walks around there were pleasant and indicated after so much driving. Wandered over with Douglas Culverwell to have a look at a pranged Fortress and to the edge of the plateau where we admired the view enhanced by the soft twilight. Later we attended the camp cinema and then to bed.

Another early start was made the following morning. The weather now changed and it was drizzling besides getting colder as we moved north. We did not go through any large town that day and stopped for the night at a camp set in a huge wood. There saw a good flick *A Body too Many*.

At 6.30 am on the 6th April 1945 found us on our way once more heading into a wet dreary chilly day. We were approaching Paris but, of course, detoured around and passed by the Compiègne Forest where the Armistice had been signed twice. Then we commenced passing places famous during the First World War, Ham, Pérrone, Cambrai and soon we were in Belgium and our immediate destination just beyond the latter town. We travelled 155 miles that day. The CO went forward for orders whilst we settled down for the night and serviced our vehicles for the morrow.

With our final destination known, the Squadron could now make its own way and we ceased to follow the convenient Gold Flake signs and reverted to map reading and our own traffic control.

We were hauled out of our flea pits at the unearthly hour of 5 am to continue on our way. The weather behaved and was sunny in spots. Kept going past more famous battle grounds and by midday we were skirting Brussels, passing by the exhibition grounds. Pulled up by the wayside for lunch, consisting of spam sandwiches. Scottie, following on Marion's tail, produced his patent brew can that he had fashioned from a fire extinguisher and a 3.7 shell cartridge case with which it was possible to boil water in under four minutes and we brewed up some tea. This helped push down the dry sandwiches.

The CO had fixed things fine [6 April 1945] and we drove into the beautiful grounds of an old chateau, surrounded by a moat, that was to be our temporary abode. It was in the village of Oostmalle, a little place not far from Antwerp.

Gracious Living and Glorious Beer

With Bill Bolam and Ted Sloan took over a swell room on the first floor overlooking the moat. We found to our joy that we even had real electric light, a luxury we hadn't enjoyed for years. No sooner cleaned up than we headed for the village and looked up the Town Major. He proved to be a Belgian and a decent type and promptly invited us in to partake of a cup of coffee.

After that set off to sample the local beer and found it was wizard stuff made by the Trappist Monks; trust them to turn out something good.

The author in front of the Chateau at Oostmalle
Photo courtesy of the Estate of A. C. Young via VF.

Settled down to enjoy three days of gracious living in that elegant chateau with its spacious beautiful dining hall, oak panelled walls, and bright electric lights.

Managed a couple of trips into Antwerp, not too far away, and ate and drank at the Excelsior and Continental Hotels where we ran into some old friends, Air OP types and other odd characters, such as a blonde Londoner who had parachuted behind the lines and worked with the underground, as also several of her tough pals.

For the second time since we came into action the Squadron was united and there was some attempt to return to Army life and the odd Squadron parade was held. Duty Officers were instituted but nothing too orthodox was tried and life there never failed to be peaceful and pleasant.

Vehicles were inspected and repaired. Wireless equipment put in tip-top shape and all generally made ready for the impending renewal of hostilities. The battle was raging furiously not so very far away.

In which I Adopt Holy Smoke VII

The order to move was not long in coming and on the 11th April 1945, at the reasonable hour of 9·30 am the Squadron convoy got under way. I was driving Marion and pulling the trailer. It was a pleasant day as we wended our way via Turnhout and Tilburg to a large aerodrome on the outskirts of Gilze, where we were to pick up our new war planes.

Were thrilled to find we were to have the company of a squadron of the famous and extremely hush-hush jet planes that would go screaming along the runway and disappear into the distance travelling at a great rate of knots.

Our planes were being stuck together and I did not receive mine until the 15th April. She proved a lovely little job, an Auster Mark V, and No. TJ526 and was to be my last trusty steed in this War. Took her up into the blue and she behaved beautifully. Checked her stalling speed with and without flaps and chucked her around the sky a wee. She stuck together fine and all was well.

Next day the Squadron moved once more, heading for an ALG near Doetinchem. This time Spedding drove Marion as I, of course, had to fly Holy. At 10 am, taking advantage of the huge drome we were on, 'A' Flight took off in formation. Bob was in the lead, I to his right rear, Ted left rear and Aubrey tail-end Charlie. Bradshawed our way via Tilberg, Hertogenbosh, Nijmegen and then along the Rhine Salmont. From there south to Kleve and we were over German soil for the first time. This round-about route was considered necessary for the very good reason that otherwise we would have to fly over enemy held territory and we did not want to risk scratching our new planes.

Still flying in formation we turned north for Emmerich, nicely smashed up, and a little later we saw a beautiful green field beside a Country Club that was to be our ALG. In peacetime this set up was used by people with private planes to drop in and make use of the pleasant little Club which boasted two swimming pools as well as the usual sports.

We arrived way ahead of our transport and while we waited a crowd of Dutch boys and girls joined us, all pleased as punch and very friendly.

That evening the BBC gave out the sad news that president Roosevelt had died.

We Seek 'B' Flight Lost in Battle

'B' Flight had flown off to do battle the previous day and nothing further had been heard from them. The CO was worried as their chosen ALG was right in the middle of the area where a heavy German counter-attack had been launched that morning and which had caught the 21st Army Group napping. The few reports that came out were confusing and nobody really knew what was happening.

It was decided to send somebody off to look for them, or at least bring back some first-hand information on what was going on, and I had the doubtful honour of being chosen for the job.

Nobody knew where the front line was, not even what way it faced. The weather was dirty, ceiling down to 800 feet, and this would force me to keep well within range of any and all guns in the hostile areas we were sure to fly over. Not a job to be relished.

Holy Smoke VII and I took off on our first quest as soon as we had had our elevenses. To be on the known safe side, at least to start off with, flew towards Arnhem before turning due north for about 15 miles towards the original map reference of 'B' Flight's ALG

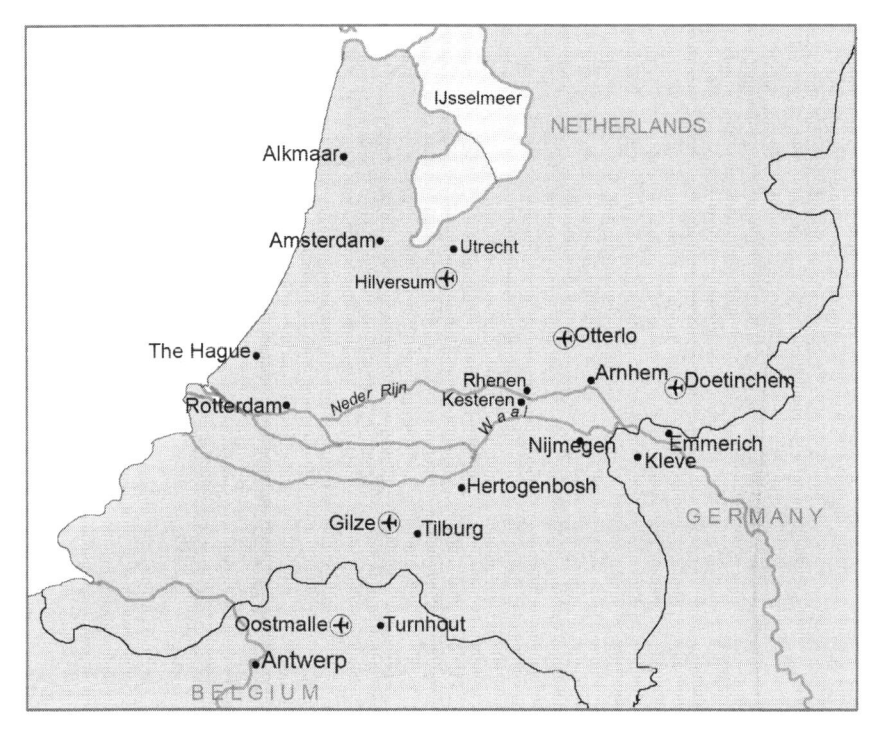

Locations in Belgium, Holland and Germany

While still well away it became apparent that something was happening. A large area of this flat ground was covered in a dense smoke screen, beneath which anything could be brewing. Visibility was hopeless. As this was Holland the ground was really flat as a pancake without any prominent feature to act as a reference point and soon we were truly and properly lost. Flew haphazardly over the murk and through sundry smoke-screens waiting for the sign of tracers coming up which would, at least, indicate the wrong side of the elusive front. But nobody obliged.

This was hopeless so headed south on a compass course until I could see Arnhem and, starting from scratch again, tried to fly directly to the map reference given. Once I guessed I was over the spot descended into the smog and flew round and round, at tree top height, in an ever increasing arc. By sheer good luck I was able to glimpse signs of an Army camp in a gap in the smoke. By rapid maneuvering managed to haul Holy round without losing sight of it. They were British all right and then I saw an Auster picketed down.

I still did not know what the position was and obviously had to land to find out. It was impossible to find out where the landing strip was in all that smoke and fog of war and any fancy landing procedure was out of the question. Made a snap decision, pulled down on my emergency flap and came in to land straight ahead hoping to goodness nothing solid would appear. Our luck was in and nothing did. Taxied towards the main group of vehicles which I could now see more clearly and just then a couple of Erks ran out to meet me each grasping a tommy-gun and looking somewhat scared.

George Riley, their CO, was up front somewhere, nobody knew exactly where and the rest of the crowd hadn't a clue what was going on. The noise of heavy firing could be heard from too many points of compass and the situation was confused, to say the least. However, as far as I could gather a large unit of Germans, reputedly 2 Divisions, had been by passed by the 21st. Army Group without them realising it, and they had chosen this morning to attack the Headquarter area, causing a large deal of alarm.

Having now accomplished my mission, I arranged for wireless contact and lost no time in climbing into Holy Smoke to escape from this mess. The Erks pointed out the direction of the strip and I shoved on full throttle and headed into the smoke. Kept climbing until we were above it all then headed back to our more peaceful Country Club to report.

A Spot of Exploring

'A' Flight, considered the crack Flight of the Squadron says us, were chosen to work with the 1st. Canadian AGRA (Army Group Royal Artillery) possessing a tremendous weight of firepower with their heavy guns. However, they were not yet in action so, therefore, we had to await their pleasure.

Taking advantage of this enforced idleness Bob Barrass, acting CO at the time, and I went off by Jeep to reconnoitre a new ALG

Loosdrecht Lake — Friendly Natives

Loosdrecht Lake — Pleasant aftermath

just south of Otterlo. We headed south to start off with and entered German territory for the first time, travelling through Emmerich and Kleve, both very much destroyed. There were hardly any civilians to be seen. From there we turned back into Holland and reached Nijmegen in time for lunch at the Officers' Club. Then on to Arnhem over the famous Nijmegen bridge, scene of bitter fighting not so long before. We then traversed in nervous haste a forest reputedly containing snipers, but nothing happened and we reached the other end safely.

On nearing the assigned area came upon a nice looking field that would be just the job for our next ALG and pinpointed it on the map. It was by then 16·00 hours and time to head for home.

A quick wash and wandered over to dine with a friendly Dutch family and it was interesting hearing about their war-time adventures whilst under the occupation. Many of their stories were unpleasant.

Taking advantage of our really first class Mess and the lovely ball room that formed part of the Country Club, we organised a Squadron Dance, inviting all the pretty girls in the neighbourhood.

And just as I was getting poshed up and all ready to tread a dainty measure, was detailed to chase off and find 661 Air OP Squadron, stationed somewhere in Holland as also 'B' Flight and deliver some urgent mail. Without wasting time had Holy wound up and off we went. Discovered we were up against a stiff head wind and, in order to move faster, came down to the deck and had great fun hedge hopping and leap-frogging cows. Located 661 without trouble, landed, handed over the mail to the first chap I saw and took off again to find 'B' Flight. This latter mission was slightly hazardous on account of their occupying an ALG near Barneveld towards the front end of a spearhead thrust then battling its way forward, which meant that the enemy was near at hand on either side and feeling bellicose. To be on the safe side headed for their HQ flying up their main advance road.

Found the map reference I had been given but there were no planes to be seen. To find out where they had gone I landed in a bumpy field and was immediately surrounded by a happy crowd of

Occupied Germany

locals. A beauteous blonde put her head through the side window to welcome her liberator! A nice wee girl tied a lucky fox's tail to one of Holy's struts, a lucky charm that was to fly with me till war's end. Luckily a 'B' Flight type had seen me land and came across and I was able to give him the mail bag. Had not turned off the engine and could take off right away. Asked my local friends to clear a way for me, bumped to the far end of the field, and sailed away to the cheers of the happy crowd there assembled.

I had accomplished my mission with celerity and dispatch, so much so that the party had just about got really under way when I was able to join in and have a jolly good time. A real band had been impressed from somewhere and the beer was good. The general atmosphere, supplied largely by the friendly natives attending their very first liberation dance, was really terrific.

Into Action with the 21st Army Group

On the 21st April 1945, three weeks from the day we landed at Marseilles, we packed up regretfully and abandoned our beautiful Country Club for our first battle ALG on this front. Our transport left in the morning in the rain. Bob, Ted and myself, Aubrey being away in England on leave, took off after lunch and made our way to Otterlo where we landed rather trickily in the midst of a veritable squall.

Our new strip was beside an ex-radio station which was housed in a comfortable edifice which we took over as our Mess.

The next day we were officially in action with the 1st Canadian AGRA but the weather proved so bad that nothing could be done. I found that I had been detailed to work independently from the flight and cooperate with a Composite Brigade formed to eliminate a dangerous concentration of Jerries on the left flank of our advance. Went along with Bob in Elsie to contact the people I was to work with.

Our private little battle-ground was to be the island area between the Waal and the Neder-Rijn, west of Arnhem and Nijmegen. All the enemy in the area had been squashed back into this area and the Composite Brigade I was to work with consisted mainly of the 1st Canadian Armoured Brigade plus the 98th Field Regiment and a troop of the 1st Canadian Medium Regiment and last, but not least, Holy Smoke VII and skipper in support.

Met Colonel Palmer who was in charge of this little front, became acquainted with the situation and their needs and after selecting a suitable landing ground as near as possible to Brigade HQ returned to our Studio Mess for lunch.

We Fight Sedately and in Comfort

On the 23rd April 1945 Holy Smoke and I sailed off to do battle once again after a respite of exactly one month and one day.

My first job was to have a good look at the island to see if anything showed, but nothing did. Jerry was lying low and well camouflaged.

Landed beside Brigade, strolled over to the command post and had a chat with Colonel Palmer. It seems there was little doing at that moment. After a cup of tea took off and had another look at the front but nothing stirred so went home for lunch.

Later returned to my private landing ground after taking time off to have a look at the famous Arnhem battleground. Flew low over scores of Horsa gliders lying broken on the ground where they had crashed landed on that memorable day.

This time the Colonel had a couple of jobs for me. A registration shoot on a railway junction and another on a cross road. This made me the first pilot of 'A' Flight to go into action with the British Liberation Army.

Returned to my little strip with my mission accomplished and had tea at Brigade. Then home to our comfortable Mess, having done five sorties.

And so it kept on. I'd fly over after a leisurely breakfast and have a look at the front. If I saw anything interesting I would engage. Then down to Brigade in time for elevenses. If things were quiet would not fly again till after lunch, then I would either come down for tea at Brigade or fly straight home.

On the second day Jerry had the cheek to commence firing a gun whilst I was up and this I promptly engaged with the 98th's 25 pounders.

To lighten my task would take Wilson along on the first trip and he would remain all day and would service the plane and start her up when needed. I did not use him as an observer as I considered that a Jerry fighter could easily swoop out of the sun or from below without being seen by either of us and why risk two lives. Besides, my weight was quite enough for our little planes.

On the 25th April 1945 the tank boys planned to shoot up Rhenen and Kesteren. I provided cover by flying over and ahead of them as they advanced but the enemy made no retaliatory move whatsoever. Did four sorties that day and really things were so quiet, at least from the enemy's side, that I would have been bored if it wasn't that I enjoyed peaceful flying.

I became friendly with one of our neighbours and it turned out that he had given shelter to an Argentine RAF type who had bailed out thereabouts and hidden him for quite a while. Eventually a captured Jerry bomber landed nearby to pick up this lad and two others and ferried them safely back to England. I never found out his name but wondered who he was.

Ours was not exactly a vital battle and provided we kept the enemy properly cooped up and out of mischief our mission was fairly accomplished. To be on the safe side however, it was decided that our infantry would then attempt to challenge and have it out with their opposite number and I was asked to help reconnoitre the attack line. When I arrived that morning I met Brigadier Perón (no relation) of the Belgian Army, ex War pilot with four rows of medals up and commanding the infantry detailed for the job. Discussed our flight plan over a cup of tea.

Not to give the show away we had to survey the whole front although the attack was to go in on the south flank. The principal factor for worry was whether any vital bridge had been blown.

Took off with the Brigadier, a hefty type, in the rear seat and weaved our way towards the front and over. No 88 mm's had been reported in this area but, no doubt, the sight of a much hated "lame duck" stooging around at a low altitude would be too much for the chaps underneath who could be depended upon to have a go at us with whatever weapon came to hand. Hence our flying was most erratic. We were lucky, or they were bad shots, because no holes appeared. Not having the comfort of an armoured seat, taken out to compensate my weight, caused me some anxiety.

Brigadier Peron was pleased with the results of the reconnoitre so quickly and efficiently accomplished thanks to the Air OP. He asked me to take up one of his officers after lunch. This proved to be a tough paratrooper, another Belgian by name Captain Pitot who would also like to have a look at the attack area. Despite his toughness, after a short period of erratic flying, horrible gurgling noises were to be heard strength five coming via his larynga-phones as he became violently sick. However, he just had to last out the flight until everything had been checked. I could not afford to pity him nor fly any straighter with my unprotected posterior floating so invitingly over the enemy.

The Infantry attack never went in. Orders came through that we were to respect Dutch property. We were not to fire unless fired on and eventually, that we were not to fire in the Rhenen area. The War became really sissy and we smelt a rat. The Jerries were on the run on all fronts and the Russians were fighting in Berlin. Rumours had it that they were trying to surrender and eventually we found out that the order not to shell any movement seen near Rhenen was to allow the Dutch civilians to receive foodstuff dropped there by RAF bombers.

Then the whole of 657 Squadron was grounded and we knew the end was nigh. There was no object in remaining on in this area and tried to hurry up a spot of leave.

Meanwhile there was no alternative but to make the most of things and enjoy life. Explored the area and visited friendly units where we had parties and guzzled lots of "moose milk", a Canadian specialty.

And so it happened that my leave ticket came through and I bade Holy Smoke VII a temporary farewell.

A Spot of Leave and VE day

And so it came about that using our RAF flying crew prerogative we wangled airborne transport for our leaves. On the 3rd May Scottie and self were deposited by Elsie onto a large aerodrome near Nijmegen and after hanging around for some time eventually managed to squeeze ourselves into the 16·30 Dakota for London. The weather proved duff on the way over and we had to circle through a gap in the low clouds to sit down in Croydon.

We dined together in London and then I headed for Grove Park where I received a grand welcome and found them all well.

Then I commenced to enjoy my leave going into London most days and meeting many old friends including J. E. Walding, Harold Dougall, Godfrey Cooper, etc. and exchanging news and experiences.

Sent a cable to Mother in Buenos Aires to let her know that I was safe and sound in London. Due to the strict censoring, now relaxed, she never knew exactly where I was nor what I was doing. Promptly received a reply with good wishes which pleased me no end.

This leave had all the makings of a wizard one there being no doubt about it that the War was virtually over. We kept expecting Churchill to make an announcement at any moment and on the strength of a rumour went into town with my cousin Cathie on the 7th May and mingled with the huge crowd awaiting the fateful news in Piccadilly Circus. It was expected over the 6 o'clock news.

It was a happy and noisy crowd which hushed when Big Ben tolled out the hour and the news commenced; but this wasn't it.

Next day surely would be the day and 6 o'clock [*8 May 1945*] found us once again plus a huge crowd outside Buckingham Palace. This time it was true and the wonderful news that the War had finally ceased in Europe was given by Winnie himself. The crowd did not become wild right away. There was an atmosphere of thankfulness and relief as also sorrow for those who had not survived to welcome this day. Soon, however, sheer happiness prevailed and people started calling out for the King and the Royal Family to appear. After a while they all came out and the crowd really went wild cheering.

It was a lovely sunny day as we walked through St. James' Park. Had tea then saw *Private Lives* at the Apollo and then dined at Young's. To finish off an historical day we roamed around the centre of London mingling with the crowd and enjoyed seeing the lights go on in London for the first time in six years. An attempt had been made at flood-lighting the more important buildings and although no doubt the results were feeble, the change from the previous strict blackout was so great that it was awe inspiring. Wandered around Trafalgar Square and saw some sailors bathing in the fountain fully dressed. The crowd was fairly sober, there not being enough beer to more that whet their whistle, but that did not seem to make any difference.

By a stroke of sheer luck we happened to be passing the Ministry of Food building when who should appear on a balcony but Winston

Churchill himself. He had just concluded a round of visits to all the Allied Embassies and, no doubt, he had been well and truly toasted at each and every one of them. By then he was undoubtedly properly lit up and full of beans. A terrific roar went up from squares around when he was spotted and a speech was demanded. A mike had been hooked up and he started. It was a speech of homage to the Londoner and I have yet to hear anything so perfect or so moving. Truly the Londoner had "taken it" in many disagreeable ways and it was their steadfast courage that had set an example and helped keep the morale of the whole Empire to a high pitch in the days when all seemed black.

He finished his speech and somebody with a squeeze-box started up *For He is a Jolly Good Fellow* which was roared out by everybody. Next *Roll out the Barrel* was started but did not go at all well. Then Churchill grabbed the mike and ordered all to stop. Now "Follow me" he said and using his cigar as a baton he conducted the crowd through half a dozen popular songs before he had to leave for some other celebrations, which he highly deserved.

Spent the rest of my leave sightseeing and enjoying myself until it was time to head back to my Squadron. Said farewell to the Grove Park folk on the 12th May and made my way to Croydon to catch my plane.

WITH THE OCCUPATION FORCES IN GERMANY

Aftermath to War

The Squadron had moved on VE Day [*Victory in Europe, 8 May 1945*] into Holland and found a terrific welcome awaiting them. I had missed all this but then, London on VE Day had been something unforgettable.

We were now occupying a lovely little weekend chalet near Loosdrecht Lake inside a pine wood and quite near Hilversum. And the natives were friendly indeed. We were soon put to work running a mail route from Hilversum, HQ of the Canadian Army, then on to Rotterdam, up the coast past The Hague to Alkmaar where Squadron HQ resided and back home via Amsterdam. This we called the "milk run" and carried out twice a day. It was usually a pleasant trip but landing at Rotterdam nipping over a six story building into a small football field was interesting. The evening run, usually carried out when one was in a socially inspired hurry, would be done with some risk, without refuelling in an hour and a half. One of our little pranks on these runs was to dive at and do a twisting turn a few yards from a sailing boat sailing peacefully along and cause it to heel over sharply caught by our wash.

Parties at the Hooyland Hotel, now our Officer's Mess, sailing on the Loosdrecht Lake in wizard B.M. boats [*Berckmeyer Yachts*], plus trips to Amsterdam, Utrecht, etc., made life extremely pleasant especially after rather a grim session of war. Sometimes, highly contrary to standing rules and regulations we would fly a girl friend to Amsterdam, land on a street on its outskirts, pay a small boy to look after the plane and catch a tram into the centre to do a flick.

We were privileged to see the *rot moffen,* the Dutch unflattering name for Jerry, sneaking out on their flat feet through our wood on their roundabout way back to the Fatherland. They did not dare herd them along the more direct route for fear of reprisals from the populace that had suffered so much under them. In consequence, they had to walk north and cross over the dyke that joined

With the Occupation Forces in Germany 283

The Vanquished German Army, Loosdrecht, Netherlands May 1945

the two extremities of the Zuiderzee, now IJsselmeer. They walked unguarded on this lap and we were given the job of keeping an eye on them, to see they did not get up to any monkey business and to keep the traffic flowing, especially over the long 20 km dyke which had to be traversed without a stop, and it was a long walk. In the end the Allies relented and allowed them transport for this journey. To control this part we would carry an Army photographer and photo all the concentrations of troops we could spot. These photos would then be used to identify the troops and check their progress.

An Amazing Coincidence on my Birthday

Another birthday [*25 May 1945*] caught up with me but this time there were no *disparos de bombas* as on my previous two. Instead I was detailed to fly an Intelligence type into Germany on the track of some spy or other.

Captain Wilson, the cloak and dagger chap, came along in a Jeep and picked me up in my summer residence. We soon had Holy Smoke VII wound up and sailing through the peaceful sky on a pleasant sunny morning. I map-read my way to Rhede in Germany, after some practice I had learned to fly straight and level. We landed in a rather small field which my passenger assured me was landable. It was, just. A Jeep came roaring up and we piled in and headed for the town and his local Headquarters.

Drew up by an old fashioned chalet where Wilson had to report to his chief. Rather than leave me hanging around he suggested I come up with him and meet this chap. We climbed a staircase walked into a small room and who should I find sitting behind the desk but my old pal Beacroft last seen some fifteen years previously in Paraná, Entre Ríos, where he worked for the local Branch of the London Bank. He was now a Major in the Intelligence Corps.

We promptly headed for some beer to double celebrate. By his girth he still liked it plenty, and we had a jolly good time yarning about the good old days and comparing experiences.

The 25th of May was a Friday. After lunch at his Mess I suggested he should come back to Hilversum with me and spend the weekend.

He joyfully accepted my invitation and gathering his togs together we headed for the small field where Holy awaited. Now it so happend that Wilson also had an errand back in Holland and had to be carted too, the which caused me a little bit of worry. Bea was a hefty type and had put on plenty of weight. I was not exactly tiny. Wilson was just normal but, plus the two suitcases poor Holy would be grossly overloaded and would have some job to get us all airborne from off that rather small grass field.

Paced the field and found it was just long enough to warrant a risk being taken and short enough to make me worry like hell. However, we had a bit of a breeze and the ground was firm.

We pushed the plane until her tail was up against the hedge. Then I swung the prop telling Bea what to do in the cockpit. She started up easily and we piled in. Wilson and baggage at the back, a tight squeeze, and Bea and myself in front, another tight squeeze, leaving me little room to swing the stick and kick the rudder bar.

Warmed up the motor thoroughly, checked mags carefully and having stroked my fox's tail for luck, pushed the throttle wide and released the brake. We went forward reluctantly and the tail wheel rattled along for a long, long, time before that part came up. Applied all the tricks I knew, such as not applying take off flaps till the last minute to decrease wind resistance. Found we were all swinging our bodies forward urging old Holy onwards, as if that helped. She eventually did pick up speed nobly and when the other fence was very near, yanked down on the flap lever and felt her rise like a bird, well, like an overfed vulture anyway, and we were on our way.

Beacroft remained with us until the following Tuesday when Ted flew him back to Rhede as I was on the "milk run" that morning.

We Move into Germamy

On the 20th June 1945 the Squadron upped sticks and headed for Germany. I, however, had other plans having timed another leave very nicely. They left me at Apeldoorn drome where I managed to persuade the RAF types to fly me per Dakota to Biggin Hill, the famous fighter drome, and then went by bus into London. Us Air

OP types were famous by then and we never had any trouble in persuading the blue types to cart us most anywhere. Being considered aircrew, we wangled aircrew's leave which came round every eight weeks, to the envy of the ordinary brown types who had had to fight the war the bloody way in high discomfort.

When I arrived at Grove Park heard of Harold Dougall's nasty prang and went out to Sherborne post haste to find out if he was still all in one piece. He was, if stitched up a bit and cross eyed real awful; but luckily the eye later clicked back into place.

Had a pleasant leave meeting many old friends including Lewis Massey and J. E. Walding. Stayed at Grove Park most of the time.

My time was soon up and managed to fix up a passage with the Canadian Air Passage people. At an unearthly hour of the morning took off in a Dakota landing at Brussels for a cup of tea and arrived at Apeldoorn at 12·30.

A lonely Auster sat on the field and later Scottie turned up. By 14·00 we were off. Our destination was Brunswick, quite a distance away, and it was necessary to land twice to refuel. The first time at Munster and the second at Oscherleben where we were unpleasantly surprised to find the drome deserted and no petrol available. Luckily a wandering RSM [*Regimental Sergeant Major*] turned up in a Jeep and obliged us with a Jerrycan full.

We finished off the trip flying through some rain squalls and landed at a huge Luftwaffe aerodrome to find 'A' Flight comfortably installed in a large building. Picked out a nice little upstairs room, with electric light and running water. Quite a luxury.

We Meet the Master Race

The move into Germany was made with some foreboding, imagining what it would have been like in England, had the tables been turned. We expected trouble with a capital T, sabotage, sniping, booby-traps and the odd stab in the back on a dark night. Our Jeeps were fixed up with wire cutting uprights in front to save the driver's head from being chopped off by a wire strung across the road.

With the Occupation Forces in Germany 287

Brunswick, Sept. 1945. Arrol typing the beginning of this story in Brunswick

Brunswick - Arrol, Bob Barrass and Aubrey Young in Aubrey's room.
Photo courtesy of the Estate of A. C. Young via VF.

288 Warlike Sketches

Brunswick – Hitler's escape plane, a long range Condor.

German Air Force Crests

This dreaded situation did not materialize and the Germans, far from being hostile, were decidedly and rather disgustingly docile. Churchill's statement that the Germans were either at your throat or at your feet proved to be too true.

The building we occupied was in a mess from our bombing and we had not been there a day before a glazier and a chimney sweep offered their services, to be paid for in food and cigarettes. No less than an ex SS sergeant offered his services as mess-waiter and a Jerry OR as orderly-cum-dishwasher. They were cleared by the Town Major and instituted. Neither proved good at cooking so they enrolled a *hausfrau* to do her stuff in the kitchen. This turned out to be a pleasant elderly dame and we commenced to enjoy food.

By the simple expedient of asking the local German Mayor we furnished our Mess with elegant arm chairs and a good wireless set. The Jerry who accompanied us on our requisitioning expedition advised us where to go to pick up the best bits of furniture!

The Jerry mentality soon became evident in our little Mess setup. The ex SS Sergeant took over the discipline of the kitchen corps. He, known as Walter, forbade Willie, the OR, never to step across the threshold of the Mess dining room whilst any of us were present. The *fat frau* had to remain in her kitchen and not be seen. Walter, dressed smartly in a white mess coat would receive his orders from us, pass them on to Willie who would retransmit them to the cook. When whatever had been ordered came back, Willie would hand this over to Walter on the very threshold of our Mess and we would then be served with due ceremony. I just cannot imagine any of our lads accepting a position such as this with their ex-enemies.

An artist type came along one day and offered to paint the walls of our Mess with crayons for his keeps and a packet of cigarettes. He stayed a week, fed well, and did some really first class stuff on the walls, including a curvaceous, but reasonably discreet mermaid.

In other words there was nary a sign of the dreaded werewolves that had threatened to appear as soon as the Allies overran the Fatherland, and just as well too! It is one thing to fight a nice steady war with the enemy in their right place but quite another to live perpetually scared stiff that they should infiltrate into our midst and start being objectionable in a really nasty way.

Peaceful Jerries

Aftermath of the War

With the belligerent part of the war over, a useful job was found for us and we turned into aerial taxi drivers at the beck and call of all Brass Hats. This suited me down to the ground. It kept me flying which I enjoyed, and gave me a splendid opportunity to roam around a fairly large part of Europe.

The procedure was simple, Divisional HQ would ring up and advise that General, Brigadier, or what have you, so and so, wished to travel from A to B on such a day and hour, and one of us pilots would be detailed to carry out the mission, weather permitting. Destination was usually a Regimental HQ, Battle School or the likes, and on arrival the Brass Hat would be whisked off to do his business and we would be escorted to the Officers Mess there to be regaled with drinks and if timely, lovely grub. As Air OP pilots we had played a decidedly useful supporting role during all, and I mean all, battles and skirmishes in which these Regiments had been committed over the last couple of years, and our hovering presence had not been forgotten by the poor sods who fought dangerously down below. Hence we were always made welcome and properly looked after.

One mission I particularly enjoyed was that of flying General Hull's aide-de-camp all over the Hartz Mountains looking for a suitable hunting lodge for his personal use. We flew over that beautiful scenery circling low whenever we came upon a likely looking estate; and there were some marvellous ones to be seen, mostly belonging to the Nazi hierarchy. As soon as we had chosen a few and made a note of their map reference, we headed back to Holtzminden, landed at the Battle School, borrowed a light truck, and drove into the mountains to check on our findings.

All were marvellous residences in beautiful surroundings but the third one we inspected seemed just the job. It was built halfway up the mountain side, in a sort of hollow, allowing space for a well kept garden and a view that extended for miles. The residents, a middle aged couple with two children plus an old Frau were highly indignant when they were told they had to lend their chateau to the Army and Captain Hilton had to be really firm with them and stood for no nonsense. They were ordered to vacate the premises without removing a stick of furniture, but were allowed the use of a couple of rooms in what probably was the servants quarters.

Some of these trips were tricky. One day in September with Major Payne as passenger, flew off to attend a gymkhana in Heinsberg, too far to reach in one hop and had to stop at Lippspringe to refuel. Was surprised to find the aerodrome deserted, the which caused a problem as we certainly couldn't carry on to our destination. Luckily, spotted some sort of army camp on the perimeter and walking over found it was a RASC [Royal Army Service Corps] Depot. They were able to supply us with a couple of jerry cans of petrol. It was a good thing that our planes weren't too fussy and flew on ordinary MT stuff.

When we eventually arrived over Heinsberg, flew over the indicated landing strip and didn't like the looks of it at all. It seemed far too short and worse, tall trees grew on the approach side if I wished to land into the wind. Although landing down wind is a highly frowned on procedure, decided to do just that, it being the only possible way of getting down, and managed it fine with full flaps and brakes full on but even so overshot and ran into high grass. Paced out the strip and found it was only around 125 yards long, far too short for safety.

Luckily my passenger was staying there so was able to take off lighter and into the wind, away from the tall trees, and had no trouble. This time landed at München Gladbach [now Mönchengladbach] to refuel and was back in Brunswick in time for tea.

Flying over this part of Europe was an unforgettable experience as frequent rain storms and high winds, also low clouds, called for a high degree of plane handling. We faced many frightening moments flying along narrow valleys, unable to rise above the surrounding mountains as dirty black clouds hid their tops. Our map reading had to be pretty good not to get lost, as of course, we could not fly on a compass course, the usual method of getting from one place to another.

It must be remembered that we carried no radio and were very much on our lonesome as we bumped around the sky in heavy turbulence and, to make things more difficult, with hardly any forward visibility when it was raining, the plane possessed no windscreen wipers. But it was all very interesting and, in retrospect, enjoyable.

Speedy Gymkhanas and Bagpipes

Monty had decreed that horse-racing was taboo. Many race horses had been "liberated" as we overran Germany. With the traditional love of horses and horse racing that lies in the heart of every Englishman, it did not take long for the Army to organise things. With the new prohibition in force I found I was being called upon to transport sundry Generals and Brigadiers to gymkhanas where horses were expected to run as fast as they could around an oval track.

On one occasion I was asked to fly Colonel Snowball, famed CO of the Seaforth Highlanders, to Verden to attend a grand farewell show staged by the elite 51st Highland Division. The setting was a large and modern football stadium. The grass was lovely and green and the day bright and sunny, it was early September. It was all really magnificent and I felt privileged to view that stirring scene. A massed band consisting of Cameron Highlanders, Black Watch, Seaforth's etc., in total more than 120 men, put on a stirring show as they marched and countermarched to the skirl of the bagpipes and the martial rhythm of the drums, thrilling the large crowd present, consisting mostly of "vanquished Jerries." I wonder what they were thinking.

Some time later Colonel Snowball invited the Officers of 'A' Flight to the farewell party given by his Regiment, the 6th Battalion Seaforth Highlanders. Bob Barrass and I flew our plane to Göttingen and then Jeeped it to a lovely chateau set in a beautiful glade high in the Harz Mountains that had belonged to Herman Göering. It was a fantastic party. Champagne cocktails were available in bountiful quantities and the food that followed was stupendously prepared by the best Chefs in Germany. There was wild boar set up in such a way that the animal seemed almost lifelike although it was completely carved and ready to serve. There was venison, turkey, wild duck, roast beef and lots of side dishes such as I had never seen before, nor likely to see again.

When everybody was thoroughly mellow, pipers appeared marching up and down the green glade in front of the large picture windows, playing those soulful and thrilling tunes that stir the heart of all Scots; and I felt truly proud of my ancestry. Many a tear was shed by those tough guys that had battled steadily and courageously all the way from El Alamein; probably giving thought to the many friends left on the way or, more probably, thankful to be alive and heading for home. It was another unforgettable experience.

Berlin Episode

I took off from Brunswick at 7.30 on the 1st August 1945 to ferry Bob and Aubrey to Berlin, they were starting their leave, hoping to wangle a lift to England in an American transport plane.

The weather was lousy. We ran into rain before reaching Magdeburg and had to navigate carefully, following the autobahn, so as not to overstep the narrow permissible corridor that joined Berlin with the rest of occupied Germany. Any deviation from that route could cause trigger happy Russians sitting down below to have a go at us. The flight took just over an hour and we found Gatow aerodrome without difficulty, taking time off to gaze down in awe at the thoroughly destroyed ex-Capital of Naziland. 'C' Flight was stationed on the drome and we soon spotted one of their Erks signalling us in. Their Mess was in a pleasant red-roofed house across the road from the aerodrome perimeter and there I was made welcome. Bob and Aubrey had been whisked off to the Main Control area and had no difficulty in persuading a Yank to fly them home in one of their DC-3's that were shuttling back and forth with supplies.

Had a pleasant evening chatting with my old pals and hearing harrowing tales of screams in the night as Russian soldiers prowled around the neighbourhood chasing all the women they could find, not being at all fussy with regard to age or beauty.

Next morning borrowed a Staff car and with Captain Rigby as guide headed for the centre of Berlin. The main roads were clear but side ones were still piled high with rubble from destroyed houses. There I witnessed the start of the German Miracle seeing hundreds of women, some wearing elegant clothes, clearing the rubble by hand, brick by brick. Here it should be stated that unless they worked they could not claim meal tickets, hence the reluctant enthusiasm. At every main intersection smart and fairly pretty Russian policewomen controlled the traffic by means of an impressive system of signals using small flags. They were a vast improvement on some of the other lady soldiers I had seen floating around on their flat feet in clumsy top boots and swathed in shapeless uniforms, each carrying a revolver on one side, and like as not, a tommy gun slung from a shoulder looking real tough. Wouldn't have liked to tangle with them.

We drove along the famous Unter den Linden, past the Adlon Hotel still standing fairly whole and on as far as the Brandenburg Gate, the limit of the Allied Zone. On the left were the skeletal remains of the Reichstag and beyond the garden where, I had been told, flourished a thriving black market. The Russian Army had received no pay of any sort for ages and, with the war finished, they thought it was about time they did something about it. The Allies had invented an Allied Reichmark and all transactions were carried out in this currency; including our Army Pay whilst in Germany. The Russians borrowed the plates and proceeded to print millions of notes of all denominations which differed from ours only in that a hyphen was placed before the serial number. They then proceeded to hand out large quantities of this money to their troops who, as they doubted their value back in Russia, tried to get rid of it as fast as possible by buying any small easily transportable item they could lay their hands on, such as jewels, watches, etc., and quickly expendable items such as bottles of booze, for which they paid any price.

Now I am not averse to doing a spot of business myself and when a couple of Russians came up to me and pointing to my watch made signs that they wished to acquire it, I entered into the game and we commenced to haggle in dumb language. The watch was a fairly cheap job, it must have cost me the equivalent of three pounds in Casa Escasany, but it made a good healthy tick and this enhanced its value in this market.

We sat down on a fallen tree trunk, a Russian on either side of me, whilst we haggled. Rigby stood aside and having a camera slyly took some photos. I started with a going price of 5.000 marks but eventually brought it down to 4.000; at that time the equivalent of 100 pounds, and at this price we did business. I handed over the watch receiving in exchange a wad of freshly printed notes, all with their tell-tale hyphen. Feeling prosperous we then headed for the Chancellery, guarded by a couple of Red soldiers seated comfortably in arm chairs outside the imposing entrance. In a comradely spirit they agreed to allow us in and, in a gesture of true fraternity

296 *Warlike Sketches*

Brandenburg Gate, Berlin. 2 August 1945

The photographs on this page and the next were taken on 2 August 1945 and are courtesy of the Estate of A. C. Young via VF.

Rigby's photo of Arrol after selling his watch for £100 in recently printed paper to the perplexed Russians.

With the Occupation Forces in Germany 297

Russian guards at Hitler's Chancellery

In front of Hitler's Chancellery

The skeletal remains of the Reichstag

Arrol standing in front of the Reichstag

one of them awarded me a high Nazi decoration. We explored that place of horrible memory, going through huge rooms strewn with rubble and empty medal boxes. It was here that, not so long before, Hitler had committed suicide and his body burnt. It was an historical spot all right, where the scourge of the earth, having caused the death of millions of people, had finally succumbed to his evilness.

There was little else to see in this chaotic mess that had been the mighty city of Berlin. In any case I had planned to return to Brunswick by lunch time, so we headed back to Gatow. Collected my things from the Mess crossed the road to reach my plane, when I was stopped most rudely by the point of a bayonet held by a Russian soldier who kept saying *niet* as if he meant it. My plane was but 20 yards away and by it sat an Erk looking quite forlorn. He had been caught unawares when the Russians spread their guards around the perimeter with orders that nobody was to leave or enter. There is no way of arguing with these Russian types who are completely and utterly dumb and seem to lack any reasoning power. The poor Erk had been marooned there for hours and eventually I managed to persuade the Red type to allow him to receive some sandwiches and a mug of tea.

The Potsdam meeting had just taken place between Churchill, Truman and Stalin. Stalin was heading for Rome via Gatow and although it had been agreed that this was an Allied drome, the Russians took it over without any by-your-leave, in their usual high-handed way.

Making the best of it, settled down in 'C' Flight Mess and was treated to a good lunch, then went into Berlin again to have another look around. When we returned in time for tea found that the Russian soldiers had disappeared and things were back to normal.

Rang up Control Tower to advise them I was leaving. DC-3's were landing and taking off all the time and only getting near the slip stream of one of those planes would have turned us upside-down. To avoid any trouble, not having a radio I could not advise Control my precise moment of take-off, did so off to one side and I'm sure nobody noticed. Despite it being definitely off-limits flew over the Potsdam Palace, scene of this historic meeting, and took photographs of the place. Then flew carefully down the middle of the access corridor and so back to Brunswick in time to take Smokey, my wee dog, for a walk around the aerodrome, hunting for mushrooms which we later turned into tasty omelettes with the help of a primus. Our favourite after dinner snack to accompany the wizard beer, then available in goodly quantities.

A Tentative Berlin Blockade

Our Mess was right alongside the Autobahn leading to Berlin and the famous 2nd Armored Division (US Army) better known as "Hell on Wheels", had discovered us. The convoys, heading for Berlin with provisions for our Troops, were wont to call a halt here and come into our Mess for a couple of beers and if lucky a mushroom omelette.

The beer was really first class and every evening we would open a 25 litre barrel and although we were only five residents, with willing help we usually managed to finish it off before midnight. Apart from genuine beer, we were also supplied with a whole series of excellent liqueurs, such as Benedictine, Kaffekalter, Curaçao, etc., all *ersatz* to be sure, but marvellous nevertheless.

Hell on Wheels was then committed to supplying the Allied Garrison stationed in Berlin and to do so were driving huge MAC trucks along the autobahn.

The first attempt by the Russians at blocking Berlin was tried out on the 26th of July 1945. Fortunately they picked on a Hell on Wheels convoy with a tough American Lieutenant in charge, and this is the story he told us on his return.

On reaching Helmstedt, the start of the Berlin Corridor, he found the barrier down and the sentry on duty would not let him through. His demand to see an officer was met by a further series of stubborn *niets* and in an increase in the number of burp toting soldiers. The Lieutenant was faced with quite a problem. His orders were to get through but was reluctant to use force, which could start another war, although he had plenty of men with him. The convoy consisted of six fully laden trucks with trailers.

He observed that there was quite a traffic of Russian vehicles heading towards West Germany with many Brass Hats visible and he thought up a sure way of solving his problem. He ordered his six trucks to straddle the Autobahn. With those mastodons strung across the road he created an efficient road-block of his own. To avoid any misunderstanding he had his men out with tommy guns at the ready. Traffic started to pile up, and so did the Brass Hats. The atmosphere became tense. When confronted by the by then angry officers by sign language he made it clear that he would gladly clear the road if they would only raise the barrier and allow him to proceed. The Russian officers then attempted to persuade the sentry on duty to do this but to no avail. Luckily one of the staff cars had a two way radio and contact was made with the Berlin Russian HQ. The counter-order seemingly went all the way down the line and eventually, after a wait of around two hours, a troop carrier drove up, the guard was relieved, and new ones conditioned to allowing Allied vehicles through, installed. This was probably the first attempt to establish a blockade by the Russians. As will be recalled the second attempt was more successful and overcome by a massive and expensive airlift.

The Powers that Be had little illusions about our "gallant allies" and on the 11th September I was ordered to fly Col. Falkner of Army Intelligence along the boundary line on the look out for anti-tank and AA guns pointing our way. The front was already thoroughly wire-netted by the Russians with lookout towers at frequent intervals. We would wave gaily to the Russian types manning the towers as we flew at tree-top height, and they would wave gaily back. We found nothing that time but it was evident that Allied HQ was highly suspicious and had little trust in Stalin's avowed friendliness. Also all the vehicles supplied by the allies had disappeared and the only ones we saw were decrepit ones captured from the Germans. Were the new ones being kept in reserve should a new war develop?

Farewell Canadians

We had been attached to the 1st Canadian Army since just after the battle of Cassino and had battled with them all the way up Italy until they were called away in a hurry to help Monty and his 21st Army Group win the Battle of the Bulge. It was then they did us the honour of insisting that 657 Air OP Squadron should follow them into battle. We had followed them into Belgium and fought together until final victory.

Now the day had come when they were to return to Canada. We all had many Canadian friends. 'A' Flight had fought consistently with the 5 Regiments of the Canadian AGRA, and their farewell was a memorable affair in more ways than one.

We were stationed in Hilversum at the time and AGRA HQ was some 20 miles away. Of course we were all invited to the party and Bill Bolam, Bob Barrass, Peter Wells and self drove over in a Jeep [June 1945]. We arrived at the AGRA Mess, a pleasant Dutch house, and from the start imbibed Moose Milk, a wizard concoction favoured by the Canucks, consisting in a mixture of army rum, milk and eggs and is real smooth, and it gets smoother as the evening wares on.

We were all in a happy mood, but at the same time, sorry. I suppose our nerves were still under high tension after so many dicey hours of dangerous flying and also unbelievably thankful that we could live without danger stalking us.

Needless to say, when the Moose Milk ran out and it was time to call it a day everybody was properly spiffed, including the Corps Commander. He had nothing to worry about as they just poured him into his Staff Car and his driver saw him home. Our case was slightly different. We had to do our own driving. The others were completely out and I had them placed gently in the Jeep, with Bill Bolam beside me. He being a regular soldier could hold his likker slightly better than the other amateurs. Managed to start the engine, get into gear and off we went.

Having kept up with the rest was not exactly sober, but I usually managed to keep control. However the road back home was highly complicated with many twists and turns and our only hope of making it was to follow the sober-driven car of the Corps Commander that had started off just ahead of us.

Now the Staff Car was a Humber and the driver undoubtedly wished to get home and to bed as fast as possible. Adopting a dubious theory that a Jeep could do whatever a Staff Car could, I stuck to those rear lights and aimed at the middle of the two pairs and around fifty yards behind. We tire screamed round corner after corner, the Dutch roads are rarely straight for long, and kept grimly on trying to keep my eyes open and in focus. I remember clearly driving fast alongside a large lake, beautiful with the full moon shining on the water. Here I found I couldn't get gear shift down because Bill's neck was wedged between the gear lever and 4 wheel drive lever and it took some yanking to dislodge this obstruction. Bill subsided on the floor of the Jeep there to snore peacefully.

We did the trip back to Hilversum a darn sight faster that on the outward journey, goodness knows at what average speed, but it must have been pretty high, and Jeeps are prone to overturning; but there is a saying that is applicable to this case.

The Canadians left soon after and we never saw them again.

A Spot of Ferrying

It was towards the end of one of my many leaves, I had visited Westminster Abbey thronged with joyful crowds as it happened to be VJ Day, the day Japan surrendered, and was back in Grove Park when I received a phone call from Harry Simms of 'C' Flight inviting me to join him in ferrying a new plane back to Germany. Of course I said yes.

On the 4th September 1945 trained it to Andover and taxied out to Old Sarum, then the Air OP Training Base and found they were now trying out helicopters for our job of observing for the artillery. That evening we went into town and enjoyed seeing Margaret Rutherford as the medium in *Blythe Spirit*.

Crack-of-dawn found us up next morning and by 5·50 we were airborne. Visibility was fair with low clouds but by the time we reached Hawkinge, where we were to refuel before taking the channel crossing, we ran into a drizzly squall which made it inadvisable to attempt the crossing to France; visibility being nil.

Next morning dawned dull but un-raining and after a leisurely breakfast, took off at 8·45 and were soon over Calais where they gave us a Verey Light, an invitation to land. But we kept on. It was a brand new plane, an Auster Mark VI, and enjoyed flying along the beaches of France, mostly at ground level and waving to the many bathers enjoying the weak sun then shining. Passed Dunkirk with many wrecks dotting the shoreline, a memorial to the many victims of the historic retreat. The German fortifications were also much in evidence and, all in all, it was an interesting trip.

Landed at Knocke [*Knokke-Heist?*] around 11 to refuel, then carried on to Gilze where we had lunch. As our flying range was around 100 miles had to drop into Apeldoorn and then Minden to pickup fuel, arriving eventually at Brunswick at 17·30 in time for tea. Harry carried on to Berlin with the plane to hand it over to 'C' Flight, then resident in that city.

The Case of the Stolen Jeep

Whilst 'A' Flight was at Brunswick we were all able to enjoy many short "Dutch Leaves" and all because being Flying Personnel were entitled to far more leaves than the lowly Army types. The procedure we had fixed up was that two of us would drive a jeep to Hilversum, stay there for four days then another couple would fly down, swap the plane for the Jeep and so on, the last pair driving the Jeep back.

When we arrived over Hilversum we would rev. the plane's engine three times and the types down below would come and fetch us from the small aerodrome near Loosdrecht.

We had many good friends at Hilversum and furthermore, the Officers' Club, ex Hooylands hotel was really smashing. They had a marvellous bar, a small dance hall and a first class pianist would play popular and nostalgic tunes endlessly. They also had an Indonesian instrument, a native xylophone, excellent to dance to.

From Hilversum we would drive to Amsterdam to do a flick and then dine at the Royal Palace on the Damm Square, or would go into Utrecht to do likewise.

On this occasion we had gone in a party to Utrecht starting off with drinks at the Pays Bas, followed by a wizard dinner at Van Angeren's with champagne and a good band, ending up dancing at the Ravenna Club (ex-Esplanade) run by the Canadians. This place was really first class and sported three bands and a floor show. When the time came to head for home we walked along to the nearby car park and found the Jeep gone, evidently stolen. Luckily we had no trouble in getting a lift back to Hilversum.

Next morning went round to the Provost and reported the loss of the Jeep. A week later when I was already back at Brunswick, a signal arrived advising that the Jeep had been found. Picked up a driver and took off in Holy heading for Apeldoorn. The weather was really duff with low clouds forcing us to fly low along the Weser Valley. Landed at Bad Oeynhausen to refuel, taking off in a rain storm.

At Apeldoorn rang up the Provost and was told the Jeep was at Utrecht, so took off again and headed for Hilversum where I knew I could borrow a DKW from a friendly native to get me into Utrecht. When I eventually arrived there found out that the Jeep was a total write-off. It had been "borrowed" by a wild Canadian and smashed. Had it towed to the REME where it was officially condemned. Stayed the night at Hilversum then flew back to Brunswick.

The End of My Flying Career

After a lovely leave in the UK returned to Brunswick Aerodrome to find that 'A' Flight had flown abandoning me to my fate. They had been transferred to England, and as I was an ancient type, soon to be de-mobbbed, my place was taken by a younger person.

Nobody knew what was to become of me so thought it best to go along to 'B' Flight who were still on the drome and there was made welcome. Next day went to see G3 Air–Rhine Army and he told me I was to join the 94 Field Regiment RA then stationed at Burgdorf.

This posting did not get off the ground as, before I could do anything about it was detailed to report to the 110 Light AA Regiment then in the process of moving to Fallingbostel [Bad Fallingbostel] to look after a Displaced Person Camp, ex the Herman Göering Regiment Barracks, and housing around 18000 Poles, ex-slave labour.

This was quite a commitment. These poor sods had been "slaves" and had gone through a pretty grim time. Although most of them were good people, as was only to be expected many felt resentment, were unstable, and their morale had been undermined by many years of bad treatment. With that amount of people a certain proportion of criminals were sure to be found, and under the circumstances, the average would be greater than normal.

The barracks consisted of 12 large buildings and there was no surrounding wall or fence, therefore the inhabitants had free access to the surrounding countryside, consisting mostly of pine woods but with the odd farm dotted around. These farms were the prey to marauding parties of Poles who pillaged, raped and killed the hated Germans, then sneaked back to the barracks. Some were caught, tried and hanged, but many went undetected despite the close watch being kept on all movements to and from the place.

Several petrol pumps were installed to supply vehicles with alcohol, used in lieu of petrol. This was wood alcohol and hence highly lethal if imbibed by humans. Despite these pumps being kept locked, the DP's somehow managed to get at the alcohol and next morning would be found dead or, worse blind. The pumps were dismantled. Then we found that they still manage to get at the stuff by lowering a small container such as an aspirin tube on the end of a string down the ventilation pipe, enough to blind and kill more of these compulsive drinkers.

My job then was that of Battery Captain, consisting mostly of administrative work. Had to see that the garbage collection was carried out properly with Army lorries driven by our men but manned by German POW's. These proved to be good types and highly respectful, they would immediately stand to attention should an officer appear, and they worked well. I expect they were grateful that the horrible war was over and that they were well treated and fed.

We had a bit of a problem with our Troop's welfare. The men were not allowed to fraternise with the Polish girls as this could lead to trouble, and the German civilians kept well clear of the camp. The solution to this problem proved simple. We were not far from the notorious Belsen Camp and every now and again I would ring up Miss Montgomery (Monty's sister) and ask her to allow 80 or 100 of her "girls", ex-survivors of that horrible place, to come along to a dance. Then I would take along a couple of Army lorries to pick them up. And so I had an opportunity of seeing that hell camp. By then it had been cleaned up. All the old buildings had disappeared to be replaced by neat Jane Huts; but the evil atmosphere lingered.

The girls were counted as they entered the dance hall and re-counted when it was time for them to leave, usually around 10 pm. There was a dance band of sorts, it made plenty of noise, hot cocoa and tea was served, plus plenty to eat. Neither side could understand each other's language yet they managed to communicate somehow or other, and a good time was had by all. Found that some of the inmates of Belsen were of Spanish origin and was able to have a talk with several of them. They avoided talking of their experience in Belsen and I didn't like to ask.

Russian Interlude

As Battery Captain it was my job to keep the books of the Unit and on the 8th January 1946 I was supposed to present them to the Audit Board. However, at the last minute, I was told to proceed to Soltau there to attend a Conference with a Russian Mission. Arrived at 11 to find five other British Officers and a like number of Russians, headed by a Colonel. It was explained to us, via an interpreter, that their job was to screen all the people in our DP [*Displaced Person*] Camp to single out the Ukranians, now Russians, in order to send them back home. This had been agreed by Churchill, Roosevelt and Stalin at the Yalta Conference. It was really a wicked agreement as the majority of these people preferred not to return to a Russian dominated Ukraine, but they were given no option and forced to return.

The Conference finished after midday and it was then the Russians invited us to partake of a "cup-of-tea" in their dining room. We moved there to find a large table covered with eatables and every 10 inches or so, a bottle of vodka. The glasses were large and the Russians evidently drank this stuff as if it were beer. Then our Colonel opened the session by proposing a toast to Stalin, who was dutifully honoured. This was countered by a toast to Churchill and so way down the line. By the end of all this the British Officers were the worse for wear. Luckily most of them had drivers. I managed to drive back without incident.

The leader of the Mission, Colonel Shafanev, was made my responsibility and on several occasions I accompanied him on his rounds seeking his nationals. When I realized what he was up to, saw to it that the people were forewarned of our coming and all the Ukrainians would disappear into the surrounding woods when the Russian car, with hammer and sickle flag flying, approached.

My job was to see fair play. To allow me to do this I had a Palestinian as interpreter and he was supposed to give the gist of all that was said. The DP's had been slave labour for many years in Germany; many no doubt were married in their native land and had remarried while in bondage. According to the Colonel, if the wife or husband was not Ukrainian or Russian, he or she could not be allowed to enter Russian held territory and had to remain behind. When I protested that this policy was ridiculous and uncivilized he was incapable of accepting my point of view. Nor would he believe that a British soldier marrying a German girl would be allowed to take her to England. Being an Officer and a Colonel he was well educated by Russian standards but nevertheless had been so indoctrinated that he was mentally incapable of accepting other views than those dinned into him by the Party. He obviously was fully aware of the history of the Capitalist States and just to try him out told him about life in the Argentine where one could buy anything one wanted in any quantity or travel wherever one wished. He just wouldn't believe me and mumbled "propaganda" at these stories.

The Block Supervisors thought they had better not overdo things so several victims were brought before the Colonel for questioning and several were turned over to him for transportation to Ukraine, or further east.

Thought it would be a good idea to try and get my own back for his hospitable "cup-of-tea" after the Conference. So one day invited him into our Mess and produced two tumblers filled half way with whisky, and proceeded to toast sundry and suitable objects. He had two or three sips then refused to drink any more despite my hinting he was being inhospitable. Evidently he daren't allow his driver to see him leave our Mess the worse for drink!

Another time invited him to our Mess for lunch and he commented on our good food. Explained to him that the rations served to us were exactly the same as those served to the Troops and this he did not believe. When I asked him if the same didn't apply to the Russian Army he answered, of course not, the Officers always received better food; seemingly officers were more equal than rankers.

THE WAY HOME

A Close Shave and Farewell Germany

On the 14th January 1946 my Release Book arrived. At long last, after more than five years of adventuring, it seemed that I could look forward with some degree of hope to getting back home.

On the 21st had to go into Lüneburg to fetch money from the Bank and borrowed the Major's recently converted Jeep with my batman Riley driving. Jeeps are uncomfortable, draughty vehicles and it was customary to get some able carpenter to build a cosy body to keep out the wind and snow, and this one had been rigged out very nicely, even having glass side-windows.

It had been snowing and the temperature was below freezing, which made for slithery roads. On the way back Riley was overtaking a four-wheeled cart laden with long logs that overlapped the back by quite a bit. He was approaching at a fair speed and moved into the middle of the road to pass when he spotted another car coming. He moved back into line with the cart and applied the brakes. Nothing at all happened. The road was iced over. We sped on at an undiminished speed and I watched helplessly, the logs approaching my nose. They kept on coming and crashed into the windscreen that shattered showering me with bits of glass. Just as I thought I'd had it they stopped one inch from my face as our bumper hit one of the cart wheels and stopped with a jolt. Lucky again.

As a matter of fact the previous day had attended a Court of Enquiry into the death of a poor Gunner who had fallen out of a truck and broken his neck. He had fought all the way back from Alamein and was due to be demobbed the following week.

Managed to get a lift into Soltau and from there rang the Battery to send a break-down lorry. The Major was most displeased when he saw what was left of his beautiful Jeep.

Was given a farewell dinner with plenty of champagne and left Fallingbostel for Hannover on the 23rd January 1945, there to entrain for Ostend.

For sundry reasons the trip back took three days so had an opportunity to explore Hannover and Ostend. As I had acquired a Voightlander camera was able to amuse myself taking photos.

Made my way back to Grove Park and then reported to Woolwich where wangled a continuous spot of leave till sailing time.

A Farewell Visit to Bonny Scotland

Before sailing back home thought I'd like to have another look at Bonny Scotland. Making use of my privileged position as an officer and a gentleman, booked a first class sleeper to Glasgow; there joined Alfred Dougall, a relative from Buenos Aires, at Green's Hotel.

The following day caught a bus for Bridge of Weir and after looking at that pretty place went on to Kilmacolm there to have lunch with Aunt Bell Rogers, sister to Uncle George. I had never met her before and found her to be a pleasant person and most hospitable. Remembering that my father had a friend, by name Nigel Laird in Kilmacolm thought it would be a good idea to look him up. Aunt Bell knew of him, he was a well known character, and as he was on the phone rang him up and was promptly invited to tea. His house *Torridon* was a large ancient house built on top of a hill overlooking miles of beautiful glens and villages. The tea, as is customary around these parts, was bountiful with lots of good things to eat; I tucked in effectively while we chatted about the good old days. I found out a lot of interesting things about my father's early life. Walked around a bit though it was drizzling, and he showed me where, in ancient days, the folk around used to go curling and where many really old curling stones had been unearthed. Really enjoyed that afternoon. It wasn't only being with these good people who evidently had been fond of my father and extended this feeling to me, but the whole atmosphere was so steeped in the old Scottish tradition, the house, its furniture, the surrounding countryside and, last but not least, the typical high tea.

When I was leaving Nigel Laird invited me to have lunch with him the following day in Glasgow. Mentioning that I was with a friend from Buenos Aires he included Alfred Dougall in the invitation.

Next day we enjoyed a wizard lunch at the Royal Scotch Automobile Club and found that another friend of my father's had joined us and again was regaled with stories of their boyhood days in Kilmacolm. Thoroughly enjoyed that meal, which included real genuine haggis, helped down with good beer.

When Nigel Laird found out that Alfred was the owner of *The Standard* [a Buenos Aires English language newspaper] and a printing shop he invited us along to visit his printing shop. So we all got into a taxi and drove along for a while through Glasgow until we came upon an imposing edifice some four floors high and occupying a whole block, with a tall chimney and a flag staff bedecked with flags. This turned out to be his "shop." It was all very interesting, especially for Alfred who was quite flabbergasted by the variety and perfection of the work being turned out. This consisted mainly of beautifully printed labels in four, or even five colours, for biscuits, chocolates, whiskey and scenes for calendars, all real works of art. He showed us all over the place, gave us tea, then had us driven back to Green's Hotel in his private car.

Next day had planned a trip to Loch Lomond, the happy hunting grounds of my ancestors – and especially to have a look at Camstradden Hill after which our home in Martinez had been named. We went as far as Balloch by bus and there hired a car to take us around.

At that time was wearing my SD [service dress] uniform with an Argentina shoulder flash. Our driver, Mr McHamish (he was a Scot) on seeing that remarked that his only son had migrated to the Argentine and was happily married to a local girl. He proudly brought out a photo and who should the girl be but Lorna Matthews, a school friend of my sister's. Truly a small world.

The Macfarlanes had possessed most of the land around Luss, including Camstradden Hill, but it seems that they had sold out to the Colquhouns. The only remaining Macfarlane we could discover was the post Mistress, then well over 80 and not too lucid. [*Here Arrol was mistaken. The Colquhouns owned the land around Luss, including Camstradden Hill. Our Macfarlane ancestor was a tenant of the Colquhouns*].

Stopped for lunch at the Colquhoun Arms in Luss and there discovered that a door lintel, off the bar, was marked up with the heights of different people. It was headed by a chap called Sinclair, a mere 6' 4". Thought I had better set the record straight so called the proprietor over and made him mark up my height. As I happen to be 6' 5 ½" a Macfarlane now tops the lot.

We had an enjoyable drive round that colourful Loch. It was a beautiful sunny day with just sufficient mist to add that ethereal look that enhances Scottish scenery. Leaving Loch Lomond, we drove through Tarbet, Arrochar and as far as Holy Loch, the base for submarines, then back to Balloch and there caught the bus back to Glasgow.

A sad sequel to this story is that, some five years later, I had the opportunity of revisiting Glasgow and thought I would pay Nigel Laird a visit. When we drove up to his printing shop we saw that the flag was flying at half mast. When I enquired about Mr. Laird I was told that he had died the day before.

The Boat Race and International Rugger

I had managed to keep in touch with Sergeant Eric Hall, he was the chap responsible for us having crashed in Uttexeter some years before. He was then living in Richmond and invited me to see the famous Oxford and Cambridge Boat Race and then the England-Scotland International Rugger match at Twickenham.

So that morning found a party of us outside the Mortlake Brewery peering into dense fog where, I was assured, flowed the River Thames. The fog was low lying and effectively covered the river, but overhead the sky was clear. In fact it was quite a nice day. After a while we heard an approaching roar indicating the race was in progress and coming near. Then a helicopter flew slowly overhead. Then we saw, briefly, the white splashes of churning oars and that was that. But we read all about it in the papers.

After that we all went off to Eric's flat there to imbibe beautiful beer.

The following day a party of us went along to the Twickenham Grounds and saw a really first class game of rugger. The place was packed solid and we were right behind one of the goal posts. Despite the awkward position of our seats we were lucky in that during the first half Scotland did all the scoring in front of our noses and during the second half the reverse proved true and we were able to enjoy most of the action that took place. The final result was England 12, Scotland 8.

The Way Home

Once I knew I was sailing on the Highland Monarch, time really flew. Had to go to Olimpia, that huge place, to collect my "civvies" and found it well organised, with swarms of Army types entering one end and leaving, not much more than half an hour later, laden with a set of good shoes and socks, three sets of undies, a blue pin stripe shirt and pork pie hat. Out of one uniform and into another!

One extremely interesting day was spent on an extensive tour of the huge Ford Works at Dagenham. This invitation was wangled by Eric Wilde, an old friend, and included Harold Dougall, J. E. Walding and self all posing as South American Journalists. Of the three only Harold could claim some degree of authenticity as he was heading back to work for *The Standard* owned by his dad. This factory was immense, especially the foundry part where sparks fly wickedly all over the place and glowing molten steel whizzes by at great speed as it is squeezed between powerful rollers and transformed into recognizable car parts.

The highlight of the tour was undoubtedly the lunch break when we were entertained by the PR Manager, in a swell private dining room, and there tucked into luscious steaks, something we had not seen for years.

The day before I sailed went with Walding to the House of Commons and, sitting in the Visitor's Gallery, heard Winston Churchill give a rather nonsensical but witty speech defending the House's late working hours.

And so at long last, after saying goodbye to Aunt Dolly, Uncle George and family, and thanking them for being so kind to me during my stay in the UK, headed for Tilbury and boarded the MV Highland Monarch. It was the 13th of April 1946. Was delighted to find that she had been partly reconverted and the upper decks were back to pre-war elegance and there we could enjoy some semblance of civilized existence. The cabins were still un-partitioned and bedded around 30 of us in triple bunks.

There was a good mob on board and discovered many old friends. Better still, no attempt was made to enforce any sort of Army discipline and the voyage was pleasant throughout. Plenty of games were organised and the food was good and plentiful. Tea served in the elegant lounges, delightful. We stopped at Las Palmas, Rio and Santos and had time to explore those places. Our arrival in Montevideo was something special as George Mackern, of Alpargatas, invited all the volunteers to lunch at a place near the market where we were served tremendous *bifes* [beef steaks]. One was weighed and proved to top 800 g. He also entertained us that evening at his luxurious flat in Pocitos, and before that we were all taken to visit the Punta Carreta Golf Club, a lovely place.

On the 4th of May 1946, 5 years, 9 months and 8 days since leaving on this trip, stepped once again on Argentine soil to be welcomed by my Mother, who seemed pleased to see me back, and lots of relations and friends. And so ended a wonderful experience.

Summing up is difficult. Obviously with an interesting war going on in an area I had always yearned to visit, not going was unthinkable, else I would have suffered a sense of frustration for the rest of my life.

Having attained my most cherished ambition, that of soaring through the air in a plane, was a priceless bonus.

The return to normality, after living with a perpetual feeling of uncertainty, if not plain fear, for so many years greatly enhanced my appreciation of life. To put it simply – it was good to be alive.

THE END

THE WAR OFFICE,
London,
S.W.1.

P/222306/1/M.S.2.(A).   19th June 1946.

Sir,

I am directed to inform you that as you have now ceased to be employed on active military duties, and as you have taken up residence outside the United Kingdom, you will relinquish your commission with effect from 28th June 1946.

The requisite notification will appear in the London Gazette (Supplement) on or about 9th July 1946, when you will be granted the honorary rank of Captain.

I am Sir,
Your obedient Servant,

General,
Military Secretary.

Captain A. MacFarlane,
Royal Artillery,
A Del Valle 473,
Martinez Province,
Buenos Aires.

Glossary of Terms

AA	Anti Aircraft	MP	Military Police
AFHQ	Africa Force Headquarters	MT	Motor Transport
AGRA	Army Group Royal Artillery	NAAFI	Navy Army Air Force Institutes
ALG	Advanced Landing Ground	NCO	Non Commissioned Officer
AOP	Air Observation Post	Nissen	Arched corrugated iron hut
ASI	Air Speed Indicator	OC	Officer Commanding
ATS	Auxiliary Territorial Service	OCTU	Officer Cadet Training Unit
AT	Anti Tank	OP	Observation Post
Airstrip	Landing Ground	PBI	Poor Bloody Infantry
BOA	British Overseas Army	Panther	Heavily armoured German tank
Blower	Wireless		
Bofors	44 mm quick firing AA gun	Prang	Crash
Bradshawed	Navigated by following ground features	Pronto	Communications Officer
		RA	Royal Artillery
Brew Up	Make Tea - Burn	RAC	Royal Armoured Corps
CFI	Chief Flying Instructor	RASC	Royal Army Service Corps
CO	Commanding Officer	RATD	Royal Artillery Training Depot
Char	or Chei, Indian for tea		
DAF	Desert Air Force	RE	Royal Engineers
Don R	Despatch Rider	REME	Royal Electrical and Mechanical Engineers
EFTS	Elementary Flying Training School		
		RHA	Royal Horse Artillery
ENSA	Entertainment National Service Association	RHQ	Regimental Headquarters
		RTU	Returned to Unit (Failed)
Flack	Anti-aircraft fire	Round	One shell
Flip	a short flight	SAS	Special Air Service
GL	a secret name for Radar	SD	Service Dress
GOC	General Officer Commanding	SM	Sergeant Major
		SP Gun	Self Propelled Gun
Gen.	Information	Sortie	Patrol
HE	High Explosives	Stonk	Shell, engage with gunfire
HQ	Headquarters		
Jane hut	flat sided wooden hut	Stooge	Fly around
Jerry	German	TCV	Troop Carrying Vehicle
LAC	Leading Aircraftman	Tiffy	Artificier - Mechanic
MO	Medical Officer	VP	Vital Point

War Travels

1940	July	27 – Sailed from Buenos Aires
	Aug	22 – Arrived Liverpool
	Sep	02 – Enlisted in British Army
1941	Jan	21 – Joined Mountain Regiment
	July	15 – Moved to Wales
	July	30 – Joined OCTU
1942	Feb	02 – To Scotland, 2nd Light A A Regiment
	Mar	25 – Moved to Wick
	May	21 – To Dunfermline, Mixed Heavy AA
1943	Feb	23 – To England, Larkhill Air OP
	Apr	07 – To Cambridge, EFTS
	Aug	18 – Awarded Air OP Wings
	Aug	28 – Moved to York
	Nov	28 – Flew BOAC from Bristol to Algiers
1944	Jan	09 – To Châteaudun–657 Air OP Squadron
	Feb	21 – Moved to Tunis
	Feb	27 – Flew to Naples Italy
	Apr	03 – To Cassino
	Apr	19 – Into action at Cassino
	Aug	25 – Attack on Gothic Line
	Oct	14 – On leave, Florence
1945	Feb	25 – On leave, Rome
	Mar	30 – To Leghorn, exit the Eighth Army
	Apr	01 – Landed Marseille
	Apr	06 – Arrived Belgium
	Apr	11 – Arrived Holland
	Apr	21 – Into action with the 21 Army Group
	May	03 – On leave, London
	Jun	30 – Into Germany, Brunswick

1946 Jan 08 – Liaison with Russians
   Jan 26 – Departed Germany via Ostend
   Apr 23 – Sailed for Home, *MV Highland Monarch*
   May 05 – Arrived Buenos Aires

Grand Totals

Total time away from Buenos Aires	5 years	9 months
Time spent in the UK	3 years	6 months
Time spent in Scotland		6 months
Time spent in North Africa		3 months
Time spent in Italy	1 year	1 month
Time spent in Holland		2 months
Time spent in Germany		7 months

Flying hours total	844
Flying hours operational	421
Operational Sorties	389
Number of Artillery Shoots	263

My Tale is Told

About this 2016 Edition

The first edition of these Warlike Sketches was typewritten and held in three ring binders. There may have been two or three copies made. The original maps were large, hand drawn, coloured fold-outs. When scanned to black and white and reduced to a 9" x 6" page size the legibility suffered. To solve this problem l have overlaid larger sized digital type on the original maps. Although the author provided a Glossary I have written out many of the abbreviations in square brackets when they first appear in the text.

As this book is now offered to the present generations, who have grown up long after these events took place and who live on another continent, I have included maps showing the locations of many of the places mentioned in the text.

We were fortunate to contact Aubrey Young's nephew, Vic Flintham, an aviation historian, and through him Aubrey's son, Peter. They kindly provided scans of photographs in Aubrey's photo album and more detailed information on some photos we already had. In addition I must thank Vic Flintham for his helpful comments and corrections.

The National Library of New Zealand allowed me to reproduce the aerial photograph of the Cassino battle scene on page 107. The Museum of Army Flying at Middle Wallop UK holds the Operational Logs for the 657 Squadron and some photographs. I have obtained permission to include the scan of a page of the 'A' Flight Operational Record on page 223 and the photograph on page 111. The watercolour of the Ceprano Landing Ground that Arrol mentions on page 135 was obtained from the Canadian War Museum in Ottawa.

My grateful thanks to Heather Macfarlane for her patient proofreading. I claim responsibility for all remaining errors and omissions.

Cathy Murray
Michigan · 2016

Further reading

The Story of 657 Air O.P. Squadron RAF January 31 1943-May 8 1945 prepared by Captains Barrass and Owen and privately published in 1946.

Memoirs of an Air Observation Post Officer by Major Andrew Lyell DFC published 1985. This describes the beginning of the Air Observation Post Squadrons and the activities of 658 Squadron in Northern Europe.

The Men Behind the Medals, a New Selection by Graham Pitchfork, published in 2003 contains a chapter on Captain Aubrey Young of the 657 Air OP Squadron who was awarded a Distinguished Flying Cross in November 1944.

In this letter, sent to his great-nephew then aged 11, the author explains how he observed and corrected the fire of three regiments.

```
                                             MARTINEZ.
                                             April 18th. 1993.



Dear Martin,
             Thank you for your letter of the 1st. April. You
talkof reading all my articles but the onely ones you must have
read could only have been the book and the one about climbing.
      Yes, I tried to have the book published but they
didn't find it suitable.
      I read your "Phoenix" story but find it too complicated
and teahnical for fme to understand properly. And how did you
draw the Plasma Designer?
      I am not good at inventing stories and all I do is
write about things I have done or seen. As I have lived quite a long
time and done a lot of odd things, I have had plenty to write
about. Apart from the Book I wrote a "Family History". This I
did for Susan to read when she grows up and learn how her
ancestors lived many years ago. To this I photocopied and
included all the stories I had written so it is quite long.
      I have written quite a few stories about life in the
Province of Corrientes when that place was quite wild and many of
these stories have been published in the B.C.C. Bulletin. I will
send you some but they are not very interesting.
      Yesterday we wnt to the Nautico with Chris and Tita
and had luhch there. They will soon be going to visit you
and I may send this letter by them.
      Hope you are getting on well at school and are enjoying
life and are all in good health.
             With love to the lot of you,

                                    Arnol
```

You want to know how I managed to observe and correct the fire of up to three different regiments. It is all rather complicated but I will try and explain simply.

Each plane was in wireless communication with 5 regiments of Artillery. We all had code names of two letters and a number and I was always XX 16.

I'd be flying around over the front and, maybe, observe some guns firing. Quickly I pin-point the place on my map and take note of the map reference. To make it easier I will give you one sequence of orders and I will use one code letter for each regmt. "Hullo A.- Guns now firing. Map reference 345678. Troop Target" (That meant four guns would fire) "One gun ranging - Report when ready".
"Hullo . XX16 - Ready - Time of flight 46 seconds"
"Hullo. A - Fire.   "Hullo XX16 Shot"
Then around 40 seconds later I would look with my binoculars at the target area and if the shell fell short order.
"Hullo A - Add 400." If the next shot went over the target then I'd order "Less 200" until the difference was 50 yards then go to fire for effect that is "Hullo A.- 5 rounds gunfire" And the 4 guns of the troop would fire as fast as possible.
Then, maybe, I'd see more guns firing from a large area and I'd repeat the sequence except that this would be a Mike Target, that is all the guns of the regiment would fire.
Then if I saw another target worth engaging the sequence of orders would go down to regiment C and so on.
All that time I was flying the plane with only my feet that is with the rudder only, as my hands were busy with the map, and wireless so the plane waltzed around the sky, which was a good thing as it made it difficult to hit by gunfire.
I had a clock in front of me with a large second hand so I could calculate when I had to observe each shot. When I was doing three shoot at the same time it was quite a job remembering exactly when each shell was due to land, which target area it was heading for and what my last order to the gun had been. It was really quite hectic while it lasted.

The time of flight varied according to the distance of the guns from the target area. When firing a big gun it could be as long as 90 seconds.

Maps

- 11   Locations in England and Wales.
- 27   Locations in Scotland.
- 35   Firth of Forth and Inchkeith, the "Fortified Island."
- 42   Locations in England and Wales.
- 61   f Africa.
- 61   Sketch Map of North Africa.
- 79   Route from Châteaudun to Naples.
- 94   Arrol's travels in search of the missing squadron.
- 100   In this map the author shows the successive fronts.
- 101   The Liri Valley before the Cassino Battles.
- 105   The Gustav and Hitler Lines.
- 125   Hitler line Battle.
- 144   Arezzo Front.
- 158   Arezzo Front Detail.
- 174   The Gustav and Gothic Lines.
- 175   Gothic Line Battle.
- 186   Gothic Line Battle Detail.
- 206   The Ravenna Front.
- 232   The Ravenna Front Detail.
- 265   The Gold Flake Route April 1–6 1945.
- 271   Locations in Belgium, Holland and Germany.
- 275   Occupied Germany.

Photographs and Illustrations

- 9   On board the MV *Almeda Star* - Cutts, Makin, Wilson and self.
- 11   Fargo Camp, Larkhill, with two Barbadians and a local.
- 16   Cathie Bonner and the twins in Portpatrick.
- 17   In Mountain Battery rig.
- 23   As Cadet in Llandrindod, Wales.
- 29   Ben Nevis.
- 29   Scotland, near Kinlochleven. Mountain climbing on motorbike.
- 50   Uttoxeter plane crash.
- 54   The Ubiquitous Auster.
- 73   Bamford landed beside a station to ask the way to Biskra.
- 80   The Auster Mark III that I flew from Africa.
- 89   Naples. … balloon after balloon loomed overhead…
- 107   Observing the Battle Scene – Mount Trocchio in the foreground.
- 107   A view of Cassino, taken from Trocchio.

111	A half covered Auster in front of Monte Cassino.
113	Cassino Battle - RAF photo, Pignataro.
128	"Marion" in the Liri Valley.
131	Remains of Holy Smoke II, Bob Barrass and self.
131	Capt. Aubrey Young RA and the remains of his plane.
135	At Ceprano ALG, Scottie, Aubrey, Bob and self just back from a sortie.
135	Aubrey, Bob and Arrol at Ceprano 1 Jun 1944.
136	My "caravan" tucked into an ex-Jerry 88 mm gun pit, Ceprano.
136	Interior of my caravan!
137	Watercolour by Lawren P. Harris.
183	Our tanks were creeping up that road towards the Panther turret.
184	My Panther turret bag. "Elsie" on the right.
184	Bob Barrass
187	Aubrey Young with a 88 mm dual purpose gun.
190	Heading straight for a great white parachute.
198	Battle Communications Diagram.
223	A page from 'A' Flight 657 Squadron RAF Operational Record Book.
227	Lighthouse hopping in Cervia.
243	LAC's Wilson and Green with Holy Smoke V.
243	Aubrey Young, ground crew and Arrol
255	Me and Lofty (F/Lt A.C.G. Harding RAF).
255	Rome, Pincio Gardens — tucking in with elegance.
260	Wells, Bob Barrass, Self, Aubrey Young, Rigby and an Italian Family.
262	Apennine Pass en route to Florence, March 24 1945.
264	Harrod's Camp near Leghorn, March 24-30 1945.
268	The author in front of the Chateau at Oostmalle.
273	Loosdrecht Lake — Friendly Natives.
283	The Vanquished German Army, Loosdrecht.
287	Arrol, Bob and Aubrey, Brunswick, Sept. 1945.
288	German Air Force Crests.
288	Brunswick — Hitler's escape plane, a long range Condor.
290	Peaceful Jerries.
296-7	Berlin, August 1945.

Index

Aberdeen 26, 27
Abergavenny 24
Advanced Landing Ground
  Abissinia 201
  Barneveld 274
  Cattolica 194
  Ceprano 135
  Cervia 227
  Cesenatico 222
  Citta dela Pieve, 146
  Cortona 158
  Doetinchem 269
  Ferretto 154
  Frosinone 136
  Gilze 269
  Gradara Castle 196
  Greve 170
  N of Cortona 155
  NW tip of lake Trasimeno 153
  Orvieto 147
  Otterlo 274
  Paglieta 96
  Panicarola 152
  Piegaro 148
  Presenzano 99
  Roccasecca 135
  Rotonda Hill 115
  Tivoli 142
  Venafro 103
  Viserba 215
Africa Force HQ 62
Afrika Corps 82
Agropoli 88
Airacobras 83, 84
Alatri 139
Alexander, General 103
Alfonsine 245
Algiers 61, 169, 224
Amesbury 12, 15
Ancona 179
Antwerp 267
Aquino 114, 127, 130
Arezzo 154, 157, 158, 159, 161, 163, 174, 221
Arielli River 92
Army Co-Operation Flight 54
Assisi 176, 220
Astengo, Oscar Oneto 257
Audland, Brig. General 98

Auster Mark III 53, 80
Auster Mark IV 169, 199
Auster Mark V 244
Auster Mark VI 303
Bagnacavallo 236
Bamford, Captain J A 66, 71, 74, 77, 82, 87, 96, 99
Barham, Captain R F 109, 116
Barnett, Brig. 99
Barrass, Captain R., DFC 109, 111, 130, 140, 148, 177, 182, 185, 204, 219, 272, 293, 301
Barr & Stroud 20, 35
Batna 71
Beacroft, from Entre Rios 284
Belsen Camp 306
Benevento 97
Berlin 279, 294, 298, 299, 300, 303
Berlin Corridor 299
Bertucci, General of Cremona Gruppe 259
Biskra 71, 73, 74
Bolam, Captain J W 83, 87, 89, 145, 154, 168, 263, 267, 301
Bône 68, 81, 82
Bonner, Cathie 13, 57, 280
Bonner, Fred 17, 92
Bridlington 59
British Army Formations
  Army
    8th Army 37, 71, 79, 92, 99, 101, 102, 103, 104, 114, 133, 157, 158, 169, 171, 176, 178, 179, 180, 186, 194, 201, 209, 222, 224, 225, 231, 234, 260
    21st Army 252, 261, 270, 276, 301
  Corps
    XIII Corps 103, 114, 180
  Division
    6th Armoured 159
    51st Highland 293
    75th Division 114
    78th (Battleaxe) 104
  Regiment RA
    1st Royal Horse Artillery 150
    2nd Royal Horse Artillery 97
    15th Heavy 244
    21st Med. & Hvy Training 10
    66th Medium 139, 145, 149, 150

75th Medium 152, 172
  95th Light A. A. 27
  98th Field 276
  110 Light AA 305
  132nd Field 109, 114, 118, 121
  138th Field 153
  158th Mixed Heavy AA 26, 37, 38
  Other Formations
    2nd Fife & Forfar Yeomanry 59
    2nd Glasgow Highlanders 58
    6th Seaforth Highlanders 293
    24th Lancers 59
    27th Lancers 226, 230
    East Surrey 133
    Popski's Private Army 224, 225
British Liberation Army 277
Brunswick 286
Buchanan, Captain J. 61, 254
Buchan, Captain J. 108
Cairo, Mount 114
Caithness 31
Cambridge 43, 53
Canadian Army Formations
  Corps
    1st Canadian 92, 96, 180
  Division
    5th Canadian Armoured 92
  Brigade
    1st Canadian Armoured 276
  Artillery
    Canadian AGRA 92, 180, 197, 203,
       215, 217, 235, 247, 251, 252, 272,
       276, 301
    2nd Canadian Medium 237, 246, 251
    3rd Canadian Medium 250
    5th Canadian Medium 244
    15th Canadian Heavy 245
  Other Formations
    1st. Canadian Infantry 92
Cape Granitola 84
Capodichino aerodrome 90
Carthage 83
Casa del Guardiano 225
Cassino Front 99
Cassino village 106
Castiglione del Lago 149, 152
Castletown 32
Catania 85
Cattolica 194
Central Med. Training School 97
Charlesworth, an Argentinian 12

Châteaudun-du-Rhumel 65, 67, 75, 79
Chester 49
Churchill, Winston 280
Citta della Pieve 146
Clark, General Mark 104
Clifton 57
Conca River 196
Constantine 63, 69, 81
Cooper, Godfrey 279
Coriano Feature 194
Cowan, Captain A.A. 109, 113, 139, 146,
   147
Cremona Gruppe 259
Culverwell, Captain Douglas 266
Cutts, Charles Duncan 8
Davidson, an Argentinian 12
Dennis, Amalia 57
Derby Transit Camp 17
Desert Air Force 94, 201, 220, 221, 261
Dougall, Harold 279, 286, 310, 313
Dunfermline 37
Durrant, Captain R H 106
Edinburgh 31, 34
EFTS 74
Eisenhower, General D. 63
El Alamein 293
El Khroub 80, 81
Fallingbostel 305
Ferguson, Major 12
Finnigan, Mrs 118
Florence, City of 163, 170, 171, 220, 221,
   222
Foggia 93
Foglia River 181
Forli 261
Fortunato Feature 201
Fort William 27, 28
Fossato 177
Fosso Ghiaia 230
Free French Squadron 65, 67
French Foreign Legion 141
Frosinone 135
Gander, 61
Gatteo 216
Gibraltar 62
Gilmore, Major Sir John 59
Glasgow 31, 58, 310, 311, 312
Glaysher, 2/Lt 28
GL, gun laying radar 37, 38, 252, 253, 316

Gold Flake Route 264, 265, 267
Golfo Policastro 88
Gothic Line 129, 179, 189
Graham, Mr 40
Green, Corporal RAF 109, 188, 208, 213, 246, 259, 310, 311
Gulf of Gioia 86
Gulf of Sant'Eufemia 87
Gustav Line 103
Hall, Dennis Edwin 8
Hall, Major 58
Hall, Sgt. Eric 10, 49, 312
Handley, an Argentinian 12
Hanse, Captain 19, 20
Harding. F/Lt A.C.G.(Lofty) 253, 254
Harris, Lawren P 135
Harrods Camp 263
Henderson, Major P.H. 219
Henman, Michael Furse 8
Hickson, Major 250
Highway 6 115
Hilton, Gunner RA 109, 123, 200, 216, 246, 259, 291
Hilversum 282
Hitler Line 104, 114, 127, 135
Holtzminden 291
Holy Smoke II 111, 134
Holy Smoke III 154, 156, 199, 224
Holy Smoke IV, written off 241
Holy Smoke V 244, 259
Holy Smoke VII 270
Howard, Leslie 62
Inchkeith, 35
Indian Army Formations
  8th Indian Division 92
Ingram, Major J R 64, 69, 86, 92, 155, 219
Invergordon 39
Italian Partisans 160, 165
Jesi 177, 178, 220, 222
Kerosin Predictor 28
King, Captain R.J. 145
Kinlochleven 28
Kinross 31, 39, 40
Korba 83
Laird, Nigel of Kilmacolm 310
Lake Comacchio 248, 259
Larkhill 10, 13, 16, 39, 42

Leese, General Oliver 176
Leghorn 262
Liri Valley 103, 108, 114, 121
Llandrindod Wells 25
LST 177 , U.S. Navy 263
Luftwaffe 13, 56, 83
Lysanders 56
Mackern, George of Alpargatas 314
Maison Blanche 62
Makin, Leonard St John 8, 10
Marseilles 263, 276
Marshall's Aerodrome 43
Martin 61
Massey 15
Massey, Lewis 286
Matafou, Cape 62
McCallum, Lt Ian W. of BsAs 226
McCorquadale, Lt D. 218, 219
McHamish, Lorna née Matthews 311
Melley, Lt 48
Messina 86
Metauro River 180
Mickleborough 61
Mickleburgh 93
Monastery Hill 114
Montgomery, Miss (Monty's sister) 306
Mount Belvedere 103
Mount Blow, 268 Baring Rd 13
Mount Trocchio 112, 119
Naples 88, 92, 113, 244
Nebel [Nebelwerfer] gun 150, 195, 202, 207, 209, 211, 217, 218
Newydel Camp 24
New Zealanders 170, 221
Nichols, Colonel 129
Oostmalle 267
Ouid Farara Vehicle Dump 68
Packard, Brigadier 140
Paglietta 98, 99
Palmer, Colonel 276
Pantelleria 83, 84
Parry-Evans, Dr 52
Peniakoff, Vladimir alias Popski 222, 224, 225, 226, 230, 259
Perkins, Frederick M and wife 177
Peron, Brigadier (Belgian) 278
Philippeville 63
Picatello River 219

Pignataro 119
Pitot, Captain (Belgian) 278
Pitts, Lt 63
Plum, Captain 10, 41
Pompeii 92
Ponte Olivo 84
Porter Force 226
Portpatrick 16, 23
Powell, Gunner 109, 134, 153, 188, 213, 214, 225, 250, 259
Presenzano Military Cemetery 109
Purvis, Major G3 Air 219
Rabat 62
Radcliffe, Captain M. B. DFC 70, 87, 90, 91, 92
Rapido River 112, 115, 118
Ravenna 224, 226, 232, 238, 244, 252, 259
Rigby, Captain A.S. 205, 261, 294, 295
Riley, Captain G W 113, 219, 272, 309
Rimini 192, 197, 201, 205, 215
River Arno 171
River Plate House 40
Rogers, Aunt Bell 310
Rogers, Dolly née Macfarlane 10, 13, 40, 314
Rogers, Uncle George 310, 314
Rome 140, 170, 221, 226, 253, 255, 256, 257, 298
Rosyth, Naval Base 38
Route 6 103, 130
Royal Air Force
  Squadrons
    651 Air OP 92, 96, 124, 168
    657 Air OP 64, 71, 79, 103, 176, 223, 234, 279, 301
    659 Air OP 57, 60
    661 Air OP 274
    663 Air OP 261
Royal Navy Ships
  HMS Aphis (river gunboat) 191
  HMS Scarab (river gunboat) 191
  HMS Undine (destroyer) 191
Russi 239
Sahara 71, 72
Salerno 88
Salisbury 54
Sangro River 92, 96
San Marino 194, 197, 199, 200, 204

Sant'Apolinare in Classe 231
Santarcangelo 150, 208, 209
Scalea 87
Scott, Captain A. R. 115, 130, 140, 143, 146, 152, 156, 157, 169, 176, 177, 189, 194, 195, 204, 208, 209, 220, 233, 234, 244, 267, 279, 286
Shafanev, Colonel (Russian) 307
Shoot
  Divisional 120
  Mike Target 150, 164, 215, 216
  Victor Target 164
  Yoke Target 180, 195, 203, 219
Sicily 83, 84, 218
Simms, Captain Harry W., DFC 179, 302
Snowball, Colonel 292
Sorrento 88
Souk-el-Khemis 82
Spedding, Gunner 259, 262, 269
sugar factory 231
Talbot, War Correspondent 62
Tanner, F S 96
Taranto 95
Taylor, Captain ex BsAs 58
Tiger Moth 43, 49, 53
Trasimeno, Lake 150
Tunis 81, 82
USA Army Formations
  2nd Armored Division 299
Uttoxeter 50
Vasto 93
Veroli 136
Walding, J. E. 43, 199, 286
Walker, Johnny 94
Walrus amphibian 83
Ward, a Barbadian 12
Washington N.C. 37
Way, Robert E 22, 47
Weedon 18
Wells, Captain E. 219, 235, 244, 263, 301
Welsh, Colonel 97
Whitleys 55
Wilde, Eric 313
Wilson, Captain 284
Wilson, L.A.C. 109, 155, 188, 208, 213, 277
Wilson, Wilfred Mervyn 8
Wright, Major 246

Yataiticalle 211
York 57
Young, Captain Aubrey C, DFC 108,
    109, 111, 115, 130, 140, 142, 151, 152,
    153, 167, 169, 170, 177, 178, 192,
    195, 204, 220, 221, 222, 225, 226,
    234, 246, 247, 250, 251, 262, 269,
    276, 280, 294
Young, Major 248
Yunnie, Captain 225, 226

Printed in Great Britain
by Amazon